Gauchos
and the
Vanishing Frontier

GAUCHOS
and the Vanishing Frontier

Richard W. Slatta

Georgette M. Dorn

University of Nebraska Press
Lincoln and London

Portions of Chapters 5 and 7 have previously
been published, in different form, as "Pulperías
and Contraband Capitalism in Nineteenth-
Century Buenos Aires Province," *The
Americas* 38 (January 1982): 347–62, and
"Rural Criminality and Social Conflict in
Nineteenth-Century Buenos Aires Province,"
Hispanic American Historical Review 60:3
(August 1980): 450–72.

Library of Congress Cataloging in
Publication Data

Slatta, Richard W., 1947-
Gauchos and the vanishing frontier.

Bibliography: p.
Includes index.
1. Gauchos—Argentina—Buenos Aires
(Province)
2. Buenos Aires (Argentina:
Province)—History.
I. Title.
F2861.S53 1983
305.5'63'0982
82-20014
ISBN 0-8032-4134-8

In honor of
my mother, Amy I. Solberg Slatta;
and in memory of
my father, Jerome E. Slatta

Contents

Acknowledgments

I wish to thank the many persons and organizations whose guidance, criticism, and financial support facilitated the completion of this study. The late Thomas F. McGann provided the original impetus and direction for the research—and, moreover, his warm friendship. Richard Graham helped me to understand what good historical thought and writing should be. Others who contributed their critical appraisal or other assistance include: Luis Arocena, William H. Beezley, Jonathan C. Brown, Harley Browning, Roberto Cortés Conde, Joe B. Frantz, Carlos Antonio Moncaut, Hugo Nario, the late Luis C. Pinto, Ricardo Rodríguez Molas, Carl E. Solberg, and William B. Taylor. Research was made possible by fellowships granted by the Social Science Research Council, the American Council of Learned Societies, and the Fulbright-Hays Doctoral Dissertation Abroad program.

Material in Chapter 7 has appeared previously in altered form in the *Hispanic American Historical Review*. My thanks to Duke University Press for permission to use the copyrighted material. Small sections of Chapter 5 appeared in *The Americas*, and I thank the Academy of American Franciscan History for permission to reprint those sections. Translations of foreign-language passages are my own unless otherwise indicated.

Finally, a word on what remains to be done in the study of nineteenth-century rural Argentine history. Although I touch briefly upon these topics, major research efforts are needed on internal migration from the interior provinces to the littoral and from rural to urban areas; formation of the ranching elite and development of the ranching economy in general; land tenure patterns; real wages and prices throughout the century; and the position of women in rural society. I hope that my work will provide direction and fuel continued debates that will spur others to add pieces to the historical mosaics of Argentine, frontier, and ranching life of the past century.

Gauchos
and the
Vanishing Frontier

Introduction

During the last third of the nineteenth century, gauchos—migratory ranch hands and horsemen of the Argentine pampa—ceased to exist as an identifiable social group. A juggernaut of legal and political continuities and inexorable social and economic changes forced them to abandon their accustomed way of life and brought frontier life on the pampa to an end. The gaucho, exploited even when deemed useful as a seasonal ranch worker or soldier, faced the relentless oppression of successive administrations acting on behalf of a powerful landed elite that sought to eradicate rather than educate him to twentieth-century life. Established customs of a firmly entrenched gaucho subculture conflicted sharply with the new rights and concepts of private property inherent in Argentina's burgeoning export capitalism.

Vanquished from his beloved pampa, the gaucho gained immortality in the poems and prose of gauchesco writers who wistfully depicted rural life and employed gaucho dialect. This literary and symbolic heritage notwithstanding, the gaucho's extinction epitomized the results of policies pursued by rancher-dominated administrations when throughout the nineteenth century, conflict between the interests of the ranching elite and those of the rural masses formed a central dynamic of Argentine history.

Nineteenth-century Buenos Aires province, the focus of this study, provides an appropriate unit for analyzing the social dynamics of rural society in Argentina. In that century, provincial leaders pushed back hostile pampean Indians and expanded the frontier to encompass some 308,000 square kilometers (119,000 square miles). By 1881 the province's 30.4 million hectares (75 million acres) of rich pasturelands nourished 58 million sheep (86 percent of the nation's total) and 4.8

million cattle (40 percent of the national total). By the early twentieth century, the expanding rural economy had diversified to include 2 million hectares (4.9 million acres) of wheat farms producing 40 percent of the nation's wheat crop. Buenos Aires province, the most politically powerful and populous of the provinces, was the hub and focal point of national history, development, and often controversy throughout the nineteenth century.[1]

This rich, growing province held a gaucho population that is virtually impossible to enumerate. Like other frontier types, wary gauchos avoided census takers and other officials, so government statistics often omit them. Ricardo Rodríguez Molas, Argentina's leading scholar of the gaucho, estimates that the first national census of 1869 may have undercounted the rural population, especially the gaucho, by some 30 percent. Population estimates indicate a growth in the provincial countryside from about 32,000 persons at the onset of the century to between 184,000 and 200,000 at mid-century. The 1869 census recorded 317,320 persons in the Buenos Aires countryside. Perhaps a reasonable estimate would be that one-quarter of the rural population at any given time until the 1870s could be classified as gauchos. Thereafter gauchos disappeared as an identifiable social group, and only ranch workers (peons or *jornaleros*) remained. A census of 1908 recorded only 93,000 men working year-round on provincial ranches and a total of 219,138 men in the countryside counting temporary seasonal ranch hands (mainly sheep shearers).[2]

Although the actual number of gauchos is difficult to discern, their general social condition is much better documented. An accurate portrait of the gaucho and of rural Argentine society has been slowly emerging against a backdrop of often polemical historiography. The predominant so-called liberal interpretation of the Argentine past has described rural society in terms of the conflict between "civilization and barbarism"—between the civilizing *unitarios*, Europeanized leaders in Buenos Aires, and federalist caudillos leading barbarous rural masses in the interior provinces. According to this view, the latter half of the nineteenth century, after the overthrow of the dictator Juan Manuel de Rosas in 1852, represented an era of progress during which backward Indians and gauchos were subdued and supplanted for the national good. Conflict between the elite and the masses did indeed dominate rural social relations during the past century, but not precisely in these terms. The nineteenth century in Latin America has been provocatively reinterpreted by E. Bradford Burns as *The Poverty of Progress*, wherein Europeanized elites progressed at the expense of rural "folk" who unwillingly paid the high cost of uneven "modernization." My findings for Buenos Aires province support Burns's vision of the elite-folk conflict as a central motif in nineteenth-century Latin American history.[3]

Jonathan Brown posits greater economic progress and social justice on the nineteenth-century pampa than most other recent studies of the Río de la Plata region have indicated. Though he admirably supports the case that some economic growth and diversification occurred during the era of traditional technologies to about 1860, Brown erroneously extrapolates his economic data into the social realm. In place of the civilization versus barbarism model of liberal historiography, Brown presents a consensual model of a harmonious rural society in which cowhands, farmers, and ranchers great and small enjoyed considerable progress and well-being. He correctly notes that cowhands on the traditional ranch or *estancia*, enjoyed a degree of economic leverage. They possessed needed equestrian expertise that commanded relatively high short-term wages during roundup and branding seasons on the labor-short pampa. However, Brown incorrectly concludes that this economic advantage was translated into a better social and legal condition for the gaucho. On the contrary, because of the gaucho's economic leverage, ranchers successfully utilized a variety of repressive mechanisms to force him to work. I accept the accuracy of Brown's economic portrait of the pampa but reject his presentation of rural social conditions. Brown failed to consult the critical justice of the peace and police archives and the voluminous correspondence housed in the Secretaría de Rosas archive at the Archivo General de la Nación in Buenos Aires.[4] These sources provide the key to rural social relations.

Brown excepted, most modern students of the rural Río de la Plata present a mosaic of discord, oppression, and social conflict. Ricardo Rodríguez Molas thoroughly documents the genesis of the legal repression of the gaucho during the colonial era in his *Historia social del gaucho*. Land tenure and the formation of the ranching elite await fuller treatment, but studies by Miguel Angel Cárcano, Andrés Carretero, Jacinto Oddone, James R. Scobie, and Carl E. Solberg point in the right direction. John Lynch's recent biography of Rosas adds significant evidence of the dictator's manipulation and exploitation of the rural masses and his furtherance of rancher elite interests. Reid Andrews' lucid analysis, *The Afro-Argentines of Buenos Aires*, documents the discrimination suffered by blacks during the nineteenth century. Many of his observations on elite treatment of and attitudes toward blacks apply equally well to gauchos (who were usually of mixed blood). For neighboring Uruguay, the admirably thorough research on rural history by José P. Barrán and Benjamín Nahum corroborates my findings for Buenos Aires province.[5]

The liberal orthodoxy, long the leading interpretation of the Argentine past, has also come under fire from Rosista scholars who have rehabilitated the dictator as a nationalist hero. Unfortunately, the cost has been high because Rosistas at times distort historical fact to suit present political expediency. The conflict between Rosistas and liberals (during the past century on the battlefield and today in historiographical debates) has obscured the significant continuities of Argentine history. I do not see a sharp break at the fall of Rosas, but rather, continuities in the successful maintenance of rancher political power, in land tenure, and in the rural social relations that persisted before, during, and after the Rosista dictatorship. These continuities, not just the impersonal market forces of so-called modernization, doomed the gaucho's way of life to extinction. To be sure, the socioeconomic changes produced by Argentina's successive intergration into the world market system militated against the gaucho, but those impersonal forces also had a human dimension. A powerful landowning elite shaped the nation's destiny through purposeful legal, economic, military, and political actions. This book seeks to provide a fuller vision of the continuities and changes of Argentine rural society during the past century—a vision unencumbered by the contemporary political and polemical pressures that often constrain Argentine historiography.[6]

Politically charged debate envelops the social origin of the gaucho and the etymology of the term. During the eighteenth century, gauchos developed as a distinct social group of wild cattle hunters who rounded up and slew livestock for their hides. The vast lush grasslands of the frontier pampa, which nourished seemingly endless herds of cattle, horses, and game, molded a unique equestrian lifestyle and subculture and a nearly self-sufficient existence for these skilled horsemen. Pampean history is largely the chronicle of the subjugation and displacement of Indians and gauchos by *terratenientes*, large landowners bent on monopolizing the rich land and its resources. Chapters 1 and 2 define and describe gauchos and their pampean frontier environment.

Responding to changing European market demands, the rural economy and hence the nature of ranch work changed drastically during the nineteenth century. By the independence years, 1810 to 1816, the primitive slaughter of wild cattle for hides and tallow (*vaquería*) had given way to production for the *saladero*, a crude industrial plant that processed hides, by-products, and dried meat (*tasajo*, or charqui). By mid-century, ranchers had diversified into wool production, and merino and other breeds of sheep displaced cattle in better pastures near Buenos Aires. Fencing and farming quickly followed, moving the pampa from a largely pastoral society toward a more complex, mixed economy. By 1900 the *frigorífico*, or modern meat-packing plant, had superseded the saladero and generated a demand for high-grade beef. These myriad rapid changes forced rural workers to learn new skills or to migrate in search of employment, and they reduced or eliminated many tasks performed on the traditional estancia.

Equestrian, macho values of the gaucho subculture shaped rural social relations, but women contributed substantially to the economy and provided what stability the precarious rural family enjoyed. Usually occupied with domestic chores and child-raising, the women also sheared sheep, served as healers and midwives, and filled other essential roles. The same political and juridical continuities and socioeconomic changes so destructive to the gaucho's working life also inhibited the formation of stable family ties on the pampa.

Like ranch work, material culture also changed greatly over these years, except for diet and housing. Outside forces usually imposed the modifications while the gaucho struggled futilely to retain his accustomed way of life. His one-room adobe and thatch hut and his diet of quick-cooked beef and *mate*, or highly caffeinated Paraguayan tea, changed little. But traditional handmade apparel yielded to imported machine-made boots and textiles. The ranching elite worked assiduously to eliminate the old-style dress, diet, and customs in a successful effort to reduce the gaucho's status from self-sufficiency to peonage. Chapters 3, 4, and 5 delineate changes in rural life on the pampa during the nineteenth century.

Restrictions on personal and economic freedom are at the heart of the gaucho's persecuted existence. Argentina's nineteenth-century ruling elite, whether *unitario* or federalist, liberal or conservative, viewed and legally defined gauchos as criminals and forced them into peonage or military service. Landowners expanded latifundism, and successfully directing national and provincial policies toward their own interests and against those of gauchos and other landless rural inhabitants. Chapters 6, 7, and 8 trace the continuing power of the terratenientes, who had managed to eliminate gauchos as a distinctive social group by the 1880s.

Part of the plan of the elite for modernizing the pampa included supplanting and mixing the native population with European immigrants. The wave of millions of foreigners that rolled onto the pampa during the last third of the nineteenth century further eroded the gaucho way of life, skewed the sex ratio toward males, and altered the racial and cultural composition of rural society. Although they were seldom in direct economic competition, gauchos and gringos (a derogatory term that referred to Italians—as well as to other foreigners) sometimes clashed because natives viewed immigrants as harbingers of unwanted change—fencing, farming, railroads. The starkest example of the gaucho's xenophobic reaction was manifested in the massacre of seventeen foreigners in the southern *partido* (county) of Tandil in 1872. Chapters 9 and 10 focus upon the massive socioeconomic changes that, combined with the continuities discussed earlier, doomed the gaucho.

As modernization and massive immigration reshaped the littoral, the Argentine intelligentsia experienced a sense of loss and fear. Argentinidad, the essential Argentine character, seemed in danger of inundation by the foreign floodtide. Nationalists resurrected and rehabilitated the much-maligned gaucho, who became an ideological weapon against the more threatening demands of immigrant workers. As the historical figure receded into the endless pampean horizon, his stylized, romanticized counterpart, subordinated and domesticated, moved onto the literary and symbolic stage—a transformation delineated in Chapter 11. The ruling elite that waged a successful battle to eliminate the gaucho participated in enshrining him in Argentine mythology. As with other figures of history, disdained in life, the gaucho became far more appealing after his passing. His true historical role and significance are described herein. His continuing influence in the constant redefinition of argentinidad gives him transcendental importance in the nation's cultural and ideological formation.

1
Who Was the Gaucho?

The definitive social origin of the gaucho lies shrouded in the mists of the early colonial pampa and mired in the quicksands of academic polemics. The debate over the social origin, that is, the "birthplace" of the gaucho as a distinctive social group, divides roughly into two camps—the Hispanists and the Americanists. The argument strongly resembles the debate over the growth of North American democracy, between proponents of the "germ" theory that focused upon European origins and the frontier interpretation that stressed New World experiences as formative.

Hispanists emphasize either Andalusian or Arabian roots of the pampean equestrian culture. In 1886 Federico Tobal argued that in dress, customs, character, tribal fraternity, and physiology, "everything in the gaucho is eastern and Arabic." Even his music, poetry, "simplicity and democracy" bore an Arabic stamp passed through Andalusia and thence to the pampa. Other Hispanists ignore remote Arabic influences and focus on the Andalusian pastoral culture. Ernesto Quesada, a nationalist writer, asserted in 1902 that gauchos of Argentina were "Andalusians of the sixteenth and seventeenth centuries, transplanted to the pampa." Quesada insisted upon the Spanish heritage carried by the early conquerors as formative and definitive. Eduardo Olivera, prominent rancher and founding member of the Argentine Rural Society of large landowners, and Martiniano Leguizamón, noted folklorist, also concur with the theory of Spanish roots for the gaucho.[1]

Americanists stress the autochthonous development of the gaucho, whom they view as the product of a unique New World frontier environment. Their ranks also bifurcate. Indianism, a minority position best articulated by Vicente Rossi, traces the gaucho back to fierce, nomadic guarani warriors (*hauchús*) of the Banda Oriental, (the "east bank" of the river), the nation of Uruguay since 1826. Rossi sustains his argument with etymological evidence, positing the origin of the term "gaucho" as the Guarani words *hauchó* or *hauchú*. Pablo Blanco Acevedo also supports the Indianist position, citing the *Charruas* of the Banda Oriental as the central influence in the early social formation of the gaucho. The gaucho's use of the Indian *boleadoras*, or bolas, and his addiction to mate, long used in South America, bolster the Indianist argument.[2]

Most Americanists, however, emphasize the gaucho's mestizo heritage—a racial and cultural blending of Indian and Spanish components on the pampean frontier. Though they concur on his New World origins, they diverge greatly on the precise birthplace. Blanco Acevedo, Rossi, and the Franco-Argentine writer Paul Groussac posit the Banda Oriental as the cradle of the gaucho. Emilio R. Coni, a fervent anti-*porteño* federalist (porteño pertains to a resident of Buenos Aires), insists that the province of Santa Fe was the gaucho's homeland. Other writers locate the birthplace on the Argentine littoral amid the vast herds of wild cattle and horses that thrived during the colonial era. In 1601 an anonymous traveler watched bareback riders lasso horses on the pampa near Buenos Aires. Accounts as early as 1730 describe vaquerías in which horsemen rounded up and slew wild cattle for their hides. Manuel Gálvez and Carlos Octavio Bunge distinguish between the *campesinos*, or peasants, of Salta and Jujuy in the interior, who customarily rode mules, and the gauchos of the pampa, who rode horses. It seems likely that gauchos first appeared along the Argentine bank of the Río de la Plata as wild cattle hunters seeking livestock that spread along the river from Asunción, Paraguay, during the late sixteenth and early seventeenth centuries.[3]

If the social origin of the gaucho remains a mystery, the etymology of the term represents an equally complex and refractory question. The word first appeared in the 1743 journal *Noticias secretas de América*, written by two Spanish scientists and navigators, Antonio de Ulloa and Jorge Juan y Santacilia. Describing inhabitants of the mountainous region of Chile, approximately eighty leagues (about 250 miles) from Concepción by their estimate, they referred to "gauchos o gente campestre," using the term generically for rural people. In Argentina, the term first appears in a complaint of 1774 by government officials of gauchos or cattle thieves operating in the Banda Oriental—a wild, largely ungoverned frontier region.[4]

The root of the term inspires lively debate among proponents of Arabic, Andalusian, Basque, French, Gypsy, Hebrew, Portuguese, Quechua, Araucanian, and even English origins, among others. The English painter Emeric Essex Vidal offered the first known, if unlikely, etymology in 1820: "All countrymen are called by the inhabitants of Buenos Ayres *gauchos*, a term, no doubt, derived from the same root as our old English words *gawk* or *gawkey*, adopted to express the awkward, uncouth manners and appearance of those rustics."[5]

Proponents of an indigenous origin form a majority, with most favoring Araucanian. The Araucanian term hauchú and the Quechua word *hauk-cha*, both meaning orphan, seem the likeliest antecedents. Usually the etymological debate, like the conundrum of social origin, smacks more of political and ideological fervor than of scholarly interest. Hispanists and Americanists divide over etymologies, favoring roots consonant with their ideological predispositions. The Argentine historian Antonio J. Pérez Amuchástegui placed the question in perspective: "Surely the gaucho worried very little over the provenance of his generic name."[6]

The gaucho changed greatly over the course of two centuries of hunting and tending livestock, and his name was considerably altered as well. Government officials used the term *gauderio* in 1746 and gaucho in 1774 to describe men who illegally killed cattle for hides and tallow on the pampean frontier. A synonymous term, *changador*, appeared earlier in documents of the Buenos Aires *cabildo*, or town council, in 1729. The changador, often an enterprising peon who went into business for himself by killing and marketing hides without the required license, or *acción*, might be considered the individual precursor of those who later developed into a social group with distinctive values and an equestrian lifestyle: the gauchos of the Río de la Plata frontier.[7]

The whimsical postal inspector Concolorcorvo (pseudonym for Alonso Carrío de la Vandera) frequently refers to gauderios in a guidebook he wrote in the 1770s. In one case, he describes them as idle youths in and around Montevideo who play the guitar "very badly" and sing "out of tune," dress in "ragged underclothes and worse outer garments," skillfully wield lasso, bolas, and knife, and live primarily on handouts. Later he criticizes gauderios in Tucumán who spin tall

tales and sing "obscene verses" accompanied by "badly-strung and
untuned guitars." According to Concolorcorvo, "these farmers, rather
gauderios," who lived miserably in rude huts, formed the majority of
the Tucumán population. He also railed against "rascal gauderios"
who accosted and robbed unwary travelers. Like many colonial
officials, he employed the term gauderio generically to refer to the rural
poor, held to be untrustworthy at best and criminal at worst. In the
1780s the Spanish scientist Félix de Azara used gauderio and gaucho as
synonyms meaning escaped criminals who stole cattle in the Banda
Oriental. Living in frontier regions with captive women, the cattle
thieves ran stolen livestock across the border into neighboring Brazil.
Azara also used several other terms, including peon, *jinete*, and
camilucho, as synonyms to mean rural workers (*jornaleros campes-
tres*). Flexible, shifting connotations and definitions are typical of most
late eighteenth- and early nineteenth-century usage.[8]

The term gaucho meant different things to different social classes.
In general, authorities until the Rosas era imputed a pejorative sense to
all terms applied to cattle herders and the rural landless. To the colonial
bureaucratic eye, with its monopolistic, legalistic viewpoint, anyone
who profited from livestock, except for the few holding royal licenses,
was a criminal. By the late colonial era, smuggling had become a
widespread economic activity; hence, officials considered nearly the
entire rural population to be criminal.[9]

The failure of the English invasions of Buenos Aires in 1806 and
1807 prompted Sir Walter Scott to write a few humorous ethnocentric
lines describing the gaucho of the late colonial era. Near Buenos Aires,
he observed, resides a "sort of Christian savage called guachos [sic],
whose principal furniture is the sculls [sic] of dead horses, whose only
food is raw beef and water, whose sole employment is to catch wild
cattle . . . and whose chief amusement is to ride horses to death. . . .
Unfortunately, they are found to prefer their national independence to
cottons and muslins" from England.[10] The gaucho's martial role in
twice defending the port city against British attack, coupled with later
heroism against the Spanish, marked the beginning of his climb toward
respectability, or at least grudging acceptance by the porteño elite.

During the revolutionary wars of 1810 to 1816 gaucho cavalrymen
fought fiercely and skillfully for the creole patriots. Most gauchos
entered military service because of *levas*, or forced recruitment, rather
than out of patriotic zeal. Black slaves, lured by the promise of freedom

for service, also sometimes joined. High desertion rates for blacks and whites show that patriotism was not foremost in the hearts of many common soldiers, but victory colored the independence era with romance and mythology. Politicians erroneously cited massive battlefield deaths among black patriots that supposedly reduced Afro-Argentine numbers sharply; in fact, desertion accounted for most of those missing from the ranks. But the gaucho troops of Martín Güemes held the Spanish at bay to the north in Salta. Their efforts were rewarded with special privileges, or *fueros*, and they were enshrined in the pantheon of independence heroes. The colonial stigma of contraband cattle hunter and vagabond gave way to an aura of bravery and patriotism. The liberating general of southern South America, José de San Martín, employed the term gaucho in two different communiqués to refer to valiant patriot forces. The porteño creole elite, however, substituted the term *patriotas campesinos* (peasant patriots) for gauchos when publishing the messages in the official *Gaceta ministerial*. To them and to government officials, the gaucho remained unworthy of the patriot forces.[11]

Foreigners exhibited mixed attitudes toward the gaucho but always identified him with the pampean frontier and generally with cattle herding in particular. Henry Marie Brackenridge, who traveled to South America on orders of the United States government in 1817, described gauchos as "those half horse half men" who cared for cattle on estancias or "grazing farms." Alexander Caldcleugh, a Scot who visited Argentina two years later, remarked the healthfulness of the "gauchos, or countrypeople, [who] seem perfectly free from diseases of any kind." During the nineteenth century, the term gaucho became generalized to refer to all native rural workers. Rural inhabitants from wealthy ranchers to slaves were denoted by J. A. B. Beaumont as gauchos, "a general appellation of the country-folks of South America." Foreigners often used the terms gaucho, *paisano* (countryman), and campesino, as Juan and Ulloa had nearly a century earlier, to mean any rural resident. Some derogatory connotations became inured in the use of the term, but these often stemmed from the observers' ethnocentrism, class, and ignorance of pampean life.[12]

An English mining official who journeyed from Buenos Aires to Peru in 1823 recorded various uncomplimentary reactions to the Argentine rural native. He termed gauchos, or natives of the pampas, as "savages . . . an uncouth barbarous race . . . extremely addicted to gambling'' and knife fighting. But he conceded and admired their great skill with the lasso. Another mining entrepreneur noted in 1826 that "the gauchos, or inhabitants of the endless plains called pampas, are, in appearance, a fine race, but, in comparison with the peasantry of England or France, little better than a species of carnivorous baboon."[13]

In 1832 the chargé d'affaires for the United States reported on Argentine rural life and the gaucho. Gauchos lived

> in the incipient stage of civilization—a pastoral people watching the immense herds of cattle horses and sheep which feed on these plains—untaught either in letters, manners, religion or morals:—always mounted they never quit the back of the horse except to throw themselves on a hide to sleep:—they hear mass and hold their convivial meetings on horseback—In some respects they are the most efficient Cavalry in the world—dismount them they are nothing, for they are scarcely able to walk:—constantly engaged in ham-stringing and slaughtering cattle they have engrafted the ferocity of the butcher on the simple habits of the shepherd and are both ignorant and cruel.[14]

Charles Darwin recorded more favorable impressions of the gaucho in his 1833 journal as naturalist aboard HMS *Beagle*. He defined gauchos as "countrymen" and "those who dress in their manner & lead their life," opining that "the gauchos or country people are very superior to those who reside in towns. The gaucho is invariably most obliging, polite & hospitable. I have not met one instance of rudeness or inhospitality." Darwin also commented on the gaucho's penchant for knife fighting, which frequently resulted in bloodshed.[15]

During Rosas' rule from 1835 to 1852, and under his instigation, the term paisano became synonymous with gaucho and referred to all rural residents of the pampa. Shortly after Rosas' fall from power, a writer in the *Agente comerical del Plata* of February 12, 1852, called for an end to the Rosista terminology: the derogatory terms that Rosas had popularized for foreigners (gringos) and for city dwellers (*cajetillas*) carried a stigma that needed to be eliminated. The writer urged that the term paisano be extended to include not only the rural population but all Argentines who loved their country.[16] But the call went unheeded, and paisano continued to refer only to country people.

The antipathy between the urban and rural populations played an important role in defining the gaucho's identity. To the gaucho the city epitomized oppression. The United States minister to Argentina during the 1850s recognized the geographical and social conflict dividing the nation: the "country population are a race peculiar to this country, and may be properly described as those averse to all civilized improvements, and at all times in opposition to the city population." Domingo F. Sarmiento, president of Argentina from 1868 to 1874, interpreted this conflict as one between urban civilization and rural barbarism in his anti-Rosas polemic *Facundo*, written from exile in Chile in 1845. For Sarmiento and many porteño centralist politicians, gauchos represented the barbaric military might of rural federalist caudillos: these ferocious *montoneros*, or irregular cavalrymen, raided, murdered, pillaged, and kept the "gauchocracy" of backward military chieftains in power. To the urban cosmopolitan of Buenos Aires, the gaucho or montonero held the nation's progress ransom with his frontier primitivism and violence. The city dweller and the frontiersman shared a mutual distrust and aversion.[17]

Thomas J. Hutchinson, British consul in Rosario during the 1860s, painted an unflattering portrait of the gaucho in two books of reminiscences published in 1865 and 1868. He stressed gambling as "the moving spirit of existence and enjoyment in the real gaucho." According to Hutchinson, the gaucho spent his life smoking, sipping mate, and riding from one country store and tavern (*pulpería*) to another to drink liquor and gamble. Disputes over cards often ended tragically, with a gaucho "ripping up somebody with his knife after a dispute of the most insignificant nature." But the British consul rejected the image of the gaucho as simply a bloodthirsty, ferocious brute and acknowledged some worth and productivity (albeit slight) in his existence.[18]

During the 1870s, when José Hernández published a two-part poetic defense of the gaucho, *Martín Fierro*, sentiment toward gauchos began to change for the better, a rehabilitation furthered greatly by the poem. Though the elite continued to equate them with vagabonds, outlaws, and montoneros, others stressed their marginal, oppressed condition. As the historical figure faded from the pampa, and the open range frontier closed in the latter decades of the nineteenth century, symbolic and literary evocations arose. The gaucho was lauded and romanticized by nationalists and traditionalists; nevertheless, he became indistinguishable from other rural inhabitants in the minds of many. Paul Groussac broadly defined the gaucho in a lecture to the Chicago World Columbian Exposition of 1893, terming him "any countryman fitted for the riding and breeding labors." Reflecting an idealized vision of the gaucho of old, he noted that, though gauchos still existed on the great Argentine plain, they had been "weakened and impoverished by the contact with civilization."[19] The image of the gaucho as a noble savage, overtaken and debased by urban life, gained considerable currency at the turn of the century.

Discussing the gaucho and his dialect in 1893, the linguist Frederick Mann Page listed several synonyms: " 'Gauchos,' the *hijos del país*, the *criollos*, the *paisanos* of pure strain as they love to name themselves." According to Page's character sketch, based on a racial interpretation, "the average gaucho is generous, crafty, liberal, irreligious, ignorant, immoral, ferocious, hospitable, brave, 'moderately' honest, fond of display, eager for novelty, a natural gambler, libertine and dandy." Unlike many commentators, Page recognized the formative influence of the gaucho's marginal socioeconomic status and noted that the gaucho could have become a "superb specimen of humanity" had he but received the assistance required to make the transition from traditional to modern life.[20]

Definitions and characterizations of the gaucho shifted over time. Racial definitions predominated during the late nineteenth and early twentieth centuries, the heyday of Spencerian and positivistic thought. Leopoldo Lugones, a leader of resurgent Argentine nationalism, considered the infusion of Indian blood in the mestizo gaucho a negative ingredient that resulted in an "inferior subrace" destined for subservience to whites. Juan José de Lezica also disapproved of the debasing mixture of Indian and black blood that weakened the "true creole, descendants of the Spaniards." To Lezica, the mestizo or mulatto paisano of the late nineteenth century was but a "pale, weak, prematurely old shadow" of the gaucho *criollo*, or Argentine rural native. And Groussac welcomed the massive wave of European immigrants, whose influence "completes the purifying" of mestizo blood and thus eliminates the gaucho. Most authorities of the time, including Bartolomé Mitre, Alvaro Barros, and Alonso Criado, defined the gaucho as a mestizo.[21]

Mixed blood probably coursed through the veins of most gauchos, but juridical, cultural, and social rather than racial considerations defined the boundaries of his existence. Sir Francis Bond Head described gauchos who transported his mining equipment nine hundred miles across the pampa in the 1820s as "all colors, black, white and red." Twentieth-century writer Adolfo Bioy Casares recalled that one of the "gauchos most gaucho" he had known was a French immigrant named Cipriano Cross. The man's speech, mannerisms, equestrian and work skills, values, and character, not his ethnic origin, determined his standing as a gaucho. Gauchos were a distinctive social group with a particular subculture—not a separate race.[22]

In Marxist terms, gauchos might have been considered a "class in itself," lacking the class consciousness of a "class for itself."[23] The individualism and dispersion of gauchos across the pampa and the sporadic, seasonal nature of the rural work cycle precluded the formation of either class solidarity or class consciousness. Gauchos do not fit into a schema of slaves, serfs, proletarians, and peasants, however, and thus they represent something of an aberration in classical Marxist theory. Like the serf, the gaucho controlled some of his own labor power and some of the means of production, but he lacked the clearly defined legal rights and obligations inhering in the master-serf relationship. Paid partly with "keep" (room and board, such as it was), and sometimes using his own equipment (mounts, lasso, knife, bolas), the gaucho does not qualify as a proletarian, either. But his hybrid status moved steadily toward that of a proletarian as economic change and the power of the landed elite reduced him to a wage peon who owned none of the means of production.

Ezequiel Martínez Estrada, writer and social critic, provided a useful insight for defining the gaucho. He termed gauchos a "class of the unclassified," thereby emphasizing their social marginality. In reality, the gaucho shifted from one socioeconomic and legal category to another. When contracted as a seasonal ranch worker, paid either by the day or by the month, the gaucho was a wage-earning *peón de campo* (cowhand) or jornalero. That status ended when the work contract ended. When unemployed, which was usually most of the year, he was legally classified as a vagrant. Gauchos were often draft evaders or deserters, generally shunning military service when possible. But a distinctive sociocultural pattern persisted regardless of the gaucho's temporary legal status. His single-mindedly equestrian life shaped his values, and even physiology (permanently bowing his legs). His life reflected a powerful equestrian predisposition, developed over generations of adaptation to the frontier grasslands. Without the horse there could have been no gaucho.[24]

The gaucho partially defined his world and his position in it through personal preferences based on this equestrian subculture. The self-definition created a sense of distinctiveness among gauchos, who scorned those from the city or foreign lands who lacked their skills. But externally imposed aspects of his existence also shaped the gaucho's world—particularly the legal and political structures imposed by the ranching elite. In addition, his environment, the pampean frontier with its distinct topography and peculiar ambience—and, especially, its abundance of livestock—strongly molded his character and is integral in defining him.

2
The Pampa
and Frontier
Abundance

"All grass and sky, and sky and grass, and still more sky and grass."[1] The seemingly interminable pampa sharply molded the lifestyle and character of the horsemen who lived on it, exerting powerful psychological and economic influences over its inhabitants and leaving an indelible stamp that persisted into the twentieth century. The pampean frontier and its abundance of livestock molded the gaucho and shaped those powerful forces that first nurtured and then doomed him.

The sweeping Argentine grassland, or pampa (from a Quechua word meaning "plain") extends from the Gran Chaco region in the north to the Río Colorado, which separates the pampa from Patagonia in the south. It runs more than a thousand kilometers (620 miles) west from the Atlantic Ocean to the Andean foothills. Sloping gently upward to the west to an elevation of some 600 meters (2,000 feet), the pampa in Buenos Aires province is broken only by marshy depressions or *esteros* and by two ranges of hills in the south—the Sierra de la Ventana near Bahía Blanca, some 1,300 meters (4,300 feet) in elevation, and the Sierra de Tandil, rising to about 500 meters (1,640 feet). The eastern or humid pampa receives up to a meter (39 inches) of rainfall per year, but the drier western plains receive only one-fourth that amount.

Early travelers registered vivid impressions of the great grassy plains of the Río de la Plata. Many commented on the violent, unpredictable weather, especially the blustering windstorms or *pamperos* that rained dust, hail, and even insects upon the land. Thomas A. Turner, a British visitor, felt awed by the "mighty wind" from the south, "driving before it myriads of insects, and queer, winged things, and clouds of dust."[2] The pampa, with its endless horizon, broken only by tall grasses, rustling thistles, occasional _ombú_ trees, and decaying bones, seemed an appropriately mysterious haunt for the fascinating "half horse half men" who lived there.

In the 1770s Concolorcorvo described the Merlo Chapel Road leading out of Buenos Aires province to the northwest, the main route to Chile and Peru. Near the port city, there was mostly "pasture country, with an endless number of thistles" used for fuel on the nearly treeless plain. Beyond the village of Luján, with its sixty souls, stood the picturesque town of San Antonio de Areco, astride a meandering stream and surrounded by "many farmers and spacious fields in which all species of cattle are raised." Another traveler who crossed the pampa to Peru in 1789 described a similar scene near Arecife, where he saw "orchards of peach trees, which are the only trees that grow in the pampas."[3] Only the twisted ombú grew on the pampa before the Spanish introduced peach, olive, and other trees for fuel and building material during the seventeenth and eighteenth centuries.

A half-century later, in 1823, an English mining official named Robert Proctor found the pampa near Buenos Aires little changed— "partially cultivated country with fences of prickly pear and aloes." Peach trees grew on some ranches. The narrow track westward from the port was lined with "beautiful clover" but took on a macabre appearance where myriad animal bones filled bogs and deep ruts. "The pampas," recorded the Englishman, "are immense plains extending as far as the eye can reach, with scarcely any diversity of surface, covered with long grass and high thistles, which are so tall as in summer to give the country the appearance of a low forest." The wealth of flora and fauna extended far to the south, broken finally by the granite and marble hills above what is now Tandil (450 kilometers, or 280 miles, southwest of Buenos Aires). The fertility of the southern plain impressed provincial governor Martín Rodríguez, and in 1823 he founded Fort Independence, which later became the city of Tandil. General Rodríguez extolled the "beautiful pastures" of richly carpeted, well-watered coarse grasses, excellent for grazing. The nearby slopes offered shelter from the cold, harsh Patagonian winds. Given the natural abundance of the area, the general predicted that profitable Indian trade would spur the growth of a "populous and rich city."[4]

In his "rough notes" from journeys across the pampa in the mid-1820s, Francis Bond Head delineated three natural regions of the great plain. Radiating westward in an arc of nearly 300 kilometers (190 miles) from Buenos Aires, rich clover and tall thistles flourished on the prairie. During winter, the large, leafy thistles resembled a vast "turnip field," but in spring the plants soared to ten or twelve feet in height and bloomed. The giant weeds formed an impenetrable barrier along the narrow paths on either side of them; then, during the summer, they shriveled and dried, rattling in the wind. In a second large arc of *monte*, extending some 700 kilometers (430 miles) from the port city, long, coarse grasses marked the end of the humid pampa. Beyond lay the dry pampa, covered with low trees and shrubs. As another Englishman observed in 1826, "no lawn was ever laid down with greater precision by the hand of man, than this vast interminable plain has been by nature. Not a stone is to be seen on its surface."[5]

The eccentric ombú (*Phytolacca*), transplanted from the foothills of the Andes by the Spanish, attracted frequent comment and gained a prominent place in gaucho folklore. This giant shrub, not really a tree, grew to girths of forty or fifty feet. As the Anglo-Argentine writer and naturalist William Henry Hudson noted, "the soft and spongy wood [was] utterly unfit for firewood, for when cut up it refused to dry, but simply rots away like ripe water-melon." Its poisonous leaves and unsuitability as a building material render the ombú useless except as shade for man and beast. The huge shrubs also serve as landmarks on the otherwise featureless plains.[6]

Creole and European ranchers added new varieties of orchards to those planted by the Spanish. In 1852 Pedro Luro planted the nation's first eucalyptus trees on his ranch near Dolores. The trees gained great popularity and became fixtures on larger estates by the end of the century. In 1854 an English artist, Robert Elwes, found the pampa not "so utterly destitute of trees as I expected. Many of the roads are lined with weeping willows and poplars, and the hedges are made of huge aloes (Agave)." Watching the sun set over the pampa, he saw "nothing but thistles, dark purple in the distance, then reddish and brown in the foreground; but nothing else for miles and miles."[7]

Except for the addition of more varieties of trees, the physical features of the pampa changed little through the 1860s. George Catlin, a North American painter of frontier subjects, notably Indians, visited Argentina late in the 1860s. His portrayal differs little from those of forty years earlier, as he describes the "vast level plains, not unlike the great prairies of the Platte and Arkansaw, excepting that they are covered with high weeds instead of short grasses; and amongst those weeds, of which there are many kinds, there are wild flowers of all colours."[8]

Part of the pampa's fascination and mystery stemmed from the startling mirages produced by its great distances and flatness. Elwes recalled seeing "a good deal of mirage floating about, and sometimes they appeared to be skirting a large lake; sometimes the plain seemed bounded by steep cliffs, reflected in the water; then all would change again and vanish." George A. Peabody, a Massachusetts gentleman on a shooting expedition to the Río de la Plata in the late 1850s, felt transfixed by the ghostly images. He recorded in his diary: "We could see what it was impossible not to believe to be lakes; the water was perfectly distinct & also the shores, & when we approached, the whole thing melted away . . . Animals feeding upon the pampa were distorted into the most enormous size, or were turned upside down & some little stunted bushes turned into large trees."[9]

Besides creating elusive, baffling mirages, the pampa also played strongly upon the sojourner's emotions. Near Azul in the late 1840s, William MacCann, a British investor, "awoke during the night, and beheld the moon shining forth with a softened splendour, while a stillness so absolute that the pulse of nature seemed to have ceased to beat, reigned around. A sense of inexpressible grandeur and solemnity pervaded my mind." Others echoed MacCann's metaphysical musings and evoked, many through maritime imagery, the absolute isolation, mystery, and profound silence of the great frontier grassland. Robert B. Cunninghame Graham, author of numerous telling sketches of Argentine life, conveyed the mysterious telluric force of the pampa, where "all was spacious—earth, sky, the waving continent of grass; the fierce and blinding storms, and, above all, the feeling in men's minds of freedom, and of being face to face with nature, under those southern skies."[10]

In pondering the power and influence of the pampean frontier environment, Frederick Jackson Turner's classic interpretation of the frontier in the United States comes readily to mine. In 1893, this young Wisconsin scholar delivered a seminal lecture on "The Significance of the Frontier in American History." He attributed the "individualism, democracy, and nationalism" of the American people and the peculiarities of the nation's legal and political institutions to the effect of successive frontier experiences. In Turner's eyes, the frontier molded the American into a new being, with sharp antipathy to control . . . coarseness and strength combined with acuteness and inquisitiveness; that practical, inventive turn of mind, quick to find expedients; that masterful grasp of material things, lacking in the artistic but powerful to effect great ends; that restless, nervous energy; that dominant individualism, working for good and for evil, and withal that buoyancy and exuberance which comes with freedom—these are traits of the frontier, or traits called out elsewhere because of the existence of the frontier.[11]

The imagery and influences Turner evoked with his nebulous term "frontier" resonate closely with evocations of the pampa by the Brazilian-born French writer Emilio Daireaux in 1888. Daireaux, who owned land near Caseros in Buenos Aires province, foreshadowed in his thinking some of Turner's notions about the impact of a plains frontier environment. He attributed great formative influence to the plains, steppes, savanna, pampa, and other flat grasslands of the world, which gave rise to equestrian subcultures. The gaucho, Mongol, Cossack, and cowboy, according to Daireaux, developed a "passion for independence" and accepted material misery as the price of liberty. Strongly individualistic, of robust constitution, and indifferent to material well-being, the plainsman, like Turner's frontiersman, stood apart from other men. In short, the plains imprint a similar character upon their inhabitants around the world. In 1845, well before either Turner or Daireaux, Domingo Faustino Sarmiento had linked the importance of the pampean environment to the peculiar characteristics and lifestyle of the gaucho, in *Facundo*, his influential anti-Rosas polemic.[12]

Turner has been soundly criticized for lacking clarity and precision in his frontier theory, and Daireaux could be faulted for overlooking cultural and temporal differences among the horsemen he described. Nevertheless, the formative influence of the frontier or plains cannot be dismissed lightly. David M. Potter, in a provocative interpretation of United States history and national character, refined Turner's vision of the frontier, arguing that the western geographical frontier remained a central factor in American development only so long as it represented the nation's main source of abundance. The natural resources and potential wealth in open frontier lands, not the frontier per se, shaped American character during the nineteenth century. The United States government promoted quick settlement of the west through generous land laws, and the acquisition of land in pre-industrial America provided a means of upward economic mobility for many settlers. The immense natural wealth of the continent in varied forms strongly molded the values and national character of Americans. Walter Prescott Webb pushed further the importance of abundance by postulating that the land, gold, and silver of the New World acted as a motor driving a four-century economic boom for the European metropolis.[13]

Like the western plains of the United States, the livestock-rich pampa also held great natural riches, but the frontier in Argentina functioned differently than in the United States. Blessed with vast expanses of fertile, open land, hard-pressed Argentine governments chose to lease and sell public lands as political rewards rather than to encourage settlement and population diffusion through small land grants. The extensive nature of ranching also encouraged landowners to spread herds widely across large tracts of pastureland. Speculators and wealthy terratenientes, ably supported by local officials, monopolized the open range and quickly incorporated public lands into private holdings. Some land subdivision (mostly near Buenos Aires) occurred among sheep ranchers and farmers, but vast tracts, often up to 300 square kilometers (74,130 acres) in size, remained common on the pampa. Among smaller ranchers, rental agreements with large landowners—not individual ownership—persisted throughout the nineteenth century. These great cattle estates discouraged and retarded settlement rather than promoting it. Population expansion did not accompany the nation's territorial expansion, and except near Buenos Aires, the plains remained largely devoid of human residents. As Ezequiel Martínez Estrada observed in his *X-Ray of the Pampa*, "cattle do not require populations—they are the population. They are contrary to society and displace and dissolve it."[14] None of the effects imputed to the frontier by Turner, sometimes erroneously or in exaggerated fashion, functioned on the Argentine pampa.

Although the frontier did not operate precisely according to the Turnerian thesis, either in the American West or on the Argentine plains, the natural abundance of both areas did exert powerful but diverse influences. Europeans who visited North America marveled at the largess enjoyed by the inhabitants. Concerning the American diet, William Cobbett noted in 1817 that "you are not much pressed to eat and drink, but such an abundance is spread before you . . . that you instantly lose all restraint." Alexis de Tocqueville remarked Americans' "love of equality and of freedom; but God Himself gave them the means of remaining equal and free by placing them upon a boundless continent."[15] De Tocqueville saw abundance as promoting both democracy and individualism.

Frontier abundance also played a central but very different role in shaping the character of the gaucho. The pampa abounded in wildlife—ostriches and other game birds, rodents like nutrias and *vizcachas*, armadillos, pumas, and leopards. The rich grasslands also permitted the few head of livestock that strayed away from the Spanish during the sixteenth century to multiply rapidly into immense, prolific herds. From the colonial era onward, visitors expressed awe at the plentiful supply of horses and cattle on the pampa. Thomas Falkner, a Jesuit missionary who proselytized among Indians of Patagonia and southern Buenos Aires province, noted the effect of nature's bounty upon the inhabitants: "this great plenty of horses and horned cattle is supposed to be the reason, why the Spaniards and the Indians do not cultivate their lands with the care and industry which they require, and that idleness prevails so much among them."[16] Agricultural and manual labor found little rationale or favor in the livestock-rich Río de la Plata where sustenance in the form of beef was there for the taking.

Throughout the colonial era, the rural population lived a miserable life in earthen shanties, suffering from the continual threat of Indian raids and irregular supplies of such food as wheat for bread. But the unlimited supply of free or cheap meat prevented anyone from starving, a circumstance enjoyed by few peoples in the world. Such was the excess that meat had no commercial value until the late eighteenth century, when saladeros began processing jerked beef for export to slave plantations in Cuba and Brazil. Concolorcorvo reported that meat was so plentiful in Buenos Aires that, should a quarter of beef fall from a cart headed for market, no one, including the driver, would bother to retrieve it. Not even beggars had to scavenge for meat because *mataderos*, or slaughterhouses, gave it away. Although he recognized the surplus of meat, Concolorcorvo could not overcome the cultural and economic values of his native Spain. He criticized the gauderio for wasting meat by skinning animals for their hides, which had commercial export value, and leaving the carcasses to rot. Such seeming waste, unthinkable in Europe, made economic sense on the cattle-rich pampa.

Another visitor of about the same time described the influence of plenty upon the character of the rural population:

> The abundance of the necessaries of life encourages, among the lower orders, a propensity of idleness, which has given rise to another order of strollers, called *Gauderois* [*sic*]. Their mode of life resembles that of the *Gypsies*. They are badly clothed; their whole dress consisting only of a coarse shirt, and a worse upper garment. These articles of dress, together with horse furniture, serve them for bedding, and a saddle for a pillow. They stroll about with a kind of small guitars, to the sound of which they sing ballads.[17]

This accurate if ethnocentric observation identified the nexus between the colonial rural lifestyle and the ready sufficiency of life's sustaining elements available on the frontier without regular conventional labor, in European terms.

Based on his observations during the 1780s, Félix de Azara also criticized Río de la Plata residents for idleness. He deplored their "natural inclination to kill animals and cattle with enormous waste, repugnance toward all occupations not involving running and mistreating horses, gambling at cards, drunkenness and robbery." Most Europeans recognized the remarkable largess of the pampa but rejected the logical consequence—a lifestyle premised upon playfulness and leisure, not work; upon plenty, not scarcity. A dour work ethic like that ingrained into the Puritan settlements of inhospitable Massachusetts never developed on the Argentine plain. To many foreigners, cattle workers appeared to be cavorting rather than laboring as they raced about on horseback, yelling, herding, and lassoing horses and cattle. According to Henry Marie Brackenridge, a United States diplomat, gauchos, "the name given to the country people in general," drove horses more for sport than for profit. "Horses are so abundant and cheap that the best can be had for only a few dollars"; hence their care represented no pressing economic need. The American recognized his own prejudice in deeming the gaucho wild and indolent; "but it must be remembered that we also of the north, are reproached by Europeans for our carelessness of time, and our lazy habits." Many other travelers also acknowledged the centrality of the pampa's abundance in molding the gaucho's lifestyle. As Sir Edmond Temple observed, gauchos "are indifferent about any thing that is beyond their reach, and set no value on that which is hard to be acquired."[18] If left alone, they lived humble but contented lives.

Darwin recorded many acute perceptions about pampean life in his journal, but he could not overcome his own cultural conditioning. Near Mercedes in 1833, he asked two men why they did not work. "One said that the days were too long; the other that he was too poor. The number of horses & profusion of food is the destruction of all industry." Steeped in the Protestant work ethic, Darwin could not accept idleness as a valid condition even when nature's bounty supplied most necessities. William MacCann better understood the different conditions that obtained on the pampean frontier. After killing a branded heifer for food, he explained that such an action was "so common on the frontier, particularly when travelers are benighted, or unable to obtain other food, that the morality of the deed is measured by a very different scale to cattle-lifting in Britain."[19] Wild cattle continued to roam the pampa through the 1860s, providing free meat for the taking.

A further aspect of frontier abundance, the profusion of wild horses, played a central role in shaping the gaucho's way of life. As MacCann noted, "the natives, when without a horse . . . simply assert that they are 'without feet'; whatever work is to be done, either in collecting, marking, driving, or taming cattle, must be done on horseback." An anonymous couplet made the same point humorously:

> My wife and my horse
> have gone to Salta.
> My wife can stay,
> but I miss my horse![20]

Visitors expressed amazement at the gaucho's determination to perform every possible task on horseback. A Scot recorded, in the 1820s: "The Buenos Ayrian is continually on horseback: the nets in the river are drawn from the saddle, and the Gaucho bathes from the horse, and swims round it.—The mounted beggar stands at the corner of the street, and asks charity; his horse is no more proof of his being undeserving of alms than the trowsers of the English mendicant."[21]

Gauchos hunted on horseback, whirling boleadoras with great accuracy to catch ostriches and other small game. They also developed a novel method for catching small birds, such as partridges, without dismounting. As Vidal recalled in 1820, the rural Argentine, "who never stirs but on horse back, provides himself with a noose of twisted horse-hair, at the end of a long Paraguay cane, or bamboo. From his elevated position he sees the birds running; as he approaches, they crouch and suffer him to pass close to them, when he drops the noose over their heads, and raising the bamboo, secures his prize." Captain Joseph Andrews, British merchant and mining speculator, enjoyed a tasty meal of partridges, each snared by the neck and "drawn up like a fish" by a galloping gaucho with pole and noose.[22]

William Henry Hudson, who grew up on ranches in Quilmes and Chascomús during the Rosas dictatorship of the 1830s and 1840s, knew rural life firsthand. A fervent admirer of the gaucho's horse-manship and a skilled rider himself, he described the great transforma-tion that occurred when a gaucho dismounted. Bowlegged from a lifetime in the saddle, the gaucho "waddles in his walk; his hands feel for the reins; his toes turn inwards like a duck's." Recalling Darwin's criticism of the gaucho's seeming laziness, Hudson disagreed. The gaucho literally never learned to walk or developed appropriate musculature. His entire physical and psychological being focused on riding. This "supposed indolence," in Hudson's view, derived from observations of gauchos afoot. As Don Segundo Sombra reflected bitterly in the novel by Ricardo Güiraldes, "a gaucho on foot is fit for nothing but the manure pile."[23]

Many Argentine writers recounted the preeminent position of the horse in rural society. Juan María Gutiérrez, inspiration to the brilliant anti-Rosas intellectuals of the Generation of 'Thirty-seven, wrote, "My horse was my life, / my wealth, my only treasure." In 1838, future Argentine president Bartolomé Mitre published "The Gaucho's Horse," the story of an aging gaucho who wished to die when his horse did. Sarmiento, in exile in Chile in 1842 because of the Rosas dictatorship, recalled the chagrin and disgrace of Angel Vicente Peñalosa, nicknamed El Chacho, the fierce caudillo of La Rioja province. Forced to flee on foot over the Andes to Chile after defeat by a rival chieftain, El Chacho was asked how he fared. "How can you ask, friend!" he replied. "In Chile and on foot!"[24] To the caudillo, being unmounted was as much of an ignominy as having suffered defeat and exile.

Travelers at mid-nineteenth century recorded many colorful aspects of equestrian life on the pampean frontier. One observed the traditional manner of drawing water from a *jagüel*, or well: "A woman on horseback with a lasso attached to her saddle, let down a hide bucket, and then riding away, drew it up to a man, who emptied the contents into another vessel; but these people can do nothing without horses."[25] An American who walked across the pampa learned that a man on foot was such an oddity that cattle might mistake him for "some unknown beast of prey" and attack or run away in fright.[26] An Englishman witnessed a funeral procession in which the corpse, "dressed and placed by his comrades in the usual position on his horse," rode to his own burial.[27] The determination and imagination of the gaucho to perform all tasks on horseback appeared boundless.

The gaucho not only remained mounted whenever possible, he also assiduously avoided any labor on foot. Alfredo Ebelot, a French engineer who helped construct Adolfo Alsina's long ditch, designed to hinder Indian raiders on the southern frontier, sensed the displeasure of the six hundred men digging the enormous trench. To them such "servile" footwork suited only immigrants. Regular pay and rations helped assuage the workers' qualms, however, and they labored well, if grudgingly.[28] In general, a clear ethnic division of labor developed on the pampa. Natives performed mounted ranch work, and foreigners occupied themselves with such footwork as digging ditches, fencing, and other mechanical and agricultural pursuits.

Wilfred Latham, an English rancher whose long residence on the pampa made him an astute observer, captured the excitement of riding across the great plain:

> I cannot conceive anything more exhilarating than a gallop across the plains of Buenos Ayres on a bright, clear morning, or in the cool of the afternoon or evening; a cloudless sky of deep azure, an atmosphere marvellously light and pure communicating a sense of indescribable buoyancy and pleasurable existence—a soft breeze flowing, as it were, over the vast plain, boundless as an ocean—contribute to engender an irresistible feeling of joy.[29]

Had the gaucho, unlettered and uncultured, possessed Latham's facility with written language, he probably would have expressed similar sentiments about his frontier habitat and the equestrian life.

In addition to its economic and social significance, the horse occupied a prominent position in pampean folklore and superstition. No gaucho, for example, rode a mare. Mares carried gear as pack animals, pulled carts or stagecoaches, or met their fate at the slaughterhouse, valued only for hides and by-products. The gaucho aspired to own a *tropilla* (herd) of a dozen or so horses, matched in color if possible. An Englishman recalled in 1823 that "the gauchos or natives of the pampas are particularly choice in the colours of their horses, the most esteemed being roan and pyeballed." This was not a silly affectation: the color matching developed in a frontier region where neither fences or legal boundaries delineated land and animal ownership, and where an owner could more readily identify a lost, stray, or stolen horse if he had a matched herd. Juan Manuel de Rosas extended this notion by recommending that bulls of the same color be purchased and bred to facilitate identification.[30]

The gaucho's *pingo*, the hardy, compact creole horse of the pampa, went the way of his master as the open frontier disappeared in the late nineteenth century. Purebred and mestizo animals (mixed European and native) supplanted purely native stock. On January 21, 1900, *El pueblo* of Azul lamented the disappearance of the *caballo criollo*, which was rapidly being displaced by imported English breeds. The newspaper suggested the need to preserve the creole horse and the creole man—the gaucho—both endangered species on the pampa gringa, filled with immigrants. Twentieth-century horse fanciers led by Emilio Solonet did establish an organization to breed and perpetuate criollo horses.[31]

As the gaucho and his pingo yielded to foreign imports, so too did the pampa itself change. Coarse natural grasses that had fostered the tremendous abundance so formative to the gaucho's character gave way to the plowman's alfalfa, corn, and wheat. The Spanish philosopher José Ortega y Gasset reflected on the sad paradox of life on the great Argentine plain. "Those promises of the pampa, so generous, so spontaneous, many times go unfulfilled . . . In truth, the creole spirit is filled with broken promises and radically suffers a sublime discontent."[32] Once central to the ranch economy and (as a frontier cavalryman) to its defense, the gaucho became an anachronism and a pariah. The closing of the frontier in Buenos Aires province also ended the demand for and acceptance of the gaucho's skills, values, and lifestyle. Argentina's land invited new forms of exploitation—sheep raising and agriculture—as the pro-European elite pushed for economic integration into the world market system. Rural labor and working conditions changed markedly as the pampean economy diversified and modernized.

r

3
Gaucho to Peon: Changing Ranch Labor

As ranching modernized, workers who were already buffeted by seasonal fluctuations in the labor demand found even fewer employment opportunities. Large ranchers took restrictive legal actions against the gaucho to insure an adequate supply of workers at wages they wished to pay during peak seasons. Wages rose during the century, but drastic alterations like these legal sanctions and shrinking economic opportunities dictated a deteriorating quality of life for the gaucho. The fragmented Argentine labor movement did not successfully incorporate rural workers.

Labor requirements on the traditional cattle ranch of the colonial and early national periods seldom exceeded one worker per thousand animals. Extensive herds of semi-wild cattle ranged over unfenced natural grasslands, frequently crossing hazily delineated property lines. In 1800 Félix de Azara estimated that a single foreman and ten peons could handle a herd of ten thousand. Two years later, Miguel Lastarria agreed, asserting that a foreman with four workers could tend four to five thousand head grazing over three leagues of land (20,000 acres). According to Emilio Daireaux, in 1888 fencing and other modifications in the ranch economy had reduced labor needs to a single foreman and one peon per 10,000 hectares (24,710 acres).[1] In effect ranch labor demand had been reduced by a factor of five.

As frontier militiamen (usually conscripted gauchos) pushed back the frontier and reduced the threat of Indian incursions, the number of ranches and the area under grazing in the province expanded. Sheep raising also added jobs in the rural sector. But these expanding elements in the pastoral economy did not fully offset the decline in the number of workers needed because of modernizing changes. To be sure, the number of cattle hides exported from Buenos Aires rose during the first half of the century. During the decade of the 1820s, the figure rose a modest 8.6 percent from the decade before. The 1830s showed a larger but still moderate rate of increase (28 percent) over the 1820s. During the 1840s, however, exports nearly doubled over the previous decade. Not surprisingly, the Rosista dictatorship took harsh, repressive legal and military measures to subdue gauchos and force them to work on labor-short provincial estancias. During the modernizing period beginning in the 1860s, cowhands faced bleaker, more variable prospects. Between 1866 and 1875 the number of cattle in the province declined from 6 million to 5.1 million, and the number of sheep fell 24 percent from 60 million to 45.5 million. The sheep flocks recovered to 57.8 million by 1881 but fell back to 51.6 million in 1888. Cattle herds fell to 4.8 million head in 1881 before surging to 8.7 million head by 1888.[2] To offset the cut in labor requirements due to modernization, however, herds would have to expand five-fold, and this did not occur.

In addition to the trend of falling ranch worker demand in the nineteenth century, abrupt seasonal changes also plagued laborers. José María Jurado of the Argentine Rural Society detailed shifting labor requirements on the traditional estancia during its waning days in 1875. After day laborers had rounded up herds on the open range, a reduced force of permanent salaried workers handled them. During the first week, when the cattle still acted wild and frisky, three peons per thousand head rode herd during the day. Eight men per thousand rode nightwatch *(ronda)* and another four served as a relief crew. During the second week, as animals became tamer and more accustomed to grazing within a given area *(aquerenciar)*, the work force was cut in half. Still later, just two men per thousand rode nightwatch, and by the second or third month, a single rider tended a herd of one thousand day or night. Jurado counseled ranchers to round up their herds during the late autumn months of April, May, and June because spring roundups conflicted with sheep shearing, thereby provoking serious labor shortages throughout the countryside. Most workers found employment for only a few days or weeks at any one ranch and then had to move elsewhere.[3]

The marked seasonality of ranch work persisted on the modern ranch. A skeleton crew handled the routine day-to-day chores, and special labor-intensive tasks fell to a floating pool of migrants paid by the day or by the task. With the aid of herd dogs, one man in an enclosed pasture *(puesto)* did the work of four or five on the open range.[4] Frequently unemployed, the worker on the modern ranch also enjoyed fewer supplementary economic opportunities as wild cattle and other game became increasingly rare and as fencing and legal restrictions eliminated pursuits of the old pampean frontier.

In 1886 Florentino Ameghino, one of the nation's foremost scientists, urged in vain that landowners utilize workers during the off season. Peons could plant trees, build watering tanks, and alleviate water drainage and retention problems that plagued the pampa during severe cycles of drought and flood. He saw two advantages to such employment: workers would be occupied productively instead of being condemned to a forced life of idleness, and needed environmental improvements would be completed.[5]

According to a 1908 rural census, only 42 percent of adult male livestock workers found year-round employment in Buenos Aires province. Half worked only during the brief summer shearing season. Women and children performed many of the routine, unmounted tasks on the modern ranch, and they accounted for 42 percent of the year-round ranch labor force even though they comprised only one-quarter of all ranch workers, who numbered 293,114. In neighboring Santa Fe province, 70 percent of the adult males worked year-round on ranches, considerably better than the low figure for Buenos Aires province.[6]

Given the fluidity of demand and the short-term nature of many ranch jobs, worker turnover was high on the traditional ranch. At two of Rosas' holdings in San José de las Flores, the "Rosario" and "San Benito" ranches, the quarterly turnover rate for peons generally ran from about 40 to 50 percent during the early 1840s. Foremen *(capatazes)*, who usually earned 50 percent more than a common peon, remained on the job longer than did monthly ranch workers. For the eighteen-month period ending in June 1844, only 24 percent of the peons at work in December 1842 remained on the two ranches, whereas 65 percent of the capatazes retained their jobs. The number of foremen remained nearly constant at 26, but the number of peons rose and fell with seasonal demands. Employment peaked at 66 for the two ranches during the first quarter of 1843, dropped for three quarters, rose slightly at the end of the year, and bottomed at 40 during the first quarter of 1844. Quarterly fluctuation ranged as high as a 22-percent increase and

Table 1:
Worker Retention Rates and
Labor Force Fluctuations, Rosas Estancias, 1842–44

Quarter	Workers Remaining at End of Quarter				Change in Peons (%)
	No. Foremen	%	No. Peons	%	
4th/1842	26/26	100	46/54	85	—
1st/1843	19/26	73	37/66	56	+22
2d/1843	21/25	84	31/58	53	−12
3d/1843	25/27	93	44/51	86	−12
4th/1843	23/26	88	33/53	62	+4
1st/1844	26/26	100	24/40	62	−25
4th/1842–					
2d/1844	17/26	65	13/54	24	+35

Source: Reports from María Herrera de Peredo to Juan Manuel de Rosas, 1842–44, AGN X 26 4 2.

a 25-percent decrease in the number of peons employed. The number of workers varied as much as 26 percent from the mean of 54 for the period. Table 1 indicates the percentages of foremen and peons remaining at the end of each quarter, as well as changes in the total employed. The high retention rate for peons during the third quarter of 1843 reflects a substantial pay increase granted at that time.[7]

The modern ranch reduced the total number of workers required but offered little additional security for the smaller permanent labor force. Records for two ranches administered by the firm of Farran and Zimmerman in 1911 reveal seasonal fluctuations in the labor force. At "Los Oscuros," the permanent staff peaked at 33 in January, fell gradually throughout the year, and bottomed at 22 in November—a reduction of one-third from the beginning of the year. At "Espartillar Chico," the work force varied less and remained closer to the annual average of 20. The July peak of 23 and the December nadir of 17 represent only a 15-percent fluctuation from the mean. Payment records from the Willim Walker estancia indicate seasonal fluctuations as great as those on the traditional ranch. Between May 1902 and May 1906 the ranch employed an average of 35 workers during any given month. The actual number varied between a low of 21 and a high of 51.

For example, between January and March 1903, the number of workers fell from 43 to 26, a 40-percent reduction. Between May and August 1904, the number rose from 23 to 40. Seasonal changes, combined with larger fluctuations in world market conditions, dictated economic uncertainty for the modern ranch peon. Short-term, uncertain employment plagued both the gaucho of the nineteenth century and his modern counterpart on the pampa gringa—the Europeanized, modernized plains.[8]

Paradoxically, although thousands of workers could find jobs for only brief periods during the year, ranchers from the colonial era on inveighed bitterly against labor shortages on the pampa. The politically powerful terratenientes early sought recourse through the political and judicial systems to assure themselves an adequate supply of workers at wages they were willing to pay. Vagrancy laws, labor contracts, military conscription, and passport requirements served equally well in regulating the rural work force, in controlling rural crime, and in providing cannon fodder for the army and frontier militia. Ranchers faced an additional problem created by the pampa's natural abundance: gauchos could subsist without working by felling a wild or strayed beef or downing ostriches and other small game for feathers and pelts. Rural judicial history from the mid-eighteenth century on consists mainly of attempts by ranchers and government officials to subjugate this dispersed and independent labor force, the migratory gaucho.[9]

Besides seeking restrictive labor legislation to control the errant gaucho, ranchers utilized slave labor on their estancias. The revolutionary government closed the slave trade in 1813 and set into motion several methods of gradual emancipation of slaves, but slavery persisted in Buenos Aires province until 1861. Between 1813 and 1818 some two thousand blacks from the city of Buenos Aires served in the patriotic army with the promise of freedom thereafter. The *ley de libertad de vientres*, or free birth law, of 1813 mandated emancipation for slave children at marriage or when they came of age (they were called *libertos*). These measures to end slavery reduced the subjugated labor pool of the province, thus exacerbating an already serious labor shortage, and motivated ranchers to seek further legislation to control gauchos and other rural laborers.[10]

Rosas, serving as ranch administrator for his cousins, the wealthy and powerful Anchorena family, began buying slaves for their ranches in 1822. He continued the practice of employing slave labor and freed blacks on his own holdings through the 1830s. An 1836 census of his eight ranches in the partido of Monte shows that blacks comprised 29 percent of the total ranch labor force, 54 of 154 peons. Blacks formed a majority (29 of 46) on his second largest ranch, "Los Cerillos," and made up a sizable minority (14 of 35) on the third largest ranch, "San Génaro." Two blacks and one white worked on a small puesto, "Las Viscacheras." Rosas reinstated the slave trade in 1831, during his first term as provincial governor, and the traffic in slaves continued throughout the decade. Police records also mysteriously disappeared in 1831, permitting slave owners to keep in bondage many libertos who should have been freed by the free birth law of 1813.[11]

Slavery persisted in Argentina under the Rosas dictatorship, from 1835 to 1852, and after. Rosas issued a decree on September 14, 1840, ordering all slaves owned by the opposition *unitarios* to be drafted into military service. This served the dual purpose of denying his enemies needed laborers and soldiers and of swelling the ranks of his own forces. In July 1845 he issued a decree relating to the murder of a slave named José in San Isidro, evidence of the persistence of the institution. The province had never ratified the national constitution of 1819, which abolished slavery. The new constitution of 1853 reaffirmed abolition, but the province of Buenos Aires continued the institution for another eight years.[12]

Even with the legal restrictions imposed upon the gaucho and the use of slaves, rural labor needs were not being met. Ranch workers could therefore sometimes demand and obtain relatively high wages during peak seasons, but wages fluctuated greatly from year to year. Wages in gold pesos rose gradually during the century. In the latter half of the eighteenth century, cowhands earned about 6 gold pesos per month, plus food. By 1804 the wage for peons had only reached 7.5 pesos, and at mid-century it was 10 pesos. Wages in 1864, 12 pesos, by 1904 had reached 15. Thus in the century 1804–1904, the wage for a ranch hand had doubled—an increase far less than that in pastoral export prices. Wages earned by peons on Rosas' estancias rose in terms of paper pesos from 1836 through 1846 but declined in 1849. On the other hand, in real terms the wages paid peons dropped sharply in 1839, climbed again through 1844, but then fell for the remainder of the decade. According to John Lynch, by 1850 the paper peso had lost more than half its 1835 gold value, and this deflation hurt peons who were paid in paper currency. Table 2 shows the changes in paper and

Table 2:
Peon Wages Paid by
Juan Manuel de Rosas, 1836–49

	Wages in Paper Pesos	Real Wage Index
1836	40	100
1838	50	104
1839	50	59
1842	60	66
1843	100	114
1844	150	204
1845	150	180
1846	150	125
1849	120	123

Sources: Reports by Pascual Peredo, "Rincón del Rosario" and "San Benito" estancias, 1836, AGN X 25 2 5; 1838, 1839, AGN X 25 6 6; María Herrera de Peredo, "Rincón del Rosario," 1842, 1843, AGN X 26 4 2; Dionisio Schöo, "San Martín," 1839, AGN X 25 8 3; 1843, AGN X 26 4 2; 1844, 1845, AGN X 43 2 8; 1846, AGN X 26 5 4; 1849, AGN X 26 8 4. Wage index based on conversion of paper peso to gold equivalent; conversion rates from Jacinto Oddone, *La burguesía terrateniente argentina*, p. 136.

real wages on the Rosas establishments from 1836 through 1849. The rise in wages 1843–44 occurred because of serious worker shortages on several ranches. In December 1842, Basilio Páez, manager of "Rincón del Rosario," complained of a widespread shortage of monthly peons. Many ranchers had only the services of foremen, lacking peons altogether. From "San Martín," manager Dionisio Schöo reported a hampering shortage of horse tamers, or *domadores*. Further, a serious drought limited the number of work horses available.[13]

In January 1843 Páez informed Rosas that he had advanced wages to three workers to insure their services when he needed them most. He complained of the great difficulty of finding monthly workers for mounted tasks and even more for the footwork disdained by the gaucho. April rains ended the long summer drought and permitted Páez to begin the branding of stock (the *hierra*, or *yerra*).[14] High demands for day laborers at all ranches for the hierra drove wages higher and stimulated an even greater shortage of monthly workers. Gauchos preferred to work for higher daily wages during the busy branding season.

Ranchers faced continued labor shortages throughout the 1840s because heavy demands for soldiers took many peons from ranches and put them in uniform, or drove them away to avoid the draft. Remaining workers often accepted seasonal employment at higher daily wages rather than taking permanent but lower salaried work. Rosas sometimes contracted peons from interior provinces who were not subject (in theory) to local conscription laws. Laureano Ramírez, manager of "Chacabuco," complained in May 1847 that he needed an additional forty or fifty men just to handle the routine work of the ranch and *volteadas*—the rounding up, corraling, and branding of semi-wild cattle. In June 1849 Schöo reported difficulty in finding either monthly or daily peons for the "San Martín" ranch. Workers, he felt, demanded daily wages that "their work does not justify." Because he lacked sufficient help, he had to cope with many chores shorthanded, hurrying work instead of giving each task the attention and thoroughness it required.[15]

Complaints of ranch hand shortages appeared seldom later in the century, as modern techniques and masses of European immigrants and internal migrants narrowed the gulf between labor supply and demand. The laments of Rosista managers of excessively high wage demands and worker shortages do not appear in the records of the William Walker estancias in the early twentieth century. By the 1890s, when wages fell sharply after the financial collapse of the Baring brothers' investment house in England, cowhands had lost their principal bargaining chip—high seasonal demand for ranch skills that they alone possessed. *Estancieros* were able to reduce the highest fixed cost of the traditional ranch: peon wages. Harsher, gloomier labor conditions in the interior provinces drove a stream of internal migrants to Buenos Aires province. The peon of the 1880s and after was a less vital cog in a more complex rural economy. When wild livestock no longer ranged the pampa, and the prices for staple items—mate, tobacco, and even beef—rose, the peon found himself in a disadvantaged position in the monetizing pampean economy. He worked less, thus earned less, and faced higher prices and fewer fringe benefits. The rise in wages during the century did not offset these losses and the tremendous jump in land prices.[16]

The nature and organization of ranch work changed sharply from the traditional ranch to the modern estancia of the late nineteenth century. On the primitive colonial estancia, which did not produce for the saladero market in Buenos Aires, slaughtering cattle and skinning off the valued hides were the chief labor. In spring and winter, riders thinned mature animals out of the herds. Peons skinned and staked out the hides to dry, extracted tallow, and sometimes cut the lean, stringy meat into strips for jerked beef. Until the rise of the frigorífico during the 1890s, hides represented the animals' principal value, with tallow and grease figuring as important by-products. William Henry Hudson witnessed the slaughter of cattle during the 1840s. Delighting in his work, a gaucho would sometimes leap lightly onto the back of a steer, "stick his spurs in its sides, and, using the flat of his long knife as a whip, pretend to be riding a race, yelling with fiendish glee." Riders lassoed and hamstrung an animal, then a worker on foot "thrust the long blade into its throat just above the chest." Hudson judged the slaughter as "grand sport" for the gauchos because it combined danger and entertainment in the equestrian environment they relished.[17]

In addition to the seasonal slaughter, workers on the traditional ranch castrated bulls regularly to promote weight gain and as a rudimentary form of selective breeding. Rosas, in a letter to his manager at "Chacabuco" in 1846, stressed castration as one of the three most important tasks on the estancia. The second was to round up and tame herds of wild cattle and accustom them to grazing within a limited pasturage. Rosas did not want "even one wild animal" left on his land; all had to be tamed for easier, more efficient handling. Third, he stressed the need to keep a regular supply of cattle moving to the saladero in Buenos Aires. He recognized the importance of backward integration (regularizing the supply of raw material or cattle to his industrial plant) so that workers would not stand idle and so that production would proceed smoothly. Rosas also wrote out detailed instructions for his *mayordomos* (ranch overseers) that covered all major aspects of ranch management. His correspondence shows the same careful attention to detail and concern for the most efficient and profitable operation of his ranching empire.[18]

The workday on the traditional eighteenth- and nineteenth-century estancia typically began before dawn, with peons sipping many rounds of mate to prepare for the morning chores. Riders then made the early rounds, seeking strays and gathering together herds (*recoger*). According to Emeric Essex Vidal, workers would also "ride the limits of the estate occasionally," watching for animals that had strayed from the main herds. At about eleven o'clock they returned to the peons' kitchen

to sip mate and breakfast on mutton or beef.[19] Workers gathered herds
of perhaps one hundred animals each at high, dry spots on the pampa
every morning and evening. Scratching posts attracted animals to the
chosen pastures, so that over a period of three or four months the herd
would become accustomed to gathering at the same spot, and it would
become tamer and more manageable. This gathering and taming
process meant less work for fewer peons because the cattle did not
scatter as widely over the open range as before. Hudson described an
evening roundup: " . . . the green quiet plain extending away from the
gate to the horizon; the western sky flushed with sunset hues, and the
herd of four or five hundred cattle trotting homewards with loud
lowings and bellowings, raising a great cloud of dust with their hoofs,
while behind gallop the herdsmen urging them on with wild cries."
After a dinner at sunset of the same menu as breakfast, a few riders
went out for the ronda. The night riders slowly circled the herds to keep
them from being spooked, scattering, or stampeding.[20]

   Reports by Dionisio Schöo outlined the annual work schedule at
"San Martín" during the 1840s. Workers castrated and branded young
bulls during the autumn months of March and April. Domadores, hired
by the day, tamed colts for riding. Foot workers, usually foreign-born,
tended and weeded trees and other plant growth in the *quinta*, the
orchard and cultivated areas surrounding the ranch house. In May,
newborn lambs required marking, either by branding or by ear
clipping. Around the ranch, foot peons tended peach and *paraíso*
(chinaberry) trees and prepared buildings for the coming winter.
Thatching roofs generally kept most of them busy. The castration of
two-and-a-half-year-old bulls was finished in June. During the winter
months, workers skinned and staked out hides of animals found dead
on the range from inclement weather or disease. Several times each
year, neighboring ranchers would gather cooperatively (*dar rodeo*) to
separate their animals into herds (*apartar*). They naturally strived to
minimize the mixing and roaming of animals, but storm or drought
scattered cattle far and wide as they sought water, grass, or shelter.
Ranchers would often bell a heifer (*madrina*) for younger steers to
follow in the hope of minimizing dispersal.[21]

   The yearly roundup and branding season (*hierra*) ranked as the
favorite and most storied part of the rural work calendar. The
exhausting, hectic work of gathering vast herds and separating those
animals to be branded required the addition of day laborers for up to a
month. At "San Martín," Schöo hired six extra workers to aid in the

branding in April 1847. Three peons, each with his own tropilla of mounts, worked for a week at 15 pesos per day. Three others, riding ranch horses rather than private mounts, earned half that rate. Branding traditionally began as the cooling winds of autumn swept across the pampa in April. The hierra took on a communal aspect as neighboring ranchers gathered to seek stray calves that might have been caught in the roundup. Teams of ropers lassoed each animal by the neck and feet and threw it to the ground. With a shout of "Here comes the brand!" a peon wielding the iron clearly and carefully marked each animal on the hindquarters, taking care not to singe the flesh. Oldtime brands ran up to six or eight inches across, but as fencing became more common and finer breeds proliferated, the irons became smaller. Castration often took place at the same time. Workers used the roundup and branding season to demonstrate their considerable skills. One might playfully rope a branded steer and drop him once again in a show of prowess. Following the sunup to sundown workday, the peons devoured a hearty meal and chatted and gambled around the fire. When the branding had been completed, all enjoyed a grand fiesta of special foods, gin and cane liquor, and perhaps such fruit as peaches as a special treat. A festive atmosphere prevailed during the hierra, when gauchos worked hard but also exhibited their talents with lasso and bolas.[22]

Although the ranch laborer enjoyed his job immensely as long as it involved riding, his work held considerable dangers. The rugged equestrian life resulted in numerous falls and injuries for even the most skilled horsemen. Francis Head suffered many mishaps on his trip on horseback across the pampas in the mid-1820s. He ranked falls caused by the horse stepping into animal burrows as "the greatest danger" on the pampa—worse than robbers or Indians. In one accident, he crushed his arm but had to continue because no medical attention could be found for hundreds of kilometers. Head learned that even "gauchos occasionally meet with serious accidents." Darwin echoed Head's caveat about the danger of animal, especially vizcacha, burrows: "The holes made by this animal yearly cause the death of many of the gauchos. As Head mentions, every burrow is tenanted by a small owl, who, as you ride past, most gravely stares at you." The considerable dangers notwithstanding, Darwin agreed with Head's judgment that riding across the plains was "exhilarating to the highest pitch."[23]

Routine ranch work, as well as open plains riding, sometimes ended in tragedy. In October 1842 the peon Lorenzo Ponse died from a fall at Rosas' "San Martín" ranch. Schöo reported that Ponse, riding with his knife in front instead of across the back as was customary, suffered a fatal stab to the abdomen when thrown over the head of his mount. The ranch manager sent the corpse to the county seat of Morón along with 50 pesos for church burial fees and mass. Such religious amenities were the exception, not the rule, on the pampa, where a peon seldom graced the inside of a church even in death. In July 1846 Laureano Ramírez reported other difficulties plaguing the workers at "Chacabuco." He was short of suitable mounts and had to assign peons thin, unsatisfactory horses that threw their riders frequently during the workday. Of the ten or twelve riders departing each morning, half returned on foot after having been thrown. Rosas finally had to suspend the *aparte* for want of suitable mounts.[24]

The hazards of rural life persisted on the modern estancia. J. B. MacDonald, manager of William Walker's "25 de Mayo" estancia at Monte, reported many worker injuries during autumn 1900. Peons had to lasso and down skittish cattle and treat them for hoof-and-mouth disease (*aftosa*). Many animals received injuries or died because of the workers' strenuous efforts to subdue and treat them. Several men were injured by "getting horned on their horses." MacDonald treated three men for serious leg bruises. On October 27, 1909, *El municipio* of Buenos Aires reported the death of a peon, Pedro Iriarte, in the county of Marco Paz. As Iriarte had ridden forward, drawing water from the jagüel, his horse had been startled and galloped off. The unfortunate peon fell, but his foot became tangled in the stirrup and he was dragged across the plains and mutilated. In 1912, manager Jorge MacKitchie reported to Walker from the "500" ranch that longtime foreman Rufino Roman had been injured and remained bedridden. In a fall from his horse, Roman's "foot got twisted in the lasso and he received a few nasty kicks on the body and legs."[25]

According to police reports for 1909, falls from horseback and other animal-related mishaps accounted for 9 percent of all accidental injuries and deaths in the province. Fifty-seven workers died from accidents involving horses and other animals in 1909. A higher proportion of machine-related deaths reflected the modernity of the pampa, as vehicles and machinery accounted for 22 percent of the province's accidental casualties that year.[26] Injured workers on the modern ranch sometimes received medical care and thus stood a better chance of survival than in earlier days. Gauchos on the estancia criolla had depended upon prevention, natural healing, or remedies provided by a *curandero*, or folk healer. The unlucky rider who fell alone on the pampa might simply perish amid the tall grass and thistles, a victim of the vastness and solitude of the frontier.

Except for the chores of branding and castration, many labors of the traditional estancia declined in importance or even disappeared later in the nineteenth century. The trail drive from ranches to porteño markets succumbed to encroaching rail lines. Before the advent of rail transport, a herd had required five drovers (*reseros* or *troperos*) per thousand wild cattle plus a foreman and two wranglers to handle the reserve mounts. Each peon maintained his own string of about ten horses in order to have fresh, healthy mounts ready at all times during the arduous drive. The strenuous, hazardous labor netted the resero good wages for his days on the trail. Rosas often employed additional drovers to minimize losses on drives from such ranches as "Chacabuco" to the saladero at Palermo. Generally, about six workers and a foreman guided herds of four to five hundred cattle on the six- to eight-day journey. Five or six drovers plus a foreman could drive a herd of six hundred about twenty-five or thirty miles per day. Losses on the trail could run as high as thirty to one hundred animals, especially if a night storm arose, when "the whole herd may get into motion, and scamper off in every direction for several miles."[27]

On the trail, two men rode point, guiding the herd at the front, and the foreman and two others rode behind. Remaining riders flanked the herd on either side. The cattle rested and grazed for an hour after covering fifteen or twenty kilometers (ten or twelve miles) during the first four or five hours of the morning. Riders changed mounts and resumed the drive until they stopped at lush, well-watered pastures a few hours before sunset. Two or three nighthawks, or night riders, prevented animals from straying or stampeding overnight. The foreman of the drive bore a heavy responsibility because loss, injury, or weight loss on the trail reduced the owner's profits. The foreman carried the required certificates of ownership and transit (*guías*) issued by a justice of the peace. After 1865, moving animals without proper documents could result in prosecution for rustling under the provincial rural code. The ability to buy and sell cattle and to organize and conduct a trail drive distinguished a foreman from the common peon and partially accounted for his higher wages and prestige.[28]

The resero was more skilled than the average ranch hand, but the domador stood at the top of the rural hierarchy. He was held in high esteem by the rural population, along with the others who were especially skilled—the scout (*baqueano*), the tracker (*rastreador*), and the resero. Breaking horses united the central gaucho virtues of equestrian skill, cool courage, the urge for excitement and danger, domination, and agility. The best domadores, like the hero in Ricardo Güiraldes' novel *Don Segundo Sombra* (1926), were known far and wide. Official descriptions of soldiers and criminals specified whether the individual could break horses, and Rosas prized the domador's skill in his own gaucho cavalry, the Red Rangers. He paid domadores 50 percent higher wages than the ordinary salaried peon. Although the large number of horses kept on his various estancias required a few permanent domadores, most traveled from ranch to ranch working by the task. In 1843 Schöo paid itinerant riders at "San Martín" twenty pesos per horse for taming them. Salaried tamers earned 150 pesos per month, compared with 100 pesos for peons who rode night herd or tended paddocks.[29]

Platon A. Chikhachev, a Russian who crossed the pampa in 1836–37, observed the similarities between the gaucho's method of taming horses and the methods of Kalmuks and Cossacks. The gaucho first cut off the horse's air supply with a tight lasso, then fettered and blindfolded the animal after it fell to the ground. Saddling the weakened animal, the gaucho released him and rode him to exhaustion. Although "gauchos are perhaps the best horsemen in the world," noted the Russian, "only a few break wild horses." This harsh creole method of breaking horses led to many injuries and deaths among the animals. In 1846 Schöo reported to Rosas the results of the latest session. Of seventy-five recently purchased horses, seven had died from injuries incurred during breaking at the "San Martín" estancia. Schöo salvaged the hides. The great abundance of horses on the pampa and their consequent cheapness shaped the gaucho's indifference to careful, gradual taming. Even the humblest gaucho owned a string of mounts that he could ride half-wild, so he wasted little effort in taming them fully and carefully.[30]

Observers from Europe and the United States, acculturated in societies that placed high economic value on horses, expressed horror at the brutal, destructive gaucho method of breaking them. The domador appeared utterly indifferent to the well-being of the animal, which would seem an anomaly given the centrality of the horse to existence on the frontier. Head recalled in 1826 that, after a brisk gallop, "the spurs, heels, and legs of peons are literally bathed with blood" flowing from the horses' wounded flanks; the manner of riding "all over the pampas is cruel." In 1854 Nathaniel Holmes Bishop, a North American, protested to a gaucho watching a domador at work, "How the poor animal has suffered." The gaucho replied laughingly, "Why do you pity him? He is worth but three dollars."[31]

Foreigners were not alone in their criticisms of gaucho riding and taming techniques. In a five-part series on frontier life published in 1855, *La tribuna* of Buenos Aires castigated the Argentine's indifference toward his mounts. Frontier soldiers rode their horses so unmercifully that they required months to recover. According to the porteño paper, no horseman in the world paid less attention to the proper feeding, watering, and breeding of horses than the Argentine.[32]

Foreign settlers to the pampa brought with them a greater appreciation of the worth of horses. Richard Seymour, a North American settler, criticized creole taming methods as "extremely bad for horses" because they spoiled the animal's temper and mouth. Englishmen favored breaking valuable purebred colts themselves over permitting natives to "maltreat them, as they almost invariably do." As finer breeds proliferated, more ranchers came to share the growing skepticism about native breaking methods. Purebred animals, whose value greatly exceeded that of the common creole pingo, required gentler, more patient training. In 1878 the *Livestock Journal* noted that the old gaucho domador was fast disappearing. While crediting the old-style riders with audacity and superb ability, the magazine pointed out that violent treatment had often rendered mounts unserviceable. Modern domadores, if less audacious, exercised more patience and care.[33]

As gauchos as a social group passed from rural society, a mythical counterpart sprang forth from the pens of Argentine nationalists searching for a patriotic archetype. The rough-and-tumble domador and his stocky, hardy creole mount also bowed to gentler practitioners and more refined breeds on the modern pampa. But some observers looked back wistfully upon both man and beast and viewed them in a kindlier light. In *El domador*, one of his many tracts on rural life, Carlos Lemée lauded native horses and horsemanship, noting that in the past the gaucho had been considered the "best horseman in the world," but that by the 1880s he was viewed as "a barbarian and an ignorant brute in handling horses." Foreigners held their own breeds and methods of breaking to be superior to those of the native. But according to Lemée, hippodrome standards bore little relevance to pampean ranching conditions, and the traditional methods best suited the needs of daily ranch work.[34] Lemée's defense notwithstanding, ranchers adopted more gradual taming methods to preserve their considerable investment in a blooded horse. The old creole pingo and his nemesis, the gaucho domador, both yielded to modern, foreign-inspired replacements.

Modern ranching methods began to appear on the pampa in the mid-nineteenth century and spread to encompass most of the province by the early twentieth century. The diversified rural economy dictated a new work calendar for peons, as well as the addition of many new tasks performed by immigrants. Carlos Lemée and Walter Larden outlined the range of jobs required on the modern ranch in works published, respectively, in 1888 and 1911. The heat of the summer months, from December through February, brought a new chore to the ranch: haying. The prudent rancher grew and stored hay for lean drought or flood periods, when natural pastures failed and livestock losses often ran heavy. While predominantly foreign foot peons raised hay, mounted creoles segregated the finest bulls with the cows to promote selective breeding. Rosas had practiced a rudimentary form of selective breeding by leaving only some bulls uncastrated, but modern fencing permitted a more refined level of control. Elsewhere, sheep required care. In January lambs had to be weaned from the ewes, and, in February and March, all sheep passed through dips to fight *sarna* (scab or mange), which could destroy valuable wool and kill many animals. Autumn brought other tasks, like branding; Lemée strongly counseled against the final fiesta of the hierra as harmful to worker productivity. Peons also branded, dehorned, and classified cattle into separate herds through May. In June attention turned once more to sheep, as rams had to be dipped again and castrated. Lemée recommended the traditional method of castration using the teeth (*al diente*) as the more hygienic and efficient. After cutting open the scrotum, a peon would bite through the slippery tissue holding the testicles and spit out the severed glands. Workers also cut the tails of ewes to facilitate breeding; they removed only half of the rams' tails, to identify them more readily. By late fall, especially in August, calving and lambing peaked as the cattle and sheep continued to graze and fatten. Cattle generally fed on coarse natural grasses, and sheep grazed on improved alfalfa pastures. Spring brought the ranch's busiest season: shearing, a hectic and pressured time, commenced in October or November and lasted about a month. Year-round tasks continued, such as tending sick and injured animals and repairing buildings, fences, wells, and other facilities.[35]

Perhaps least altered among all rural labors was the hierra. Branding in 1895 was much the same as a half-century earlier. Some fifty riders separated bulls from heifers, then lassoed each bull by the horns and feet in the traditional manner. Three peons on foot subdued the bull and sawed off the horns to render the animal less dangerous, causing a gush of blood to flow from the wounds. One of the horsemen dismounted, pulled out his well-honed knife, and "with surprising speed, giving only two pitiless strokes, castrated the bull" and threw the glands to waiting dogs. A large brand applied to the flank completed the process.[36]

With the many changes in work and status, the rural peon of the twentieth century more nearly approximated a rural proletarian than did his counterpart on the traditional estancia of the open range. Labor became more regularized and wages and hours more clearly established, and the rancher-worker relationship grew more formal, impersonal, and economically rational. As ranch work became more diverse and specialized, the administrative hierarchy sharpened, with the lines between peon, foreman, manager, and owner more clearly delineated.

The peón de campo, skilled at riding, roping, skinning, and butchering cattle, at herding and tending all livestock, and often at shearing sheep, still formed the broad base of the ranch work force. Some estancieros required all laborers to perform foot work as well as mounted tasks, but foot peons continued as a distinguishable group that performed the mechanical and maintenance work of the ranch. The capataz, in addition to knowing the basic skills, organized the daily work schedules, selected and formed herds for market, purchased and sold livestock, and maintained basic accounts of wages, livestock transactions, and herd counts. He had to remember the numbers and characteristics of animals under his charge. Finally, he possessed a working knowledge of the rural code, to minimize conflict with officials and neighboring ranchers. As the authority figure who was in most frequent contact with the peons, he monitored work and social habits in order to control excessive drinking, fighting, horseplay, and gambling and to insure efficient work.[37]

The mayordomo overlooked operations of the various puestos under charge of the capatazes. He arranged contracts with agricultural tenants and provided the ranch owner with periodic reports, suggestions, and questions. Rotation of herds to different pastures, timing of branding and shearing, movements of livestock to market, and other managerial decisions devolved to managers, especially those working for absentee owners. The mayordomo also set disciplinary policies and protected ranges from unauthorized entry and use.[38]

Decreasing labor requirements and an increasing supply of workers through both massive European immigration and internal migration from the interior further exaggerated the regimentation and stratification on ranches. The traditional rancher, faced with seasonal labor shortages, had provided fringe benefits such as grand fiestas and treated peons with a measure of respect to insure their services. The modern rancher could dispense with such niceties. In his ranching manual published in 1904, Godofredo Daireaux counseled ranchers to maintain strict discipline and respect among workers. The peon who left the ranch without permission, refused to perform a given task, or exhibited a lack of respect should be fired and never rehired. Daireaux also recommended hiring too few rather than too many workers, to insure a regimen of hard work rather than idleness.[39]

The daily life of the traditional rancher and his peons differed little during the early nineteenth century. A modest adobe ranch house offered few more material comforts than the humblest gaucho shack. Everyone ate the same pampean staples. Ranchers provided ample quantities of fresh meat, an item of inconsequential cost, as well as tobacco and mate. Schöo informed Rosas in 1849 that *vicios* (mate and tobacco) for the peons cost less than 2 pesos per man per month. Considering that a peon earned perhaps 120 or 150 pesos per month, the expenditure amounted to little. On the modern ranch, however, social and economic differentiation extended to diet. At William Walker's ranch in Bolívar county, peons in 1900 and 1901 ate rice, farina, rough salt, meat, and mate. The manager enjoyed extra luxuries, including coffee, sugar, fine salt, crackers, and fruit.[40] This menu—unlike the old communal roast (*asado*), where everyone sliced chunks of beef from a communal spit—reflected the greater social distance between workers and management on the modern ranch.

Table 3:
Rural Monthly Wages,
Buenos Aires Province, 1883–1914

	Wages in Paper Pesos	*Gold Equivalent*
1883	14	14
1884	14	13.7
1885	14.6	11.3
1888	30	20.4
1889	30	16.5
1890	17	7.1
1891	32.5	7.8
1892	30	9
1894	27.5	7.4
1895	20	5.6
1896	34.3	11
1897	35	11.6
1898	30	11.7
1899	33	14.7
1900	30	13.2
1901	31	13.3
1902	33	14.2
1903	33	14.5
1905	42	18.5
1906–1910	40	17.6
1911–12	45	19.8
1913–14	40	17.6

Sources: Roberto Cortés Conde, "Tendencias en la evolución de los salarios reales en Argentina, 1880–1910: Resultados preliminares," working paper 74 (1975), Centro de Investigaciones Económicas, Instituto Torcuato Di Tella, Buenos Aires, p. 20. Exchange rate for paper and gold pesos from Jacinto Oddone, *La burguesía terrateniente argentina*, p. 136.

Some modern estancieros even altered the customary laborers' diet in substantial ways. Cecilio López replaced the usual self-service asado with cafeteria-style serving lines at his "Dos Marías" ranch in Juárez. Instead of each man cutting what he desired from a roast, cooks served measured portions of *puchero* (stew), rice, soup, vegetables, and meat.

The change, according to López, yielded better nutrition, and, more important, reduced food costs 40 percent. Ranchers increasingly demanded that mate drinking be limited to short breaks at regular times throughout the day to avoid wasting time. This practice also reduced fuel costs because fires to heat water did not then burn constantly. López forbade the drinking of mate altogether. As one visitor to "Dos Marías" observed, "organization and discipline . . . reign."[41]

Ranchers could successfully impose stricter regulations on peons, alter their living and working habits, and even reduce wages because of the relative labor surplus on the modern pampa. In 1908 in Buenos Aires province, 160,000 workers found year-round employment on ranches, but another 133,000 were without permanent jobs. About 116,000 workers were employed only during the brief sheep shearing.[42] An unemployed peon could "ride the grub line," or "sundown," as did the American cowboy—a practice that entailed arriving at an estancia just before mealtime and remaining for a few days. The visitor might perform odd jobs to compensate his host, and, if particularly skilled, might gain permanent employment. More often, however, he drifted toward the next ranch, where he arrived shortly before sundown to partake of the evening meal. Ranchers accepted this custom because feeding drifters reduced livestock losses on the range. An old, unmarketable cow or sheep could always be slaughtered for meat.[43]

Ranch workers fortunate enough to gain permanent employment on the modern pampa suffered variable wages. Real wages for rural workers had jumped to 20.4 gold pesos per month by 1888. But as the effects of the Baring crisis spread throughout the dependent Argentine economy, wages fell precipitiously, to a bottom of 5.6 pesos in 1895. The first decade of the twentieth century witnessed a gradual increase from 13.2 gold pesos in 1900 to a high of 19.8 in 1911. As Table 3 indicates, it took more than two decades for wages to nearly recover the zenith level of 1888.

Ranchers took advantage of rising world market prices to reap greater profits while keeping wages down. Prices received by livestock producers rose more rapidly than did the wages they paid. Moreover, they received payment in gold or hard pesos but paid wages in paper currency, thereby gaining even further from the depreciation of paper. Between 1860 and 1895 rural salaries rose 100 percent, but the market price for wool rose 300 percent. Prices for land and other rural produce similarly outstripped wages. The years prior to World War I witnessed

Table 4:
Cost of Living Index,
Argentina, 1910–17

	Total Cost of Living	All Food	Beef	Potatoes	Bread	Clothing
1910	100	100	100	100	100	100
1911	101	98	100	118	105	103
1912	105	100	111	45	100	108
1913	108	108	129	64	100	110
1914	108	110	135	100	105	111
1915	117	120	140	136	126	127
1916	125	118	148	64	115	161
1917	146	138	149	145	152	198

Source: Alejandro E. Bunge, "Costo de la vida en la Argentina de 1910 a 1917: Números indicadores," *Revista de economia argentina,* 1 (July 1918): 46, 50–51, 54.

a growing disparity between rural wages and the prices paid to ranchers for cattle at the Liniers market in Buenos Aires. Using 1907 as a base year, with the ratio of wages to beef prices at 100, ranchers enjoyed a 67-percent increase in market prices over wages by 1914. They paid constant or falling wages and reaped rapidly increasing profits from heady livestock prices.[44]

To add to their plight, both rural and urban workers faced rapidly rising prices. Rural wages rose 20 percent from 1890 to 1895, but the cost of basic necessities jumped 100 percent. The average wholesale price of meat in 1903 had doubled by 1907 and reached 275 percent of its earlier level by 1912. At the same time, potatoes nearly tripled in price before falling back to a near-1903 level. Table 4 shows a cost of living index for the years 1910–17. Food prices rose 38 percent, including rises of 45 percent for potatoes, 49 percent for beef, and 52 percent for bread.[45]

Modernization brought hard times to the rural masses and closed off many traditional avenues of employment, but economic progress did open a few urban alternatives. Some displaced ranch workers, willing to migrate to cities, found employment as soldiers, policemen, or *bomberos* (paramilitary firemen); organized in 1887, the bomberos fought fires and also served as security forces during strikes and riots. Others accepted work as prison guards. But the mounted "security squadron" formed in 1902 best met the native's ideal of urban employment. These cavalry units maintained order during political meetings, strikes, and public demonstrations, serving on the front lines of labor repression. In 1905 the provincial government created a mounted gendarmerie to patrol frontier regions. Designed to "prevent rather than repress" crime, the itinerant patrols protected rural property and hunted down outlaws lingering in remote frontier areas on the fringes of rural society.[46]

Given the increasingly unfavorable position of ranch workers in the rural economy, it is surprising that no labor organization occurred among them. This does not indicate that rural workers were satisfied with their plight. On the contrary, many of the same forces that constrained the gaucho's life throughout the century also militated against his organizing to improve his lot. The paucity of rural labor organization stemmed from peculiarities of pampean social and economic structures, from values central to the gaucho subculture, and from the ideological orientation of Argentine labor leaders. Worker agitation and organization commenced in Buenos Aires in the late 1870s, and that city and province developed the nation's strongest unions and suffered the most strikes. Except for a few successful strikes by tenant farmers, however, the labor movement failed to touch rural society. Not until the first Perón regime of the 1940s did rural workers become a consideration in Argentine political life.[47]

What forces inhibited rural unionization in Argentina? Latifundism and the extensive nature of pampean livestock raising dictated the dispersal of workers over a wide geographical area. Short-term tenancy contracts kept both farmers and farm workers migratory and dispersed as well. In the early twentieth century, Antonio Zaccagnini, a delegate of the League of Italian Workers of La Plata, lamented the great dispersion of rural workers, which conspired against effective communication, organization, and solidarity. He urged the formation of rural leagues to organize and aid rural workers, particularly those in agriculture.[48]

As in the American west, the distinctive organization of ranch work on the pampa, its seasonality, and the excess supply of workers hindered effective organization. Cowboy unions in the United States seldom lasted longer than a few weeks, and strikers were blacklisted by ranchers. Strikers in the Texas panhandle in 1883 and in Wyoming in 1885 lost their jobs, although cowboys made some short-term gains in the latter case. No organized strike by ranch workers appears to have occurred on the pampa. The native's individualism militated against collective action. Only in rare instances, as when several foreigners were massacred at Tandil in 1872, did gauchos react collectively against the adverse changes engulfing them. Provincial ranch workers never exhibited evidence of the class consciousness central to labor organization. But perhaps an even greater barrier to a rural labor movement stemmed from the internationalist and anti-native ideologies of anarchists and, more, of socialists. Argentine anarchists, mostly Italian and Spanish immigrants, looked wistfully back to a golden age of natural existence unhampered by legal and political constraints. Socialists, mostly from France and Germany, pressed for worker adaptation to modern industrial capitalism and their party's accession to power. Both focused their energies on urban, primarily foreign-born workers, and their sporadic efforts to propagandize rural creoles met with resounding failure.[49]

In early 1891, *El obrero*, organ of the anarchist-dominated Federación Obrera Regional Argentina (FORA), unequivocally enunciated an anti-native viewpoint. According to the paper, native Argentines did "not think much" and understood neither their rights nor duties as human beings and proletarians. The native often erroneously blamed the foreigner for his problems. *El obrero* acknowledged the need to enlighten the native but suggested that efforts be concentrated on behalf of the *puestero* (usually foreign) because the native peon was resigned and accustomed to his sad lot. The official socialist organ, *La vanguardia*, revealed its anti-native bias in the initial issue of April 7, 1894: "The million and a half Europeans that have arrived join the European element already present to form the active part of the population that will little by little absorb the old creole element unable to march by itself toward a higher social type." Although socialists occasionally spoke out on behalf of oppressed native workers of the interior, such as the sugarcane cutters in Tucumán or the mate harvesters in Misiones, the general attitude was one of condescension or indifference. Socialists recognized the rural native to be the most exploited laborer in the nation but saw little hope for improving his lot. Working long hours, sleeping in insect-ridden barns, suffering from a meager diet, plagued by disease, paying prices 50 percent higher than those in the capital, rural peons subsisted under conditions far worse than those of the urban proletariat. But the rural native remained "abject and ignorant . . . stupified by alcohol and superstition, a blind and unconscious tool of the creole oligarchy," according to the socialists' press.[50]

Socialist advocacy of temperance won little sympathy among natives accustomed to swilling gin and cane liquor when income permitted. Writing in *La vanguardia* of July 6, 1895, Eduardo García stressed the need to counter the widespread abuse of alcohol by rural peons. He urged education to uplift the alcoholic rural masses. Such moralistic pleadings probably sounded hollow and ludicrous to natives faced with grave economic dislocations. In addition to their racial bias against natives, socialists displayed a remarkable naïveté and ignorance of the pampa. On January 15, 1906, *La vanguardia* glowingly described a family farm, where "healthy and agreeable work is never excessive." The paper favorably contrasted idyllic rural life with "monotonous and emaciating" industrial labor.[51] A brief visit to a provincial tenant farm would have quickly disabused the writer of this romantic vision.

The problem of the status of rural workers arose repeatedly at labor congresses. Delegates to the fourth congress of the Unión General de Trabajo in 1906 hotly debated whether to seat representatives of Obreros Rurales, an agricultural workers' union. One speaker termed rural laborers "traitors to the labor movement"; but, following prolonged debate, the congress seated two rural delegates. FORA had earlier refused to accept rural delegates at its convention. At the ninth FORA congress in 1915, the delegates held that tenant farmers (*chacareros*) occupied an intermediate position between landowners and the proletariat; the farmer did not work for a wage and thus could not be accepted into the labor movement. In June 1920, however, FORA and the Federación Agricola Argentina, formed by tenant farmers during the land rent strikes of 1912, signed a short-lived mutual support pact. Labor leaders generally voiced support for tenants and rural workers, but the groups found little common ground in organizational and philosophical terms.[52]

Writing in *La vanguardia* in 1910, José Pérez, a socialist organizer in Suipacha county, repeated the charge that creoles "unconsciously defend the government and bourgeoisie" because "with such backward workers, the chieftains do as they please." He stressed the socialists' civilizing and educational mission to uplift the illiterate rural peon, "completely stupified" by overwork and oppressive conditions.[53] Other socialists agreed. An article in another issue of *La vanguardia*, entitled "Populate," expounded the same contempt for the native evidenced by the pro-European viewpoint of the ruling elite: the nation should "attract, root, and assimilate the European immigrant" because "Argentina needs European settlers of superior quality." Progress demanded that the desert be populated, but not with "ethnically and politically inferior elements." To both socialists and the ruling oligarchy, natives were "not a factor in progress." Socialist acceptance of Sarmiento's dichotomy of urban civilization and rural barbarism partially accounts for the party's weak showing outside the national capital.[54]

Major socialist leaders such as Nicolás Repetto molded the party's anti-native ideology. Writing about Argentine laborers of the interior in 1901, he described them as "insolent and vice-ridden idlers . . . ignorant and superstitious, victims of alcohol, gambling and other vices . . . lacking any sense of home or family." Repetto understood that the *provincianos'* "miserable and exploited" condition stemmed from structural social ills, but, like most socialists, he considered them beyond help. Another prominent leader and confirmed internationalist, Juan B. Justo, foundered on the shoals of resurgent Argentine nationalism. He and many followers simplistically dismissed nationalism as merely a bourgeois phenomenon, failing to appreciate its importance among all classes as a vital force with broad appeal in the Argentine political culture; this prompted many workers to foresake socialism and form other labor organizations. These splits, added to the already deep rifts between anarchists and socialists, further fragmented and debilitated the nation's nascent labor movement. Luis Lauzet, a socialist organizer, observed in 1908 that "a divided proletariat . . . has suffered and will continue to suffer."[55]

Ranch workers, the modern gauchos, remained outside the labor movement except for a rebellion by Patagonian sheep shearers in the early 1920s, but farmers and farm workers organized and agitated for better conditions. Most agricultural workers were foreign-born, but a fair number of creoles also labored during the harvests. In 1914, native-born workers comprised about 41 percent of the provincial agricultural labor force. In August 1902 a congress of agricultural workers from Zarate, Baradero, San Nicolás, Peyrano, Alsina, Pergamino, and La Plata convened in La Plata. They focused on bread-and-butter demands, not ideological and revolutionary issues. The congress proposed guidelines governing food, rest periods, and wages for threshing crews. The laborers called for 3.3 pesos per day for threshing crews and 3 pesos per day for men harvesting on small farms. Ranch workers in 1902 earned about 3 or 4 pesos per day, so the agrarian demands did not exceed the rural wage level. The group also proposed extending their organization beyond northern Buenos Aires province to join workers in neighboring Santa Fe.[56]

Landowners reacted with horror at the prospect of a crippling strike during the critical harvest season. In early 1904, the Sociedad Rural Argentina (hereafter, the Rural Society) of large landowners proposed preventative legislation to halt this menace. The group's journal stressed that a rural strike during the wheat harvest would be a "national calamity," and that the crop had to be saved at all costs. *La agricultura*, a publication aimed at the modern rancher, also reacted against the threatened strikes, which would endanger "the nation itself" and its "eminently liberal institutions." The journal castigated foreign farm workers for biting the hand that fed everyone and called upon native workers to step in should the harvest be threatened.[57]

Early in 1905, *La agricultura* attacked the "revolutionary propaganda" being spread among rural laborers by anarchistic "professional agitators" from Buenos Aires. With rural wages high, the journal saw no justification for a strike. On the southern pampa, the daily *El eco de Tandil* agreed that high wages made strikes unjustified, and that continued massive immigration from Europe attested to the attractiveness of Argentina, where "one works little and earns much." The paper called upon the government to take effective countermeasures should strikes endanger the wheat harvest or shearing. Less than a month later, however, the paper printed an editorial entitled "The Expensive Life," bitterly inveighing against high prices. High wages meant little in the face of faster rising prices.[58]

In 1912, tenant farmers in Santa Fe and northern Buenos Aires province exploded into the largest rural strike in Argentine history centered at Alcorta. The movement represented "spontaneous and intense agitation" by tenant farmers, rather than the fruits of "outside agitation." The tenants, like the farm workers who struck earlier, made modest concrete demands for lower land rents. They did not challenge or threaten latifundia by calling for land reform or the opportunity to purchase, rather than merely rent, holdings. Justo and other socialist politicians spoke on behalf of the tenants in the Chamber of Deputies, and Justo journeyed north to address the strikers. In a speech in Rosario, he erroneously heralded the farmers' strike at Alcorta as the beginning of urban-rural socialist cooperation. He focused on the need for stability and guarantees for agrarian renters. Reasonable and secure contracts rather than massive land redistribution surfaced as the key issue in the strike.[59]

Significantly, the farmers rejected socialist overtures and formed their own organization, the Federación Agricola Argentina (FAA). Distrustful of urban politicians and political parties, the FAA sought to deal directly with provincial and national authorities to resolve their grievances. Leaders counseled adherents to remain nonpolitical. The tenant farmers achieved some short-term benefits, but the Alcorta strike illustrated the failure of organized labor to understand the needs of rural Argentina. As an Italian-language workers' paper, the *Giornale d'Italia*, charged, the urban-oriented socialists had "completely forgotten the existence of another proletariat, the rural."[60]

The Alcorta strike did nothing to reassure provincial landowners. The Rural Society cooperated fully with provincial police during World War I to counter political unrest and reduce livestock thefts. Society members furnished food, housing, and transportation to rural police units and formed their own vigilante patrols.[61] Labor unrest worried the terratenientes but failed to shake their great political power or to improve the precarious position of workers and tenants in rural society. Perhaps most disturbing, the disadvantaged position of ranch workers largely precluded the formation of stable families on the pampa. Rural males, migrant and often unemployed, left child-raising and domestic life largely in the hands of women, who usually filled those roles alone and largely unaided.

4
Women
and
Family Life

Foreign visitors to the pampa gave mixed appraisals of the *china*, or native rural woman. In the 1780s, Félix de Azara noted caustically that pampean women are "pigs," scantily and ill-clad. Cleaning, cooking meat, and serving mate occupied them, and they neither sewed nor wove textiles as did women in the interior. In the 1820s Francis Bond Head criticized the "indolent and inactive" rural women, who "literally have nothing to do." He also disapproved of what he perceived as their lax morals. "When I inquired of a young woman employed in nursing a very pretty child, who was the father of the 'creatura,' she replied, 'Quien sabe?'" (Who knows?) Head failed to realize that this noncommittal response was a standard means of deflecting prying questions from inquisitive strangers. Samuel Greene Arnold recalled that rural folk frequently answered his queries with the useful defensive phrase "Quien sabe?"[1]

Other observers disagreed that women on the pampa were idle and lazy. Alexander Caldcleugh condemned the gauchos, who "do nothing but look after the cattle," with "poor females performing all the drudgery, and waiting upon them with the greatest humility." Robert Proctor also found that "the women are much more good-humoured and civilized than the men." He usually gave cigars to men and sugar to women as presents, and he "always found the latter thankful for the attention while the former would take segars as if they were their due." Most travelers judged the mestizo women reasonably attractive, but dirty, unkempt, and prematurely aged by the harsh conditions of frontier life.[2]

Women held an ambiguous position on the pampa—excluded from the central equestrian labors of the livestock economy, yet necessary and desirable in many ways. Ranchers, however, often accepted Carlos Pellegrini's dictum of 1854: on an estancia "women are useless mouths, economically speaking." Pellegrini favored excluding them from ranches because their presence provoked jealous quarrels among the male workers. Toward the end of the century, Miguel A. Lima reaffirmed this opposition to women, asserting that they stir up disorder, jealousy, and fighting on a ranch. He suggested that only families of foremen and farmers be permitted, in addition to the estanciero's own family. Both rural authorities epitomized the prevalent elite attitude of efficiency and order above all else on the estancia. Many ranchers hired only single peons, or forced married men to leave their families elsewhere during the work season.[3]

In 1856 Bernardo Gutiérrez, a rancher from Mercedes, went so far as to suggest that families without work be forced from the countryside into towns or toward the distant frontier. He held that many families stole livestock to feed themselves, and that in towns they could find gainful employment under the watchful eye of local officials. Agustín Sosa, another estanciero, voiced support for the plan of forced relocation. Such large landowners as Rosas and his partisans often viewed families settled on the pampa as impediments to the free movement of their herds. In November 1844 Ramírez, Rosas' manager at "Chacabuco," expressed concern over the "prejudicial populations" that he believed were killing cattle on the ranch in order to market the hides. Two years later he again complained about "prejudicial populations" living on the "Rosario" and "San Benito" holdings. Though some of the settlers dated their residency back to the previous decade, under a prior owner, Ramírez objected to their obstruction of herd movements. He suggested to Rosas that they should "entirely depopulate" the countryside by moving settlers off the ranch or near the property line. Rosas instructed his manager to relocate all families to marginal areas near ranch boundaries, well out of the path of grazing cattle.[4]

To terratenientes, women and children represented obstacles to the orderly functioning of an estancia and were not welcome until late in the century, when they proved useful in agriculture. Men on horseback, not women, did ranch work, and, except for a cook and a housekeeper, ranchers kept the number of women and children on their vast holdings to a minimum. The landowner, manager, and puesteros might have families with them on the ranch, but not the peons.

The negative attitudes of ranchers and the destructive effect of rural socioeconomic and juridical institutions seriously compromised rural social relations. The dependent nature of the rural peonage left women in a vulnerable position. The Frenchman Xavier Marmier commented in the 1850s: "What servitude. The patron or his representatives could cohabitate with the daughters or even the wife of the disinherited." *La patria* of Olavarría commented in 1897 that women could not remain faithful to husbands who absented themselves for long periods to work on various estancias. One of the more cruel customs of the pampa marked the woman who was unfaithful, whether willingly or under duress: the offended husband or lover would cut off one or both of the long braids customarily worn by pampean women, then tie the braid to his horse's tail to further humiliate his betrayer.[5]

In addition to abuse by powerful males, other factors contributed to the precariousness of the rural family. Rural isolation and the lack of clergy made religious marriage difficult. Religious or civil sanction could often be attained only at great effort and expense. As a result, common-law marriages and concubinage represented normal relationships. Even middle-class families in rural society, who enjoyed a stable home life with both parents present, relied on folk rather than legal and religious rituals of marriage. Pampean folklore records a ritualized system of courting, abduction, and common-law marriage in place of the traditional ceremony. A man would first indicate his interest in a woman by hiring her to wash his clothing. With the convenient pretext of picking up his laundry, he could visit her at the parental home, drink mate, and socialize with the family. Later he might offer her gifts of sweets, perfume, or trinkets. Parents ostensibly ignored the man's attentions until one day the sweethearts eloped to his house. The "outraged" father rushed to the house and demanded an explanation from the couple. They in turn begged forgiveness and asked his blessing. The farce of seduction and pardon completed, the pair commenced their life together with familial and social sanction. Although the union was recognized as proper and moral by rural society, children born to the couple would be deemed illegitimate by the state and the church.[6] Lower class gaucho unions often lacked even this veneer of folk ritual and sanction.

Latifundism also worked against the formation of families on the pampa by limiting economic opportunities for the rural landless. An Englishman visiting South America in 1804 identified the nexus

Table 5:
Percentage of Total Adult Population Married,
Buenos Aires Province, 1869–1914

	Males		*Females*	
	Foreign	**Argentine**	**Foreign**	**Argentine**
1869	36	35	66	36
1881	44	30	72	37
1890	49	31	73	37
1895	50	32	75	39
1914	53	29	72	41

Sources: Buenos Aires Province, *Anuario estadístico,* 1896, pt. 1, pp. xi-xii; Argentine Republic, *Tercer censo nacional . . . 1914,* 2:421. Figures include persons aged 14 or older except for 1914, which includes persons aged 15 and older.

between the system of land tenure and the social consequences. The poor, unable to purchase land "granted in large tracts only," were "compelled to remain single."[7] This in turn, coupled with the seasonal, migratory nature of ranch work, reduced the growth of the rural population.

Given the demographic, socioeconomic, legal, and religious obstacles to marriage, it is hardly surprising that most rural males remained single. A census shows that only 27 percent of them were married in Tandil in 1862. Marriage rates for Buenos Aires province remained low throughout the century. Table 5 shows the percentages of Argentines and foreigners married there from 1869 through 1914. Marriage rates for native males actually declined during this period, whereas other groups showed increases.[8] Common-law and intermittent unions remained the norm for native males who were coupled.

The Argentine fertility rate during the late nineteenth century appears to have been relatively low, on a par with that of Chile, Spain, and Italy. Caldcleugh estimated that the average family of the 1820s included three children. He theorized that "the custom of suckling children for three or four years may account for this . . . low fertility." Nearly a century later, Hugo Miatello observed the same prolonged nursing among pampean mothers. He estimated that women breastfed their babies for at least twelve and often as long as eighteen or twenty-four months. Children started an adult diet of solid foods between the ages of two and three. Modern research shows that prolonged breastfeeding can be a major factor in lengthening birth intervals.[9]

Statistics available for the second half of the century indicate a secular decline in the birthrates of both the province and the nation. O. Andrew Collver estimated that the standardized crude birth rates for Argentina fell from 48 in 1860 to 43.8 in 1890 to 41 in 1910 and to 32 in 1925. Birth rates for Buenos Aires province compared closely with those of European countries, ranging from about 40 in the early 1880s to 36 by 1910. Marital fertility rates for 1914 show the same low levels as the total fertility figures. Forty-seven percent of married Argentine women had three or fewer children (compared with 42 percent for foreign-born women). Another 40 percent of the Argentines had four to nine children, and only 13 percent had more than nine children.[10]

Other factors besides prolonged nursing kept the rate of natural increase low on the pampa. High infant mortality afflicted Argentina throughout the century. In the city of Buenos Aires between 1827 and 1831, the infant mortality rate (deaths during the first year per thousand live births) averaged 284 for whites and 350 for blacks. In 1896, stillbirths and infant deaths (up to six months of age) accounted for 31 percent of all provincial deaths. Child deaths up to age six comprised 52 percent of all provincial deaths from 1893 to 1902, and 43 percent from 1903 to 1912. Diarrhea, enteritis, and respiratory ailments caused most of the fatalities. Infant deaths (to age one) ranged from 94 per 1,000 in 1914 up to 108 in 1918 and fell back to 100 in 1920.[11]

Boys began working as peons at an early age and thus suffered many of the dangers of ranch work. Henry Bird reported a fatal accident involving a boy on William Walker's ranch in 1896: "our carpenter's oldest child being kicked by a kick from a horse through carelessly approaching it too closely." Between 1893 and 1902, a total of 1,815 children up to age six died violent accidental deaths in the province. The number rose to 1,937 during the following decade.[12]

Children growing up amid the dangers of life on the pampa modeled themselves after adults, as do children everywhere. Girls patterned themselves after their mothers and learned domestic chores and artisanry. Francis Head watched as boys played with knives and lassoed birds and dogs. On horseback by age four, boys helped drive cattle to the corral and later learned to break horses and hunt larger game. Youngsters quickly graduated from roping chickens to downing

pumas and ostriches with bolas. Work and play blended as boys learned
to enjoy and excel at the skills that would earn their livelihood as ranch
workers. In his reminiscences of childhood, William Henry Hudson
evoked the centrality of nature to the child on the pampa. His early
years revolved around animals—from his beloved sheepdog,
Pechicho, to horses and vast flocks of birds inhabiting nearby marshes
or esteros. Riding horseback by age six, Hudson extended his horizons
and playground far across the plains, drinking in the fascinating flora
and fauna of the lush countryside. The distinguished folklorist
Martiniano Leguizamón recalled the idylls of a summer vacation at a
ranch in Entre Ríos. The children fished and swam in a lagoon, hunted
small game, and stole honey from bees and watermelons from a
neighboring farm. The power and splendor of the mighty pampa played
a major formative role in his young life, as it did for Hudson.
Mid-century found the pampa little changed from the 1820s. Children
still played with knives and lassos, and infants slept suspended in hide
cradles that hung from the ceiling. Boys still learned the necessary rural
skills and by their early teens had become skilled riders, hunters, and
ropers.[13]

In addition to the important duties of child-raising and maintaining
households, which women often performed alone or with only
occasional male help, women also filled a variety of other essential
economic roles. In the interior provinces, they produced important
cottage goods, notably finely woven ponchos and other wool garments.
Ceramics and cigar making occupied Santa Fe women. They also
baked bread, which young girls sold door-to-door. Lina Beck-Bernard,
wife of a French immigration promoter, enjoyed the many foods
prepared by women in Santa Fe—delicious fruit marmalades made
from lemon, peach, orange, and apricot, and the national favorite,
dulce de leche, a sweet, milk-based caramel dessert. Such domestic
tasks as carrying water from the river, sewing, weaving, and cooking
occupied much time. Although they did not perform mounted labors
associated with ranch work, women did ride horses. Beck-Bernard
observed women, with children clinging behind, riding to Rosario to
shop.[14]

Women did participate fully in one central task of ranch life, the
annual sheep shearing, or *esquila*. During the December 1838 esquila
at Rosas' "San Martín" estancia, there were four women and eight
men on the shearing team. All earned 8 pesos per 100 animals clipped.
Marcelina Guzman sheared 720 sheep, Gregoria Ferreyra 804,

Lorenza Guzman 1,009, and Eugenia Gonsales 1,252. In January 1840, manager Juan José Becán reported that five of eight shearers were women. The women clipped as many or more animals as did the men, with Manuela Bererro leading all the workers with 2,703 animals. That year the workers earned 11 pesos per 100 animals sheared. Women again participated in the shearing of 1845 and 1847, earning 15 pesos.[15]

In 1866 a Scottish traveler witnessed the shearing of some twenty thousand sheep near Chascomús. Thirty workers, mostly native women, labored from October 22 through November 20. An English sailor who had jumped ship in Argentina cooked six sheep per day to feed the hungry workers.[16] About the same time, Richard Seymour highly recommended women as shearers, "being quite as good shearers as the men, and doing the work much more neatly, seldom cutting the sheep, though they are not quite as rapid."[17]

Aside from shearing, women occupied themselves with more traditionally feminine tasks. In 1844 a cook, as often a female as a male, earned 100 pesos per month, the same wage as a ranch peon. Women also washed, ironed, and sewed clothing and served as maids and wet nurses; the latter enjoyed particularly good salaries. In 1872 the Office of Labor advertised for immigrant wet nurses at a wage of 400–500 pesos per month plus room and board. Maids, especially if foreign, commanded 300–400 pesos and were in great demand. A rural peon earned only 200–400 pesos, a farm worker slightly more, and a soldier 400, so wages for women were equal to or better than those for rural men. The scarcity of women on the pampa dictated their higher wages.[18]

Discrimination kept women out of many occupations, such as that of store clerk. The 1895 census for Tandil reveals only male clerks, usually Spanish or French immigrants. An editorial on January 21, 1895, in *La patria* of Dolores attacked employment discrimination and lower wages for women, questioning why women should be excluded from jobs including those of doctor, postal employee, and telegraph and telephone operator. Although women had entered some professions and certain areas of public administration, *La patria* urged a further widening of economic opportunities and equal pay for female workers. In 1898 Raquel Messina, writing in *La vanguardia*, condemned the "exploitation of women in the countryside," blaming the rural native male, "indifferent to his situation," for perpetuating this "oppression and misery." As long as men remained "indifferent, resigned, and unconscious," even worse conditions would obtain for women. Messina's attitude ran consistent with the usual socialist contempt toward native male workers.[19]

Women living alone or widowed, or in the absence of a mate, on occasion assumed some of the duties of ranch work, including mounted chores. Widows sometimes continued to run large ranches as managers or owners. María Herrera de Peredo managed one of Rosas' holdings in San José de Flores after her husband's death in the early 1840s. Her responsibilities included dispensing wages and assigning work to more than seventy peons on the "San Benito" and "Rosario" puestos. She also provided full accounts of ranch income and expenditures, as well as livestock counts. Judging by Rosas' replies to her correspondence, she performed all managerial duties to his full satisfaction. The 1895 census of Tandil recorded several widows, aged thirty to sixty, running ranches in the partido. Rosana M. de Gómez, widowed at age thirty-nine after twenty-three years of marriage, managed one of five ranches owned by the Gómez clan in Tandil and also raised nine children. The forty-eight-year-old widow Isabel Pereira presided over one of the ranches of that wealthy family and cared for ten children.[20]

Although the rigors of rural life and the relative shortage of women dictated a degree of egalitarianism on the pampean frontier, gauchos held sharply sexist attitudes on key points associated with their lifestyle and values. Ezequiel Martínez Estrada, one of Argentina's leading intellectuals, asserted that "the gaucho thought it humiliating to fall in love and marry, as much as riding a mare." Leopoldo Lugones, a prominent nationalist writer, contended that the gaucho held a contemptuous view of women—wives or concubines—as fit only for domestic chores.[21] But in reality, it was the pampean socioeconomic conditions and judicial strictures that shaped the gaucho's relations with women, far more than cultural factors. Faced with marginal, migratory employment and the constant threat of conscription, gauchos found few opportunities to realize more than intermittent liaisons or precarious common-law unions with women.

Gauchos held many superstitions concerning women, for example, that women should not be permitted to ride a good horse: feminine weakness supposedly debased the animal, made it disobedient, and caused it to lose its resistance and even its hair. A mount could become a "woman's horse," useless for work. A strong horse required the strength and "rigor" of a man to bring out its best. Pampean folklore recorded the tale of a peon's horse that lost its hair after having been ridden by a menstruating woman (*mujer con la luna*). A gaucho would never ride a mare, considering mares unsuitable for anything other than draft animals or mounts for gringos. A strong element of machismo suffused the gaucho subculture.[22]

In spite of their attitudes toward women and mares, gauchos did not object to feminine assistance when it was needed. During the frequent military conflicts between rival political factions and with neighboring countries, women filled important auxiliary roles. Domingo Sarmiento recalled the many necessary tasks performed by camp followers, including cooking, washing and repairing clothes, carrying provisions, nursing the wounded, guarding horses during battle, and sometimes even fighting. A swarm of carts, laden with wives, concubines, children, animals, and provisions, followed most pampean armies. During the Rosas era, military commanders permitted each soldier to have a woman as a companion who regularly received rations. This concession greatly reduced desertions and was viewed as necessary to the functioning of the unit.[23]

During his stint on the southern frontier, Alfredo Ebelot observed women of all ages and colors (except white) tagging along behind the troops. The "gauchos with skirts" tended to remain with the same battalion, changing "husbands" when their men were transferred to another unit or post. Commander Manuel Prado conceded that on the frontier "without those women, existence would have been impossible." The number of women living permanently at the garrisons appears to have been small. The 1869 census recorded only 55 women and nearly 700 men on the southern frontier at Olavarría, and 32 women and more than 400 men to the north in Junín. Of these 87 women, only 24 were married, and most labored at the predictable domestic tasks required at the forts.[24]

Among the considerable dangers facing frontier women, the possibility of capture by Indian raiders ranked high. Tales of *cautivas*, women captured and enslaved by Indians, abound in pampean literature and historical records. In 1862 the *cacique* or chieftain Calfucurá returned eight captives, including two women: Rita Díaz, taken during a massive attack in 1855, left three children born to her at the Indian village, or *tolderia*; Olegaria Flores, aged thirty-five and married, also regained her freedom and undertook the difficult task of relocating her husband and family. Justices of the peace issued circulars describing freed captives to facilitate reunion with family and friends.[25]

Given the bleakness and dangers of rural life, many women migrated to the capital or to another town in search of a more secure life. An editorial by Juan C. Varetto in *La patria* of Olavarría on March 25, 1899, lamented the loss of women to the port city. He urged the founding of commercial schools and the opening of new jobs to women to keep them on the pampa. He admitted that, for the woman who did not migrate, "a life of corruption" offered one of the few alternatives.

Both legal and illicit houses of prostitution operated in pampean towns and in the countryside, usually near a pulpería. An "itinerant madam" also traveled the plains with her girls in a huge oxcart. Their arrival would signal a fiesta, with dancing and drinking. Men purchased candles of varying lengths that determined how long they could remain with the women in small tents raised for the occasion. In 1832 Rosas combined the twin policy objectives of reducing porteño prostitution and populating frontier towns. According to Francis Baylies, an American diplomat, Rosista police seized three hundred women late at night and shipped them "off to the frontiers without any notice or investigation of their offences." MacCann corroborated the event in 1848: "A few years ago Gen. Rosas seized all the women in Buenos Ayres of doubtful character, and sent them toward this frontier, with strict orders for their detention, hoping to augment the population by that means." Tandil, on the southern frontier, received this windfall of women of questionable character.[26]

By 1877 the city fathers at Tandil were forced to recognize prostitution as an evil inherent in a growing town. They opted to limit the evil through regulation, rather than wage a futile battle to extirpate the "houses of toleration." A decade later, however, municipal intendant Pedro Duffau complained of widespread clandestine activity that escaped official vigilance. Women working at officially sanctioned houses received regular medical examinations. Some women also plied their trade at dance halls, which Duffau termed "places of corruption and scandal." In the 1895 census of Tandil, only two women listed prostitution as their profession—an Argentine and a Spanish woman both in their mid-twenties—doubtless a case of gross underenumeration.[27]

At the turn of the century, four houses were sanctioned by the city. They were run by Manuela García, Felomina Pilichutte, and Angela López, with the liveliest run by Julia Osmon. Another house existed at María Iglesia, an agricultural center at nearby Vela. Most prostitutes seem to have been Argentines between the ages of twenty-five and thirty-five. The brothels and their inhabitants and patrons figured prominently in municipal police records. Two employees of Julia Osmon's house, both Argentines aged twenty-three, were arrested for public disorder early in 1900 and again in April for fighting with one another; one of them was arrested a third time in December. Police also arrested patrons at the houses, usually for "drunken and disorderly conduct" but sometimes for beating a woman. A doctor examined the women twice weekly, charging two pesos per woman per visit. In addition to demanding health inspections, the municipality arrested women for soliciting on the streets during weekends. But not everyone tolerated prostitution with the sanguine grace of the city fathers. In 1905 Atilio Airton published a six-part series condemning the horrors of white slavery in *El eco de Tandil*. His exposé, similar in tone to the muckraking journalism in the United States at the same time, spoke on behalf of orphaned girls aged fourteen or fifteen who found life in foster homes as "beasts of burden" unbearable. Mistreatment and overwork forced them into prostitution as a means of escaping their misery. Airton lamented both the ills suffered by these young women and the loss of productive persons to pampean society.[28]

In addition to prostitution, another social ill plagued rural Argentina: a grave shortage of trained doctors. This shortage opened another field of employment to women, however, who served as midwives and curanderas. Even after professional medical treatment had become available, many rural people preferred the traditional remedies prescribed by curanderas. The number of women equaled or perhaps exceeded the number of male folk healers. The exercise of their healing arts varied, but most blended herbal cures, folk superstitions, and a vague veneer of Catholic dogma, utilizing incantations, magical rings of various metals, emetics, purgatives, and aromatic herbs that, according to Lina Beck-Bernard, either cured or asphyxiated. In Tandil in 1869 resided the curandera Ynes Rivoneira, aged forty-nine, married, illiterate, and a native of Santiago del Estero, and a twenty-seven-year-old midwife, or *partera*, Ignacia Cespedes, married, literate, and a native of Buenos Aires province. In the countryside there were others.[29]

Folk healers, though immensely popular and much utilized by the rural population, suffered constant attack throughout the province by advocates of modern, scientific medicine. In 1877 the justice of the peace of San Andrés de Giles fined a curandero 1,000 pesos for practicing medicine illegally. The provincial public health council congratulated the justice for his efforts in controlling *curanderismo*. A correspondent complained to *El oeste de la provincia* of Mercedes in 1909 that curanderos made a mockery of medical regulations. The healers allegedly exploited the public's ignorance and shamelessly demanded money while endangering people's health. Toward the end of the century, "Hipocrates" warned the readers of *La patria* of Olavarría that a new wave of faith healers and spiritualists was playing upon the superstitions of "ignorant people." Some purported to heal by laying on hands (*manos santas*), others dispensed supposedly miraculous waters.[30]

The demand for lay practitioners persisted because of a continued shortage of trained physicians. In 1896 the province had only 298 doctors, 15 dentists, and 97 recognized parteras for a population of more than 900,000. Furthermore, the doctors concentrated in the northern counties, leaving only 114 for the nearly 390,000 persons spread thinly across the central and southern plains. On February 19, 1909, *El municipio* of Tandil repeated dire warnings of thousands dying at the hands of illicit medical practitioners, but it acknowledged that the serious shortage of doctors and their refusal to make house calls forced many to rely on curanderos. *El orden* of Mercedes chastized local officials for tolerating the "alarming growth" of curanderismo and called for stricter enforcement of laws prohibiting the clandestine practice of medicine. Newspapers across the province in Dolores, Pergamino, La Plata, and Buenos Aires complained about the lack of medical care and the forced reliance on folk healers. In spite of sharp criticism, legislation, and better diffusion of professional medical services, rural residents continued to favor curanderas for the treatment of most ailments. The occupation provided status and income to many pampean women throughout the century.[31]

The position of males clearly declined as the pampa modernized, but the fortunes of women are less clear. The new rural economy, with its agricultural as well as livestock production, offered more employment opportunities for women, but many chose to migrate to towns and cities to labor as domestics or industrial workers. Those who remained in rural areas found the drudgery of daily life little improved during the course of the century. Rude housing and a simple diet remained much the same, and women, like gauchos, found little improvement in their material culture and standard of living in spite of the impressive economic strides made by the nation during the latter decades of the century.

5
Material Culture:
Housing, Clothing,
Food, Recreation

Like other aspects of the gaucho's life in the nineteenth century, his simple daily necessities changed more as the result of outside pressures than from his own volition. Housing changed least, with the humble adobe *rancho* persisting into the twentieth century. The staple diet of beef and mate also remained common on the pampa, but food consumption per capita probably fell. Handmade native clothing yielded to imported machine-made articles. Modernizing administrations outlawed some forms of gaucho entertainment and transformed others. Estancieros and politicians worked assiduously to eliminate all vestiges of the gaucho's lifestyle and to reduce his status from one of self-sufficiency to dependent peonage.

The physical layout and material conditions of the pampean ranch house changed little from the colonial era until well into the twentieth century. The dwelling usually ran north and south to offer some protection against cold winter winds sweeping up from southern Patagonia. When available, ombús or other trees sheltered buildings from the sun and wind. The venerable colonial-style house, surrounded by a protective ditch and drawbridge, featured a simple, functional design—a large central living room with kitchen and peons' quarters in one wing and family quarters in another. A second-story mirador, to provide advance warning against raiding Indians, frequently distinguished frontier homes. A *palomar*, or dovecote, which housed birds for consumption, completed the central structure. Outbuildings consisted of a modest storage shed and sometimes a separate peons' kitchen. Only a wealthy landowner could afford a large house and outbuildings as well.[1]

Ranch workers and small ranchers, who often rented their land, lived in one- or two-room ranchos that did not exceed four meters square and stood two or three meters in height. A bedroom and a kitchen, both with packed dirt floors, and occasionally a *ramada*, or porch, comprised the entire structure. Such readily available materials as adobe, thatch, and rawhide served in place of scarce wood. Bones often lined the walls of wells, and they also functioned as furniture. In 1819 John Miers, a British traveler, described a posthouse, or travelers' inn, east of Luján as a "large hut, built of rough crooked stakes stuck into the ground"; thatch topped the building, which was constructed of twigs, reeds, and mud daubed between rawhide-bound stakes. He found the stucture "most rude and miserable, resembling in everything, except its size, an Irish mud cabin." The house offered few comforts to the visitor; indeed, furniture was rare everywhere on the pampa. Most vexing was the "incredible number of fleas, bugs, and even still more disgusting vermin" that cohabited in the dwelling.[2]

During the 1820s many travelers complained of the omnipresent, omnivorous insects, rats, and other pests that plagued the filthy, barren posthouses on the plains. Robert Proctor, a Briton who crossed the pampa to Peru, recalled with horror trying to sleep as rats ran over his body. One large rodent grabbed his big toe and "no doubt expected to be able to run away with" it. Native families customarily yielded their houses to the voracious pests during hot summer nights and slept outdoors. Hudson remembered from his childhood the terrifying noises of rats running about the house at night. The horde of "vile rats and pests of all sorts" impressed the future naturalist as vividly as did the varied and beautiful birdlife and vegetation of the humid pampa.[3]

Furniture, even on more prosperous ranches, remained primitive and homemade throughout most of the century. In 1833 Darwin described a dwelling owned by a Uruguayan rancher, Juan Fuentes, near Maldonado. In spite of the owner's considerable wealth, his dirt shack had a "hardened mud" floor and was nearly devoid of furnishings. Everything inside was "filthily dirty," and Darwin found "no bread, salt, or vegetables." Cattle skulls served as macabre stools, bones as fire rings, and hides as doors and cots, if the latter existed at all. Hudson remembered morbid walls fashioned out of thousands of cow skulls discarded by saladeros that surrounded small ranches near Buenos Aires. The "heads and horns of cows and horses" also filled potholes in streets and roads. Upon taking over as manager for Rosas at "San Martín" in mid-1842, Schöo reported on the delapidated condition of the ranch house. He described the furniture and bedding as all ''dusty and dirty'' and complained of the ''dusty and stained'' chair, greasy tablecloth, broken eating utensils, and ''rats in abundance.'' He set a carpenter to work immediately to make the dwelling habitable.[4]

Some ranchers improved their grounds by planting trees for wood. An inventory in 1852 of Rosas' ''Rosario'' estancia included several varieties of trees in the quinta: 1,200 walnut, 2,600 willow, 3,900 peach, and 6,000 poplar. Hudson described the ranch of the Rosista minister of war near Chascomús as ''surrounded by an enclosed *quinta*, or plantation, with rows of century-old lombardy poplars, conspicuous at a great distance, and many old acacia, peach, quince, and cherry trees.''[5]

But such improvements marked the exception, not the rule, and mid-century travelers described pampean living conditions in the same dismal terms as their predecessors had. Many railed against the plethora of insects and rats infesting every posthouse and rancho. According to MacCann, the rancho persisted in 1848 much as before: ''The hut, built of cane-reeds and mud, was not white-washed; the walls were scarcely six feet high, and the roof was thatched with bulrushes. It contained two rooms, neither of them having a window, so far as I could discover; but the door was well hung upon iron hinges of British manufacture.'' For the workers, the all-important peons' kitchen stood nearby: ''a long hut, built of the same materials as the dwelling-house, formed a cook-house, and residence for the men-servants; at one end was a contrivance shaped like a bee-hive, but double its size, for baking bread; and a well was near at hand.'' The building lacked a chimney, so all sat on the floor to avoid the dense smoke.[6]

Although the modest rancho improved little, the dwellings of large landowners grew along with their wealth and prestige. The riches that accrued to terratenientes through soaring land values and booming European market prices for livestock and agricultural produce spurred the construction of ornate, sometimes garish, country houses designed by European architects. These great houses—some almost castles—were built according to the European fashion then current in stylish Barrio Norte, the district of Buenos Aires where the landed elite resided most of the year except during the hot summer months. Their designs stood out as ludicrously incongruent with the pampean surroundings, bearing no relation to the flat topography or to climatic conditions. On the other hand, they served as grandiose symbols of the landowners' status, influence, and European outlook. After mid-century, English sheep ranchers introduced the first impressive outbuildings on the pampa: enormous barns, called *galpones*, to store wool and to house the shearing operation.[7]

The rural masses shared not at all in the newfound opulence of the growing livestock export economy. In their widely read *Handbook of the River Plate*, the Mulhall brothers, English publishers of the Buenos Aires *Standard*, described the "wretched" huts of the 1860s and 1870s in the same unflattering terms as earlier observers had—mud walls, reed roofs, hide and stake beds, and skull chairs. According to J. V. Lastarria, writing in 1868, pampean families lived in a state of "poverty bordering on misery." As the first national census of 1869 indicated, sod houses with thatched roofs remained the rule, and only a few buildings were constructed of tile and wood. Single-room thatched structures constituted three-fourths of all housing in the province, and more substantial dwellings with tile roofs appeared only in a few northern counties. An average of more than five persons inhabited each house. In 1881, single-room structures made up 77 percent of all rural provincial housing. By 1895 housing had become even more crowded, with an average of 6.7 persons per dwelling.[8] This higher figure could reflect the fact that many rural people, particularly migratory ranch workers, had no homes at all.

Most ranch workers lacked even the coarse creature comforts afforded by the humble pampean rancho. The migratory horseman usually possessed only his saddle and a poncho to warm him against the evening chill on the open plains. The soft, flexible, multilayered pampean saddle (*recado*), with its sheepskin covering, served as a warm if modest bed—a utility not offered by the stiff, curved, horned saddle of the American cowboy. The practice of sleeping on the ground, with only saddle and poncho for protection, persisted through the end of the century. In 1887 agronomist Carlos Lemée sharply criticized this habit as unhealthful and said it contributed to such epidemic diseases as cholera and yellow fever. Day laborers, when employed, could take shelter under an open-sided storage shed or in barns. During the shearing season, however, sheep took precedence over men in the barn. Wet wool could not be clipped, so when rains fell sheep rested in the barn and the shearers faced the elements unprotected.[9]

In a revealing exposé of Argentine working conditions in 1905, Director of Immigration Juan A. Alsina condemned the pampean rancho for failing to protect against either heat or cold. The earthen dwellings, chilly and dank during the winter, heated up unmercifully during the summer. The rural family, usually crowded into a single room without furniture or other comforts, lived in conditions worse than those of the industrial proletariat, who languished in urban tenements, or *conventillos*. In July 1914 socialist deputies Jacinto Oddone and Adolfo Dickman unsuccessfully proposed legislation to require "adequate and hygenic housing" for all rural workers and for renters. Their proposal mandated a fine of 500 pesos and compliance within twenty days for rural landlords and employers. The following year, Hugo Miatello also criticized the pathetic improvised zinc and earthen shacks that housed most rural renters and laborers. He found poverty, misery, and degradation to be the norm for most rural families. Only proprietors and some long-term sharecroppers enjoyed living in dwellings that could properly be termed homes.[10]

Housing on the pampa changed little during the nineteenth century, but clothing was substantially altered. Early on, the gaucho had adopted the Indian *chiripá* (a loose, diaper-like cloth tucked between the legs) as a practical, comfortable riding garment. Lacy leggings, *calzonzillos blancos*, were worn underneath. This combination lost popularity later in the century, when *bombachas*, introduced by immigrants, invaded the pampa. These baggy trousers, closed at the ankle to fit inside the boot, had replaced the traditional garments nearly completely by the 1880s. The versatile poncho, dating from colonial times, remained popular everywhere in the country. It served as a raincoat during howling pamperos, as a blanket during cold nights on the pampa, and as a shield in knife fights—each combatant wrapped his poncho around one arm to fend off the opponent's blows. Changes occurred in the manufacture of ponchos as imported English textiles began to supplant hand-woven woolens from the interior during the Rosas era. In the 1840s, government descriptions of deserters and soldiers frequently mention an "English poncho," usually blue, among other belongings. In 1836 Sir Woodbine Parish, a British diplomat, observed the impact of European imports on the pampa, noting that "the gaucho is everywhere clothed in British textiles. Take his whole equipment—examine everything about him—and what is there not of rawhide that is not British?" Gerstaecker likewise noted that "even the gaucho is dependent on the foreigner for his most simple wants," poncho, spurs, and riding tack.[11]

The dashing horseman of the pampa captured the fancy of most foreigners, many of whom left detailed descriptions of his arresting dress. At mid-century, Xavier Marmier found the "true soldier of South America, the son of the pampa," to be a stirring figure, with his "virile face, bronzed by the sun and framed by a mass of black hair," wearing a short-brimmed straw hat, brightly colored shirt, hand-woven poncho, and red Rosista chiripá. The predominance of red Federalist clothing in 1852, even after Rosas' fall, was recalled by C.B. Mansfield: in the port city, gauchos wore "scarlet *ponchos*, scarlet jackets, scarlet leg-coverings, of the most puzzling description . . . and underneath these, white trousers of immense capacity ending in a fringe, with bare feet."[12]

About his waist the gaucho wore a *tirador*, or broad leather belt, adorned with coins and silver ornaments according to the bearer's wealth. George Peabody, a Massachusetts gentleman on a hunting expedition, met an innkeeper in 1859 who "had as many as 20 or 30 silver dollars attached to his belt, & an enormous knife with a highly wrought silver sheath & handle." The tirador served many functions, among them the provision of back and kidney support for the strenuous riding and working required of ranch laborers. Money and vital documents, such as military enrollment certificates and passports, could be tucked safely within. The tirador's size and style changed with the type of work performed, and shepherds, cattle herders, and foot peons all wore different varieties.[13]

All gauchos carried a sheathed knife, or *facón*, ranging up to seventy centimeters (twenty-seven inches) in length, thrust through the back of the tirador. The facón was vital for work (killing, skinning, and castrating animals and repairing equipment), eating, and defense. This sword-like knife, repeatedly outlawed because of the many murders committed by facón-wielding gauchos, shrank to a more modest length by the end of the century. Although firearms became common during the last quarter of the century, the facón remained the favored instrument because of its versatility.[14]

The gaucho's hand-fashioned boots, *botas de potro*, also attracted wide comment. MacCann detailed the manufacture of this unique pampean footwear. "A young colt is killed and the skin of the hind legs, from the fetlocks up to about the middle of the thigh, is taken off;

the hair is removed, and while the skin is moist and flexible, it is fitted to the leg and foot of the wearer.'' Most gauchos left the end open to permit one or more exposed toes to clutch the small wooden stirrup. MacCann judged the boot ''very light and convenient for riding.'' The fragile, thin botas were admirably suited to riding, but they served poorly for walking, a chore avoided at all costs. As wild, unbranded livestock (*ganado cimarrón*) became more scarce on the pampa, ranchers began to oppose the use of the botas de potro. In 1856, Bernardo Gutiérrez, from Mercedes, suggested outlawing them because of the ''very frequent robberies'' of livestock to make boots. Valentín Fernández Blanco, who owned a ranch at Arroyo Dulce in Bahía Blanca county, noted that a horse's value of perhaps 100 pesos made the traditional boots costly items. Another rancher, Mariano Gainza, estimated that thieves wishing to make *coronas de vaca* accounted for half of all stolen cattle. ''Hard boots'' of European manufacture replaced the hand-made botas during the last third of the century.[15]

Spurs of varying diameters, materials, and configurations dangled from the gaucho's boots or bare feet and aided him in guiding and controlling his often ill-broken mount. Gerstaecker recalled seeing spurs of three to four inches in diameter hanging loosely from riders' boots. Frequently large enough to impede walking, the spurs nevertheless formed an essential part of the gaucho's riding equipment, though the sharp rowels sometimes did their work too well. Henri Armaignac observed exhausted horses, their sides dripping with blood from spur gashes, drawing a stagecoach southward from Chascomús. Unlike the stagecoach driver of the American west, who sat atop the vehicle, the gaucho rode a lead horse and thus guided the coach. Spurs also indicated affluence and status. Ranch workers wore iron or steel spurs, and estancieros of means used finely tooled silver spurs. In addition to spurs, a *rebenque* (heavy, plaited riding whip) helped the gaucho control his horse. The whip too became more elaborately and richly decorated as social status increased. Armaignac noted in 1869 that by examining the ''rural uniform''—whip, spurs, boots, knife, belt, poncho, and riding tack—one could determine the relative wealth and prestige of the owner.[16]

The gaucho tried desperately to maintain his traditional way of life, including his accustomed dress, in spite of strong currents of change buffeting the pampa. As Francisco Bauzá, a Uruguayan writer, suggested in 1885, the gaucho's traditional dress and his own herd of mounts represented the "guarantees of his liberty." With riding gear and fresh horses, a gaucho could live self-sufficiently, kill animals for food, and sell ostrich feathers and hides at the country store to purchase mate and tobacco. Argentina's liberal elite recognized the political significance of the gaucho's dress. Sarmiento identified the dress and the entire way of life with caudillo rule and montoneros. Observing the gaucho cavalry of General Justo José de Urquiza, marching on Buenos Aires in 1851 to overthrow Rosas, the future president lamented the chiripá, poncho, and other traditional garments: "As long as we do not change the dress of the Argentine soldier, we are bound to have caudillos." Transformations in the basics of life thus signified more than superficial cosmetic alterations in fashion; change meant the loss of a customary, cherished way of life. The once formidable facón shrank to a modest blade for skinning hides and castrating bulls. New mass-produced garments from European factories pushed aside native hand-woven textiles. Bombachas supplanted the chiripá, and machine-made boots replaced botas de potro. In dress, ranch workers became largely indistinguishable from the immigrant farmer or urban day laborer except in the most traditional regions. The customary long hair and matted beard remained, but the paisano's outward appearance changed as drastically as did pampean life in general.[17]

Diet on the pampa changed only slightly during the nineteenth century. Beef roasted quickly over an open fire (asado) and copious drafts of mate comprised the basis and often the entirety of the gaucho diet from the colonial era on. Travelers in the eighteenth and nineteenth centuries commented upon the carnivorous gaucho's single-minded penchant for quick-cooked beef. *Carne con cuero*, large portions of beef wrapped in cowhide and roasted slowly by an open fire, was still more highly prized by gauchos.[18]

Other dishes existed on the pampa, but they usually appeared only at special celebrations. *Mazamorra* (known as *api* in the northwestern provinces) was cornmeal mush, sweetened with honey and sugar and sometimes eaten with milk. *Locro*, another variety of corn mush, included meat and spices rather than sweeteners. A traditional verse described the dish: "To eat locro / I need: / Corn, beans and meat / And fried chili." The most common vegetable on the pampa, *zapallo* (squash or calabash) was one of the principal ingredients in a beef soup called *carbonada*, or *caldo*. Rice, onions, and, less frequently, other vegetables also found their way into the soup stock.[19]

On a day-to-day basis, however, gauchos demanded and ate fresh beef. In 1820 Vidal pointed out the common custom of carrying a "stack of raw beef" tied to the saddle. "Filthy as this custom may appear to us," the painter wrote, "it is universal among the gauchos (countrypeople) of these provinces." Caldcleugh, visiting about the same time as Vidal, remarked the gaucho's distaste for vegetables. "The *Gauchos* view them with eyes of ridicule, and consider a man who would eat them as little superior to the beasts of the field." Three decades later MacCann found the situation little changed: "The land, though very fertile, is never tilled by them, their food being exclusively beef and mutton; they have neither bread, milk, nor vegetables, and seldom eat salt." The great popularity of beef stemmed from its abundance, low cost, tastiness, and nutritional quality. Juan Fugl, an immigrant farmer from Denmark, found beef in great abundance in Tandil during the early 1850s because of the many stray cattle from ranches owned by Rosas' enemies embargoed by the dictator. Anyone could avail himself of free meat with the toss of a lasso. Gauchos simply roped a cow, sliced off the choicest cuts (the tongue and *matambre*, the meat between the ribs and hide, were especially prized), and skinned and staked out the hide. Bones and excrement served as free fuel on the wood-short plains. Throughout the decade, meat could not even be sold in Tandil because of the free supply from stray cattle.[20]

Many travelers at mid-century found the limited, bread-free diet monotonous. Samuel Greene Arnold, a North American traveler, dined on roast mutton, puchero, and mate in the old town of Luján but could find no milk. Jean León Pallière, a French painter, termed puchero the "alpha and omega" of the Argentine kitchen because it was served so frequently. Gerstaecker ate beef and sometimes zapallo but never encountered bread on the pampa, and Burmeister, too, recalled gauchos living "almost exclusively" on beef and mate.[21]

By the late 1870s, the rural diet had improved or diversified little according to foreign tastes. Edwin Clark, an English engineer, found rural meals "substantial but very monotonous fare" consisting mainly of beef, mutton, and a "dry hard and tasteless kind of cheese." Rural families grew no vegetables and churned no butter. Carlos Lemée criticized native women for using no condiments in their dishes, except for asado, and he urged them to emulate French and Italian immigrants by adding new spices to their humdrum recipes. According to Lemée, dull food drove men to town for more palatable meals, thereby increasing food expenditures unnecessarily. Another rural expert,

Godofredo Daireaux, also found fault with the traditional diet. He held poor nutrition responsible for generations of physical debilitation, which kept the gaucho "living in misery." He counseled ranchers to strengthen their workers, just as they did their livestock, with nourishing foods.[22]

As important as beef to the gaucho was his favorite beverage, mate (*Ilex paraguariensis*). From colonial times on, the rural Argentine (and often the city-dweller as well) began and ended each day with large quantities of mate cimarrón, or unsweetened tea. As MacCann noted, Argentines "usually take mate early in the morning; indeed they are drinking it throughout the entire day." After heating water in a small kettle, or *pava*, the gaucho would pour hot but not boiling water into a small pear-shaped gourd (also called the mate) filled with tea leaves. Passing the gourd around a circle, gauchos sipped the hot, strong tea through a communal straw, or *bombilla*, usually made of silver or other metal. Lively conversation, jokes, gossip, and plans for the day's work accompanied the seemingly endless rounds as the gourd was refilled time after time. The quintessential Briton Samuel Haigh noted with great surprise that native Argentines actually preferred mate to black English tea. Wealthier persons sipped their tea through individual silver straws from silver or copper-clad wooden or natural gourds.[23]

An elaborate folk ritual and folk beliefs developed around the beverage and its preparation. Beyond the sense of intimacy, sharing, and camaraderie involved in sipping from a common straw, the composition and temperature of the tea was significant. According to a traditional poem, mate could convey a variety of messages:

Bitter mate shows indifference.
Sweet mate, friendship.
Mate with balm-mint, displeasure.
Mate with cinammon, "you're on my mind."
Mate with brown sugar, congeniality.
Mate with orange peel, "come and look for me."
Mate with bee balm, "your sadness pains me."
Mate with milk, respect.
Mate with coffee, offense pardoned.[24]

Carlos Pellegrini, in the December 1853 issue of his authoritative journal *Revista del Plata*, commended mate to estancieros, terming the beverage a necessity for the gaucho and assuring ranchers that native workers could subsist on nothing but meat, tobacco, and a pound of mate per week. As a low-cost stimulant, the caffeine-rich tea was ideal for cost-conscious employers. Armaignac asserted that "pampean shepherds" would rather exist without meat than without mate. He estimated the per capita monthly consumption as about ten pounds of leaves.[25]

Debate over the nutritional and hygienic aspects of mate raged throughout the century. Like Pellegrini, many other rural authorities deemed the tea beneficial. In 1879 the *Anales* of the Rural Society reprinted a report by a Mr. Louis Gouty to the French Academy of Sciences. The research concluded that mate was a "therapeutic and nutritional agent," salutary for the intestines, heart, and liver, and recommended it as a useful, low-cost stimulant. In a lecture to agronomy and veterinary students in 1908, Dr. Julio Lesage likewise praised the beverage's physiological effects: experiments with humans, dogs, horses, and cattle pointed to the tea's positive digestive and stimulative actions. It also dulled the appetite, thereby permitting workers to labor longer with less solid food.[26]

Mate inspired as many critics as defenders. In 1904 Godofredo Daireaux attacked the tea, as well as traditional gaucho garments such as the poncho and chiripá, as unwanted vestiges of an era when one could live without working. He acceded to a brief period for mate drinking in the morning, but condemned the beverage for wasting time and dulling the appetite for more substantial fare. His polemic assumed a political significance beyond the mere nutritional aspects of the drink. Emilio A. Coni, at the extremity of "gauchophobia," decried the tea as "an abominable and dirty vice." Juan Alvarez, writing in *La prensa* of May 10, 1925, likewise criticized the drink and urged abstinence. Julio Díaz Usandivaras, a noted folklorist, responded to Alvarez with a spirited essay entitled "Nationality and Mate." He defended the flavor of the tea, judged a restaurant coffee cup far less hygienic than the communal bombilla, and termed drinking mate an integral part of the Argentine experience and character. Marshalling impressive scientific evidence, Luis C. Pinto emphatically refuted the critical attacks on mate.[27] As with etymology, literature, and other facets of the gaucho debate, partisans used mate as ammunition in a running battle to defame or exalt the gaucho.

The academic and scientific debate had little influence on the ranch worker, who continued imbibing his favorite drink in great quantities. The beverage retained its social and entertainment value, occupying a prominent position in pampean folklore. Today's Argentine extends the tea-filled gourd in a hand of friendship, and the mate passes in endless rounds about open fires and polished coffee tables from the remotest province to the heart of Buenos Aires.

The mate ritual opened and closed each ranch workday; and many other rural festivities also patterned themselves after the work calendar. Considering the bleakness, isolation, and hardships of rural life, it is not surprising that people grasped at every excuse to congregate and celebrate. The fall harvest, or *minga*, offered one such opportunity to dance and enjoy savory delights such as carne con cuero. This celebration largely disappeared when foreign farmers, farm workers, and threshing machines ended the native communal harvest that had dated from colonial times. The hierra and esquila provided two other occasions to celebrate the end of the strenuous seasonal chores of roundup and shearing. Singing, dancing, feasting, drinking, horse-racing, and gambling characterized most rural festivities.[28]

Other celebrations grew out of noneconomic events in the rural life cycle. The death of a child inspired one such fiesta—the *velorio del angelito*, or wake of the little angel—a practice growing from Arab and Spanish roots. According to Roman Catholic dogma, a child who died before age seven passed directly into heaven without sin, an event deserving commemoration. A godmother (*madrina*) dressed the corpse in fine garments, often tying a beautiful sash around the waist. A bedsheet overhead symbolized heaven, and paper flowers and candles brightened and lighted the room. The British mining engineer J. A. B. Beaumont attended a velorio in 1826 at the home of an army major in San Pedro. He recalled the tiny corpse, "dressed out in silks and silver" and surrounded by a "profusion of flowers and wax lights." The well-dressed party-goers sipped mate "in silver cups, brought in by slaves," dined, and danced late into the night to the music of a four-piece band. The wake had evidently been in progress for several days because a slave stood by the corpse "to wipe off the moisture, as it exuded from the eyes and mouth."[29]

A half-century later, Ebelot witnessed a wake in rural Azul. The child, dressed in fine clothing, sat propped on a table, ringed by greasy, smoking candles. On the second night, a gaucho played the guitar and everyone danced. Drinking, laughing, and kissing occupied the young, and the old men gathered in a corner to smoke and discuss horses—the ubiquitous topic among rural men. Wakes always continued as long as possible. The body was kept in an airy room, free of flies, to preserve it and hence prolong the festivities. Tavern keepers sometimes rented a child's body and placed it in the pulpería to draw a large crowd of drinking, festive patrons. Men gambled and drank mate, gin, and cognac, and women baked hearty filled pastries (*empanadas*). Dancing occupied many; and the traditional "dance of the little angel" always began just before midnight. Wakes also commemorated adult deaths, but on a far less extravagant scale than those for children. Velorios sometimes got out of hand, and at least one pampean town found it necessary to pass an ordinance regulating the festivities: in March 1871 the municipality of Rauch forbade dancing at wakes because of the "abuses and immoralities committed with such a prejudicial custom."[30]

The immigrant wave that so altered pampean life even touched the traditional creole velorio. By the late nineteenth century, the once-obligatory guitar-strumming gaucho had yielded to a small Italian orchestra as the preferred entertainment for a wake. Parents who lacked funds for an ensemble could also hire a lone "Italian with his organ."[31]

Whatever the occasion—velorio, hierra, or gathering at the local pulpería—the guitarist made his appearance. Many travelers found little to admire in pampean music. Concolorcorvo listened to gauderios near Montevideo play the instrument "very badly," singing "out of tune." In Tucumán he heard Argentines play "badly strung and untuned guitars" and "bandy their ballads" and "obscene verses." In 1823, Proctor noted that "almost all the peasants in this country play on that instrument. The music of the Pampas is dull, melancholy, and monotonous, but its jingle in these wild deserts, in the absence of better sounds is not unpleasant."[32]

Many gauchos could strum a few chords and sing folksongs, but the skilled *payador*, or troubadour, stood in a class by himself. He excelled at improvisational, poetic, musical duels (*payadas*) that offered consummate entertainment and allowed participants to exhibit their full intellectual and musical talents. Quick wit, double entendre, and clever repartee were highly prized in the singing duels. The payadas between Martín Fierro and a black singer whose father Fierro had killed, and Santos Vega's losing battle with a mysterious stranger (Satan), rank among the more famous musical battles in gauchesco literature. The payador, or *cantor*, who "corresponds to the singer, bard, or troubadour of the Middle Ages," was one of the four archetypal gauchos described by Sarmiento in *Facundo*, his masterful attack on the "barbarian" pampa of Rosas. Lugones entitled his influential eulogistic interpretation of the epic poem "Martín Fierro" (by José Hernández) *El payador*.[33] According to *El correo ilustrado* of September 1, 1877, the wandering singer could always find food and shelter in exchange for a few welcome tunes. Toward the end of the century, a weekly newspaper, *La pampa argentina*, collected and printed old pampean songs to preserve them for posterity. The paper also gave budding folksong writers a medium for publishing their compositions.[34]

Pampean music often revolved around the twin themes of love and nostalgia. Sad, repetitive airs, appropriately called *tristes*, expressed tender, sorrowful, resigned feelings. Many songs evoked the freedom and happiness of bygone days on the frontier and included as Sarmiento observed, "imagery relating to the open country, to the horse, and to the scenes of the wilderness, which makes it metaphorical and grandiose." Other songs provided political and social commentary, thereby serving as a kind of musical journalism that recorded customs, history, and biography. Current events, popular culture—indeed, much of the flavor, color, and pathos of rural life—found expression in anonymous ballads. The payador preserved and enriched the traditions and culture of the pampa and extended them into the twentieth century, when folkloric and traditionalist groups organized to cherish, nurture, and perpetuate them.[35]

In addition to listening to and making music, rural people greatly enjoyed dancing. Neighbors often gathered on a Sunday, when the work schedule permitted, to dance the *gato, pericón, zamacueca, triunfo, media caña, vidalita,* and other typical steps. The pericón stood out as the most typical and patriotic of the traditional dances. Both it and the gato included variations *con relación*, with partners singing verses back and forth as they danced. A couple dancing the gato might engage in this kind of verbal duel:

He: Pretty baby with black eyes,
      And scarlet lips.
      Your parents will be my in-laws.
      Your brothers my brothers-in-law.

She: I do not have black eyes,
Nor scarlet lips.
Papa will not be your father-in-law,
Nor my brother your brother-in-law.

He: There is such fire in your face
That each eye is a hot coal.
When I get too near it
I get toasted to the bone.

She: My eyes are not so strong
To singe your flesh and skin.
More than my eyes what burns you
Is the pulpería's drink.[36]

When not dancing, party-goers joined in animated conversation. According to the linguist Frederick Mann Page, who studied the gaucho dialect in 1893, "talking and singing" ranked as favorite rural pastimes. Rural people spiced their "vivacious and ready" conversations with "vivid, voluble and picturesque" similes and metaphors from daily life and with quaint, apt folk sayings. Page admired the paisano for his "vague poetic feeling," and found him a good improvisor who was "alert, quick at repartee." Although he had a reputation for reserved, melancholic stoicism among strangers, the gaucho reveled in practical jokes, humorous stories, and animated, convivial conversation with his own kind. Stories of the country bumpkin slyly outwitting a corrupt official or a "city slicker" abound in pampean folklore. As MacCann noted, the gaucho's "pleasures consist in visiting amongst his friends on the Sabbath-day, together with dancing, card-playing, and horse-racing."[37]

Whenever rural workers gathered, gambling inevitably occurred. Cockfights (*riñas*), popular throughout Latin America, also found adherents in Argentina. As with many rural customs, cockfighting persisted despite repeated prohibition. In 1867 a cockfighting establishment named La Empresa advertised contests in *El hurón* of Mercedes; the admission was ten cents.[38]

Betting on the outcome of the fight generated part of the riña's appeal and fascination. Azara affirmed that a gaucho would gamble away his money, riding tack, clothing, knife, and even horses. At mid-century, Francisco Juldain, Tandil's first schoolmaster, expressed disapproval of the native's fondness for strumming the guitar and gambling at *taba* in the pulpería. To play taba, participants threw the knuckle bone of a cow; the resulting heads or tails (*suerta* or *culo*) determined the winner. Throughout the nineteenth century, rural workers spent their free Sundays gambling at taba.[39]

Gauchos also played a variety of card games. MacCann asserted that their "chief amusement is card-playing, and they are confirmed gamblers." *Truco*, the favorite game, included much bluffing, witty table talk, and hidden signaling among the players, providing a forum for the clever repartee so enjoyed by gauchos. Betting always accompanied card games, and knife fights frequently developed out of disputes over the fall of the cards.[40]

The widespread popularity of gambling in many forms alarmed some Argentines and prompted denunciations of the vice. In a report on public land legislation in 1856, Eduardo Hopkins castigated the many "gamblers and drunkards, who do not want to work." Every town on the pampa, he complained, harbored such a class, yet the countryside languished for want of labor. "Where is the authority," he asked, "to force them to work?" In its issue of April 27, 1873, *La voz del Saladillo* roundly criticized the social and economic evils attendant to gambling. According to "Un Campesino," gambling had reached epidemic proportions on the pampa. Oliver Aquíleo González, a Pergamino policeman writing in *Revista de policía* (Police magazine) of Buenos Aires in 1900, termed gambling the passion of the working class. He condemned the wide range of games openly tolerated at all fiestas and urged a provincial campaign to restrict gambling, especially clandestine lotteries. Two years later in May 1902, another article in the same magazine charged that a farm worker earned 10 pesos per week but promptly drank and gambled away his wages in two days. Many rural families thus lacked an income yet continued to eat, which proved to the author's satisfaction that rural idlers and gamblers stole in order to support their vagrant habits.[41] Despite moralistic pleas and some legal prohibitions, rural gambling flourished into the twentieth century.

Not surprising in the gaucho's equestrian culture, horse-racing provided a principal gambling event at most gatherings. A variety of contests offered horsemen the opportunity to exhibit diverse skills and courage. One favorite, the *sortija*, or ring race, demanded good horsemanship, a steady hand, and a sharp eye. Riders attempted to lance a small gold ring suspended by a slender thread from a high wooden arch. The agile rider who skewered the tiny ring with his foot-long lance rode away with the prize or presented it to his favorite china. The Independence Day celebration of May 25, 1854, in Tandil was climaxed with several ring races. A half-century later the race retained its popularity: in 1900, a group of young people petitioned municipal intendant Federico Demarchi for twelve rings and aid in constructing an arch. These festivities commemorated the nation's final independence from Spain on July 9, 1816.[42]

Other equestrian races involved much more danger than the relatively tame ring race. In the *maroma*, a rider dropped from a gate crossbar onto the back of a horse running below, in a spectacular exhibition of timing, strength, and daring. According to his contemporaries, Rosas excelled at the maroma and could drop onto a wild horse, force reins onto the animal, and tame him. A variation involved dropping onto the back of a steer, holding on with spurs alone, and, after a wild ride, dispatching the animal with a knife thrust into the neck. Another showy example of equestrian skill required the rider to remove layers of his saddle one by one at a gallop and drop them onto the ground. On a return pass, the gaucho leaned from his mount, grabbed each piece, and reassembled the multi-layered saddle at a headlong gallop. For the gaucho, the chance to *pialar* permitted him to exhibit several virtues of the plains: courage and fearlessness in the face of danger, agility, and horsemanship. A lone horseman would gallop through a gauntlet of lasso-wielding gauchos. The ropers would lasso the horse's feet (pialar) and throw him to the ground. The rider sought to land on his feet, reins in hand, as the horse tumbled. According to Carlos Hurtado, Rosas also excelled at this dangerous, highly gaucho game. The sport grew out of the real need for such a skill on the solitary frontier, honeycombed with vizcacha and other animal burrows that made falls inevitable for even the most experienced horsemen. The lone rider, falling beneath his horse or losing his mount on the expansive pampa, could easily perish, but falling on one's feet and controlling the horse spelled survival on the frontier.[43]

Other games also grew out of rural survival and work skills, such as the need to develop horses strong enough to pull against a wild lassoed bull, or to push an unruly animal into compliance. The *cinchada*, or tug-of-war, tested the pulling power of two horses; *pechando* (breasting) required riders to run their horses into one another head-on. The prized virtues of strength and courage in both man and mount figured prominently, and animals and riders frequently met with injury or death. Several types of races permitted large numbers of participants to compete. In 1859, the sportsman Peabody witnessed a 200-meter race between fifty or sixty riders near Fraile Muerte (now Bell Ville) in the northwest part of the province: "the track is of a certain width, & if one of the horses is able to crowd the other off the acknowledged track, he wins the race: they accordingly run down the course, each horse pushing the other with all his might, & it is frequently not the fastest, but the best trained and strongest horse that wins." In the late 1880s Thomas J. Turner reaffirmed the broad appeal of Sunday horse-races. Competitors dressed in their finest clothes gathered for miles around and provided an exciting "display of the hardihood and intrepidity of the man and the speed and endurance of the animal."[44]

Pato (duck), a modified cross-country race dating from the early seventeenth century, was the gaucho's favorite contest. Hudson described the preparations and conduct of the game: a large fowl "was killed and sewn up in a piece of stout raw hide, forming a somewhat shapeless ball, twice as big as a football, and provided with four loops or handles of strong twisted raw hide made of a convenient size to be grasped by a man's hand." The riders, ranging far across the pampa, contested possession of the duck. "There would perhaps be a scuffle or scrimmage, as in football, only the strugglers would be first on horseback before dragging each other to earth." Bartolomé Mitre summarized the spirit of the rugged game in a poem in 1839, "El pato: Cuadro de costumbre."

> Pato! strong game
> for the man of the pampa,
> traditional custom
> of a virile people.
> To temper the nerves,
> To enlarge the muscles
> like a fleet race
> of one's youthful years.

Frequent injuries, death, property damage, and scattered livestock prompted successive administrations to ban the strenuous contest in 1799, 1800, 1811, 1822, 1840, and 1899, but its popularity never waned. By the twentieth century, participants had domesticated the game, replaced the hapless fowl with a stuffed hide, organized teams and leagues, and written official rules. The vitality and substance of pato disappeared, as did the gaucho himself, but the form—properly tamed and subdued—remained as a popular reminder of bygone days.[45]

The government also made repeated efforts to suppress another favorite gaucho pastime, the *boleada*, or ostrich hunt with bolas. This recreation doubled as an important economic activity because ostrich feathers found a ready market among rural pulperos. The Indian or gaucho would hold one thong of the boleadora, or bolas, and whirl the others about his head while galloping after game or pursuing an enemy; and he could toss them with surprising accuracy. Foreigners found the dramatic boleada exciting and exotic, and some even participated in a hunt. Darwin tried his hand at whirling the bolas in the early 1830s. He caught one ball in a bush and another around his horse's leg and came crashing to the ground. "The Gauchos roared with laughter," he recorded in his journal; "they cried they had seen every sort of animal caught, but had never before seen a man caught by himself."[46]

Ranchers particularly despised gauchos who hunted ostriches because they also dispersed and poached livestock. As a young rancher in 1817, Rosas narrowly escaped being knifed to death when he attempted to chase a band of ostrich hunters from his land in Monte. His opposition to them never wavered. In September 1844 he instructed manager Laureano Ramírez that ostrich hunting "should never be permitted" on his land. The dictator demanded an end to the "scandal" and ordered justices of the peace to remit hunters to Buenos Aires "in chains." Rosas also sent Ramírez a set of stocks, "a good one," to chastize hunters captured on his estancias. In this case, as in his other policies, Rosas firmly asserted the rights of the landowning elite and pushed for the subordination of the rural poor. The property rights affirmed by Rosas and the powerful terratenientes conflicted with and ultimately eliminated many vestiges of gaucho customs and activities.[47]

After the dictator's fall, ranchers persisted in demanding the prosecution of ostrich hunters. The Buenos Aires provincial police chief issued a circular to rural justices in mid-1852 requesting more vigorous enforcement of the ban on boleadas because of numerous complaints by ranchers. A prohibition issued the following year classified hunters as vagrants and condemned them to military service; *La tribuna* warmly applauded Governor Pastor Obligado's decree as a firm step toward reducing the alarming quantity of scattered and stolen livestock on the plains. The comprehensive rural code of 1865 forbade the hunting of any fowl or quadruped on private lands without the owner's permission and on public lands without a license. Hunters were liable for damages to fences and property, and convicted poachers faced a 500-peso fine or labor on public works.[48]

Legal restrictions notwithstanding, hunting for recreation and profit persisted. In November 1871 ranchers in Nueve de Julio, Bragado, and Lincoln counties reacted with alarm to the appearance of several bands of armed gauchos hunting ostriches. Convinced that the band actually engaged in cattle rustling, estancieros demanded punitive action by Sarmiento's minister of war, Martín de Gainza. Direct losses to thieves represented only part of the ranchers' objections to ostrich hunting. Because birds often took cover in brushy areas where bolas could not be thrown, hunters set large range fires to force the game onto the open plains. Such uncontrolled blazes destroyed pasturelands and posed grave threats to rural livestock and ranch facilities.[49] Wasteful practices that had evolved over decades of frontier abundance finally yielded before the steady political pressure exerted by the provincial ranching elite.

By the 1880s, the ostrich feather industry had acquired a modicum of dignity and organization. The Rural Society urged that feather gathering twice a year be encouraged and that the birds not be killed. The traditional gaucho method of running horses to death in the wild chase, of starting brush fires to stampede the game, and of killing the prey resulted in unacceptable waste and damage. Ranchers promoted a more efficient, rational, conservationist harvest of feathers to expunge the customs of the past. Government officials responded to the powerful estancieros' wishes with new regulations in August 1883 that prohibited hunting on all public lands, permitting it on private holdings only with both the owner's and the justice's permission. The law forbade hunting during the mating season on pain of four to twelve months of labor on public works.[50] The regulated order of the modern pampa ruled in accordance with the desires of the landowners and curtailed yet another part of the gaucho's traditional lifestyle and livelihood.

In an editorial of May 20, 1883, *La campaña* of Buenos Aires accurately assessed the social causes of continued ostrich hunting in the province. What had once been a venerable recreational pastime on the open frontier had become a residual economic survival activity for the unfortunate "pariahs" on the settled, fenced pampa gringa. With land speculators and corrupt officials limiting access to honest employment, the outcasts of rural society turned to the remaining frontier regions to hunt the vanishing ostrich and earn a few coins.

As the hardy, daring participant forms of recreation disappeared and fell subject to regulation, spectator sports began to supplant them. Wild riders of the maroma, pato, and boleada perhaps became rodeo performers. In early 1909, *El orden* of Mercedes reported the close of a "bronco busting" rodeo at the Rural Society grounds at Palermo, in Buenos Aires. Riders moved to Rosario for their next performance. At mid-year, W. H. Wagner of the Sociedad Sportiva Argentina announced further competition in the capital. To celebrate the nation's centenary and to preserve the "most virile creole customs," the Sociedad sponsored a contest featuring three hundred horses and offering three gold medals as prizes. Winners were promised a trip to the United States to compete against riders from several nations.[51]

Also indicative of changing times, bicycling took pampean towns by storm during the late 1890s. Buenos Aires licensed some six thousand bicycles at 5 pesos each in 1898. Cycle clubs and velodromes sprang up in many places. "Pedal," writing in *La patria* of Olavarría, reported that Sunday races around the central plaza attracted large, spirited crowds. The fans cheered enthusiastically despite the competitors' many falls. The Olavarría cycle club planned future races against Azul and other towns.[52] Although gauchos did not exchange their horses for bicycles, the appearance of the two-wheelers in the province symbolized one more step toward a mechanized modernity that held no place for the gaucho.

From bolas to bicycles, from chiripá to bombachas, the social life and material culture of the province changed markedly during the nineteenth century. In spite of these great changes, there were certain constants, among them the fact that the paisano of the 1890s enjoyed no better housing and probably ate less beef than his gaucho predecessor of the early decades. The social changes that altered rural society resulted from forces reshaping the pampean frontier into a link in the world capitalist economy. Despite the limited economic opportunities open to him, the gaucho had developed a way of life and forms of entertainment that he enjoyed greatly and that aided him economically. Throughout the century, his economic opportunities and social life became more constricted, until finally, by the 1880s, what was uniquely and identifiably gaucho had largely disappeared. The class structure that permitted large landowners to impose their will upon rural society persisted. Latifundism and legal restrictions by the landed elite pushed the gaucho relentlessly toward conditions of dependent peonage or forced military service.

6
Latifundia
and the
Ranching Elite

Monopoly of landownership in large estates by the few, or latifundism, has characterized land tenure in Buenos Aires province from colonial times to the present. Generous grants by the Spanish crown initiated an effective monopoly for the select few and formed the basis of a self-perpetuating system. The judicious selection of a ranch site along a *rincón*, or confluence of two rivers, gave the rancher control over sometimes scarce water resources and permitted domination of a vast grazing hinterland. During droughts neighboring herds gathered at the rivers to drink, and the master of the rincón would brand unmarked animals, thereby enlarging his herds at the expense of others.[1]

A census of the city of Buenos Aires in 1744 recorded only 327 property owners out of a total population of more than 16,000. In the countryside, there were only 168 property owners among more than 6,000 rural residents. A few owners controlled vast expanses of 333,000 to 400,000 acres, where slaves slaughtered semi-wild livestock for their hides and tallow. Twenty-six ranchers dominated the fertile banks of the Río de la Plata, Paraná, and Riachuelo rivers, forming an "iron belt" that retarded the city's economic growth, built a fortune for those few, and condemned the rural masses to "moral and material misery." During the late colonial period, Juan José Sagastí protested to the crown that large grants to "powerful persons" precipitated the eviction of earlier settlers, impeded agricultural growth and commercial development, and forced many rural workers into a vagabond existence. The concentration of landownership created social problems, including "robberies, homicides, and other vices of this nature."[2]

In 1808 Esteban Romero, speaking for the porteño town council, instructed officials in Chascomús not to classify small ranchers as vagrants. Humble settlers, he stated, owning perhaps a dozen horses and a few cattle, should not be turned off lands where they had squatted because even greater social evils would result. In 1811 Col. Pedro Andrés García unsuccessfully recommended a precise survey and subdivision of sprawling unexploited holdings. He proposed the formation of small villages where those who were poor, landless, and jobless through no fault of their own could escape from their miserable circumstances. The villages and subdivision of land would also aid in safeguarding the frontier against devastating Indian attack by advancing the line of secure settlement.[3]

Such defenses of small ranchers notwithstanding, the eviction of settlers by speculators and other land grant recipients persisted into the national period. José Gallardo settled, registering a claim for land, in San Vicente in 1806. Yet in 1820 Col. Nicolás Vedia received title to the holding even though he had neither livestock nor buildings there as required by law. "How can you reject the rights given me by fourteen years of settlement?" asked Gallardo. Emphyteusis grants made by Bernadino Rivadavia beginning in 1822 evicted many other settlers as well. The land grant system provided for the long-term use of land at low fixed rents so long as the recipient kept the area under cultivation and saved it from depreciation. The national government retained title, gained rental income, and hoped to promote agriculture by utilizing Argentina's most abundant resource: land. Emphyteusis grants were legally neither heritable nor alienable, but speculators combined grants to form huge estancias. Between 1822 and 1830, a mere 538 individuals amassed nearly 7,800,000 hectares (19,274,000 acres) of pampean grasslands. The Anchorenas, cousins of Rosas, accumulated 352,000 hectares (870,000 acres), and Rosas' brother Prudencio nearly 73,000 hectares (180,000 acres). A grant in 1825 to Juan Luis Bustos displaced eight prior settlers in San Vicente. Paulino Negrete, who had settled there in 1818, Florencio Peralta, who had squatted in 1813, and several others lost their holdings. The large size of the grants, combined with easy transfers of title, encouraged further concentration of pampean landownership.[4]

The precise nature of estancias that developed on the pampa remains a subject of debate because the economic and social relations on the Argentine ranch defy convenient classification as an ideal feudal or capitalistic type. The traditional ranch of the late colonial and early national periods exhibited characteristics of both, as well as considerable internal variation. As ranching modernized during the century, the relations came to approximate more closely a purely capitalistic mode of production fully integrated into world markets. But several aspects of the traditional estancia could be termed feudalistic. Ranch workers sometimes received tokens in lieu of cash wages or worked in part for room and board. Peons remained contractually bound to a patrón and legally tied to a geographic area, either a single partido or a ranch. Several types of restrictive documents—working papers, internal passports, and military registration certificates—curtailed mobility and tied workers to an estate or region. Local justices of the peace and alcaldes, often ranchers themselves, conducted their official duties and dispensed justice from their estancias in the manner of feudal barons hearing grievances on their estates. Harsh corporal punishment and occasional paternalistic rewards, such as fiestas, colored the relations between peon and estanciero.[5]

In spite of the feudalistic flavor of rural *social* relations, evidence weighs heavily toward the essentially capitalistic *economic* nature of even the traditional Argentine estancia. On the nineteenth-century pampa, workers earned cash wages on a daily or monthly basis far more often than they received tokens, or *latas*. These metallic stamped discs usually entered the wage system only during shearing, when workers would receive a lata for each hundred animals clipped. Food, shelter, and the vicios of mate and tobacco formed an integral part of rural wages and were not a fringe benefit thrown in at the patrón's option. The landed elite directed much legislative and political energy toward formalizing and tightening labor relations in order to gain a tractable, dependable work force at wages they wished to pay. Vagrancy and work laws, as well as the threat of military conscription, coerced the gaucho into becoming a wage earner, a soldier, or an outlaw. Ranchers sought to sell their produce at the highest prices obtainable and to employ the fewest peons at the lowest wages possible. Speculation and rental also figured prominently in their fortunes because land values inflated throughout the century. Successful ranchers usually reacted quickly to changing international market demands in an economically rational fashion. They adapted production to maximize profits, shifting from hides and tallow to jerked meat, wool, cereals, and finally high-grade beef and mutton for export. While status and class considerations played a role in landowning aspirations, most estancieros managed their holdings (or, more often, paid administrators) to reap a profit.[6]

Speaking to the General Constituent Congress on May 12, 1826, Minister of Government Julian Segundo de Agüero asked rhetorically, "Who are the great capitalists of this city? The ranchers and only the ranchers." According to Agüero, persons with capital available would invest in livestock production because "they see that this is what pays." Many landowners like the Anchorena family successfully bridged the gap between rancher and merchant and operated profitably in both activities. Typically, an immigrant of the late colonial period, and increasingly in the national period, would begin in commerce and invest accumulated profits in land. The second generation would continue the commercial ventures but diversify into livestock raising, land accumulation, and meat salting. By the third generation, landowning had become an economic cushion for absentee owners who resided in luxury in Barrio Norte rather than living on the estancias. Profits and prestige merged in the halls of the Rural Society and the Jockey Club, founded in 1866 and 1882, respectively, where the landed and commercial elites mingled.[7]

In spite of frequent political rifts, Argentine ranchers displayed considerable solidarity and ably organized to further their class interests. Azara first proposed formal rancher cooperation in 1801 in his book *Memoria sobre el estado rural del Río de la Plata.* He envisioned an association of ranchers to promote the interests of the livestock industry. After independence, Father Tomás Javier de Gomensoro urged the formation of a Junta de Amigos del País for the same purpose. Both proposals went unrealized, but in early 1822 Felipe Senillosa, a prominent rancher, again urged estancieros to organize. Bernadino Rivadavia charged Domingo Olivera with the task of fostering a "rural society," and a ranchers' commission was duly constituted in July 1826. The first Argentine Rural Society faltered with the overthrow of the unitario government by porteño federalists in 1827, but the group continued acquiring assets into the 1830s. By 1830 the rancher organization had accumulated 296,000 hectares (731,000 acres) of land. In 1837 the Rural Society owned 270,000 hectares (667,000 acres) of grazing land, some 25,000 cattle, and other livestock valued at 1.8 million pesos.[8]

The estanciero organization of the 1820s and 1830s did not survive because it was not needed at the time. Large landowners, cattlemen, and *saladeristas* successfully built political hegemony without formal organization. Their low-investment, high-profit livestock and meat-salting operations raised them to economic preeminence in the province and provided the basis for their political predominance. With this leverage—and with their interests championed by Rosas, one of their own—ranchers realized favorable labor, taxation, land, and other policies without a formal and autonomous organization. Rosas—rancher, saladerista, dictator—fostered the interests of the provincial terratenientes and brought Argentine latifundism to its mature modern form. During the 1830s, Rosas encouraged the purchase rather than rental of land, and he had virtually eliminated the emphyteusis system by 1839. Thanks to this largess and political patronage, by 1840 some 825 landowners held more than eight million hectares (19,768,000 acres) of rich pampean pasturage. In 1851, as the dictator's long rule drew to a close, 382 persons held 82 percent of all provincial lands. Rosas himself owned about 330,000 hectares (815,000 acres), 179,000 cattle, 140,000 sheep, and 103,000 horses. Sarmiento, who fled from Rosas to exile in Chile from 1840 through 1852, wrote a satirical description of land policy under Rosas.

> Who was Rosas? A landowner.
> What did he accumulate? Lands.
> What did he give his supporters? Lands.
> What did he take from his foes? Lands.[9]

Rosas focused his political energies upon promoting his own economic interests and those of the commercial-financial and landowning elites that supported him. He extended the frontier to make more land available by militarily defeating and buying off hostile Indian tribes. Land confiscated from Unitarian foes became political plums for Federalist, or, more precisely, Rosista supporters. In one example of his land policy, he bequeathed 73,000 hectares (180,000 acres) near Tandil to his cousin María del Pilar López de Osornio and her betrothed, José Ramón Gómez, for their wedding in 1830. From exile in 1863, he recalled the assistance he had rendered to the Anchorenas. "I also went into public life to serve them. I served them with notorious favouritism in everything they asked and needed. Those lands they have, to a great extent they got them from me, buying them at very modest prices." The dictator had even exempted his cousins from state demands for livestock and soldiers. The Anchorenas increased their holdings in the province from 340,000 to 633,000 hectares (840,000 to 1,564,000 acres) between 1830 and 1852, and they continued to prosper after Rosas' fall. They had extended their ownership, always locating near plentiful, controllable sources of water, to 958,000 hectares (2,367,000 acres) by 1864. Pedro J. Vela of Tandil, a fervent Rosista, also maintained his fortune and power after the dictator's fall. Vela served as justice of the peace, provincial legislator, and member of the board of directors of the provincial bank. As a Tandil alcalde in 1843, he reported owning 260,000 cattle. His estate, valued at 32 million pesos, included 280,000 hectares (692,000 acres) of land.[10]

Like the Anchorenas and Vela, most prominent latifundists maintained their power and land regardless of political vagaries. Quick denunciations of the "tyrant" by Rosista landowners after the dictator's overthrow in February 1852, and professions of allegiance to the victorious Justo José de Urquiza permitted the elite to perpetuate their power and position virtually unaltered. The new administration needed landowner support and did nothing to alienate this elite. As one Argentine scholar has noted, one encounters "the same names, the same families, the same interests" dominating provincial affairs throughout the century.[11]

By 1836, large ranches of more than 5,000 hectares (12,355 acres) constituted 77 percent of all provincial holdings. Ranches of less than 2,500 hectares (6,178 acres) comprised a mere 5 percent of the total. Among the largest ranchers of the 1840s were Nicolás Anchorena, with 100,000 head of cattle in Navarro, Ysidro Jurado, with 60,000 head in Dolores, and Ysabel Zavaleta, with 238,000 head in Baradero. The concentration of latifundist power emerges clearly in land tenure patterns at mid-century. In the entire province, 200 holdings, 28 percent of the total, included 60 percent of the land in 1851.[12]

Tenancy accompanied latifundism in Buenos Aires province. In 1854 only the agricultural zone near Buenos Aires held more owners than renters (68 percent to 32 percent). In the mixed zone of ranching and agriculture further from the capital, renters outnumbered proprietors more than two to one (69 percent to 31 percent). In strictly ranching areas toward the frontier, renters constituted 59 percent of all ranch operators and owners 41 percent. The Rosista heritage of powerful terratenientes and small renters persisted.[13]

The consolidation of latifundia accelerated during the second half of the century under the nation's European-oriented, liberal elite rulers. Legislation continued to deliver huge tracts of rich virgin pastureland to speculators and terratenientes as quickly as the land could be wrested from the Indians. A sincere desire to promote smaller holdings at times motivated legislators, but the results never varied. Faulty administration, pressing governmental financial needs, and the power of large landowners frustrated every attempt at land reform.[14]

The negative effects of latifundism ramified throughout rural society. In late 1854 the *Revista del Plata* condemned the limited access to land for rendering otherwise "industrious people" on the pampa "inert". "Ragged families" subsisted in "ruined huts" because they realized the futility of building substantial homes, only to be turned out of them at the end of a rental contract. Foreign agricultural colonists enjoyed access to land denied to the "poor shepherds and laborers" of the countryside. In a note to President Bartolomé Mitre in 1863, Col. Benito Machado posited landlessness as the root of widespread rural gambling and vagrancy. He charged that the government demanded "blood when necessary" from the rural native but failed to offer him the same opportunity accorded the immigrant to acquire land.[15]

Sarmiento envisioned a pampa dotted with small family farms worked by sturdy yeomen. Writing to his close friend Mary Mann (widow of American educator Horace Mann) in 1866, he condemned the Spanish system of land tenure as one of the chief "causes of the wars and barbarism" suffered by the nation. He sought to plant the seed of the "North American system" of small freeholds on the pampa with a model agricultural community at Chivilcoy. Sarmiento's successor as president, Nicolás Avellaneda, also appreciated the tremendous social revolution that could be wrought by altering the land tenure system. Writing on land reform in 1865, the future president (1874–80) stressed the importance of making the gaucho a property owner in order to curtail his wanderings and cool his "savage passions." He condemned the prevalent rental system for its destructive, fragmenting effect on rural society. "Do you wish to curb our nomadic gaucho in his vagabond instincts? Root him in the soil with the only bond that is lasting: property." The Avellaneda Law of 1876 represented the best conceived effort at pampean land reform; but weak administration, as always, permitted speculators to acquire vast concessions without populating or improving the land as the statute specified.[16]

Writing in the first issue of the *Anales* of the Rural Society in 1866,
A. Estrada criticized "our bad social structure," based on the inequitable distribution of property. He counseled changing "the laws
that govern the feudal property of our lands" and improving "the
condition of the proletarians of today" through better education and
access to landownership.[17] Such attacks upon latifundia represented
the rare exception, not the rule, in the terrateniente organ.

Visiting the southern counties of the province in the late 1860s, a
Frenchman marveled at the great size of the holdings, estimating that
even the smallest covered at least 2,500 hectares (6,178 acres) and held
perhaps 2,000 cattle, 500 horses, and 20,000 sheep. Cattle ranches of
the 1860s commonly covered from 27,000 to 67,500 hectares (66,717
to 166,792 acres), but sheep ranches seldom exceeded 13,500 hectares
(33,358 acres). Cattle predominated in frontier areas, whereas sheep
grazed on better pastures nearer the port. In Tandil, the heirs of Vela,
the Rosista politician, maintained the family position as the county's
leading landholder with more than 89,000 hectares (219,919 acres) in
1863. José G. Lezama controlled 59,400 hectares (146,777 acres);
Felipe Arana, another Rosista, 40,500 (100,076 acres); and Leonardo
Pereira 37,800 (93,404 acres). In tax rolls of the 1870s, other
prominent family names appear—Santamarina, Lezica y Lanus,
Gómez, Iraola y Pereira, and Anchorena—with holdings of up to
77,000 hectares (190,267 acres). These great families perpetuated and
enlarged their influence through judicious intermarriage and renewed
efforts at rancher organization that bore fruit in 1866, with the
formation of the Argentine Rural Society.[18]

Rancher concern for organization had revived after Rosas' fall. In
1854, some two hundred estancieros met with Minister of Government
Ireneo Portela to discuss problems stemming from unknown and
unregistered livestock brands. Patricio Lynch presided over the
meeting, which ended in the formation of a commission of prominent
landowners to present rancher interests to the government. Such
progressive leaders as Sarmiento and Valentín Alsina, along with
ranchers Eduardo Olivera and Gervasio A. de Rosas, lobbied unsuccessfully for a rural organization during the Agricultural Exposition of
1859.[19]

A conjuncture of unfavorable economic conditions prompted
ranchers to band together in the Argentine Rural Society in 1866.
Economic dislocations touched off by the treasury drain of the

Paraguayan War (1865–70), coupled with monetary problems and a United States ban on wool imports, hit estancieros hard. Some deserted the province for virgin lands in Santa Fe and Entre Ríos. Others, led by Eduardo Olivera, whose father, Domingo, had been an organizer in the 1820s, formed the Rural Society that continues today. José Martínez de Hoz became the Society's first president. The official organ, the *Anales*, which appeared in 1867 under Olivera's editorship, came to exert a powerful influence upon provincial and national politics. Other leading ranchers, including José María Jurado, Felipe Senillosa, Leonardo Pereyra, and Estanislao Zeballos, also edited the *Anales*.[20]

As sheep ranching began to compete seriously with cattle raising for grasslands, divisions within the landowning elite occasionally arose. Those producing creole cattle for the traditional saladero markets viewed sheep ranchers as unwelcome competitors for grazing lands. Although the flexible Rural Society successfully accommodated both interests for a time, conflict emerged in 1875. José María Jurado submitted the society's official position on a pending land law. He held that unoccupied public lands near the frontier were fit only for raising cattle because sheep required such improved pasturage as alfalfa; consequently, frontier lands should be divided according to the needs of cattlemen rather than those of sheep ranchers. This criterion promoted extensive holdings, as a square league (6,672 acres) of virgin frontier land fed only 800–1,000 cattle, whereas improved grasses near Buenos Aires held four times that number. In general, cattle required five times as much pasture per head as sheep, adding weight to Jurado's argument for large parcels of land on the frontier.[21] Land tenure policies, enacted in accordance with Rural Society interests, continued to favor latifundists.

Although traditional cattle raisers continued to exert strong influence, the society evolved forward-looking, progressive policies geared toward export to European markets rather than saladero production. During the late 1870s and 1880s, many ranchers recognized the need to search out new markets, and the Rural Society supported research on beef processing and freezing. The clear-cut victory for progressive European-oriented ranchers occurred over the issue of beef shipments on the hoof. The society backed a law in August 1883 that exempted shipments of live animals and fresh meat from export duties for a decade. Ranchers who produced high-grade beef from mestizo cattle for European markets prospered at the expense of traditional saladero interests. While the society ably supported the concerns of traditional ranchers in such areas as labor control and land consolidation, it actively promoted Argentina's integration into the European market system and the modernization of the livestock industry.[22]

Terratenientes were successful in maintaining their tight monopoly on provincial landownership in the nineteenth century. Many fertile regions lay fallow and unproductive while speculators awaited a propitious moment to sell or rent. *La unión del sud* of Chascomús complained in its issue of August 25, 1872, that large areas of both municipal and private land lay idle and abandoned. The paper urged that land be opened to immigrant farmers, who would contribute to the area's growth. In one example of speculation, the Drabble firm owned but "paid no attention to" more than 16,000 hectares (39,536 acres) in southern Santa Fe province, leaving them untouched from 1857 to 1882. The firm, finally deciding to lease the land, "found *gauchos* and others squatted on the land, and had to turn them off."[23] Again the small rancher actively using the land yielded to a powerful absentee owner's claim.

Verbal attacks on latifundism and its negative social consequences continued, but no remedial action resulted. In 1876, the year of the Avellaneda land law, *La aspiración* of Mercedes aired the need for a "home for our countrymen, for the gaucho." The paper actively supported a legislative proposal for land grants on the frontier to the native-born "disinherited poor." "The moment has come when we should remember the poor gaucho," who lives a miserable vagrant existence for want of land, the editor concluded. The many "wandering families," numbering perhaps fifty thousand persons, could both secure the frontier against Indian attack and fuel economic growth if they were provided with land and draft exemption for colonizing underpopulated regions. But measures designed to promote native colonization met with frustration. Instead, a law of December 26, 1878, ceded up to 8,000 hectares (19,768 acres) of frontier land for 20 pesos per hectare provided that the buyer stock his holdings with at least 300 cattle or 1,000 sheep. Urban speculators acquired 2.4 million hectares (5.9 million acres) under the law without improving or utilizing the land. Provincial governor Carlos D'Amico nullified the fraudulent sales in November 1880 following a change in government, but this was the only case in which land sale abuses were rectified.[24]

Even the Rural Society recognized some of the negative effects of land monopoly, and in 1882 it counseled moderate reform. The *Anales* cited the precarious condition of the rural masses, living in alarming misery, as the root of "innumerable crimes" committed in the province. The "poor paisano," unable to pay inflated land rents, languished, unoccupied and unproductive. The society urged agricultural education and reform to alleviate the conditions suffered by the rural poor and to defuse the threat of social upheaval. Significantly, the *Anales* stressed the problem of high land rental but mentioned nothing about facilitating land purchase. Ownership remained the monopoly of a dynamic, adaptable directing elite that adjusted readily to changing world market conditions and wielded the political clout to assure favorable land, labor, immigration, and tax policies. This elite of Buenos Aires province joined with landowners of the interior, and their coalition formed the basis of support for the modernizing administrations of presidents Julio A. Roca and Miguel Juárez Celman.[25]

Godofredo Huss, an expert in rural affairs and publisher of the *Revista de ganadería*, added his voice to land tenure criticism in 1882. Many small ranchers had to sell their few livestock, he asserted, because they lacked adequate pasturage. He blamed speculators and rich estancieros for squeezing smaller ranchers and urged government intervention to facilitiate the sale of small parcels to the landless at a fair price. *El eco de Tandil* likewise supported land reform in late 1882. On the old open range frontier, with a purely livestock economy and the constant threat of Indian invasions, large landholdings and scattered settlements had made economic and strategic sense. On the secure, settled plain, however, latifundia impeded the growth of such pampean towns as Tandil.[26]

The provincial government finally responded, ineffectually, to the cries for reform with the Homestead Law of October 1884. In a report to Minister of Agriculture Victorino de la Plaza, Huss summarized the intent of the legislation as "an act of reparation for our gaucho, who has always been on the frontier defending the national honor and integrity." But the law, modeled on the United States Homestead Act of 1862, turned out to be a grotesque parody of that inspiration and failed utterly to promote land subdivision. As under previous legislation, speculators and terratenientes benefited at the expense of small buyers. Two years after the passage of the Homestead Law, Federico Tobal observed that the gaucho continued to exist as a landless pariah.

He urged legislation to give the gaucho "possession of the soil" and to curtail "monopolies and abusive plundering" in the countryside. Latifundists, leading a palatial existence in the port, prospered at the expense of the "poor gaucho," who, after serving his nation in war, "miserably vegetates and dies."[27]

The landowning elite continued intransigent, yielding land to neither native nor immigrant except on short-term rental contracts. In 1887 the provincial legislature passed the only law aimed at creating agricultural centers that would have given landownership to farmers. Predictably, the attempt failed, and by the 1890s officially sponsored agricultural colonization was a dead cause. Speculators, not cultivators, profited from official colonization. Roberto Campolieti, addressing the property question in 1895 in the rural journal La agricultura, recognized the danger of latifundism to rural social stability. He feared that deep class divisions, pitting the landed few against the landless masses, could erupt into violence unless redistribution occurred; but he cautioned against such extreme solutions as the collective ownership of land proposed by socialists.[28]

As the Argentine nation surged proudly into the twentieth century, propelled by its robust rural export sector, the glaring deficiencies of latifundism attracted more aggressive criticism. La patria of Dolores noted the sad irony of a foreign investor who had advertised unsuccessfully for land near a railroad or river to settle fifty to one hundred immigrant farm families. Because of the private monopoly over land, he could find no suitable property to purchase. Latifundia impeded economic development in the province and hindered population growth, according to the pampean newspaper—a serious problem for a region with a scant two persons per square kilometer (five persons per square mile). In 1903 and 1904, La agricultura published several attacks on the nation's land tenure system. The plight of the rural native was summarized by J. M. Buyo: "The poor creole class has lost all idea of the right to own land, sees it as the unalterable patrimony of the grandees, and vegetates with no other possibility than to be a soldier, ranch peon, or rustler. What else can he be?" Buyo called for a system like the single tax proposed by Henry George in the United States, which would confiscate the unearned increment reaped through inflating land values.[29]

La agricultura also harshly criticized widespread rural absentee ownership. With "no true love of the rural life," landowners left their ranches in the care of paid administrators. Resulting "miserable salaries" and poor work meant low productivity and lost income for the owner, as well as lost tax revenue for the government. The journal supported ownership by small estancieros who lived on the land and worked it more productively.[30] Ramón R. Castro, editor of the journal, urged the decentralization of landownership along the lines of land tenure in the United States. With "production monopolized by a small group of latifundists," thousands of acres of rich soil remained uncultivated and thousands of people subsisted without land or employment. Renters, lacking incentives to develop their holdings, left lands barren of trees, buildings, or other improvements. "Latifundism has continued to stifle national prosperity," concluded Castro. Carlos Girola, chief of the Office of Agronomy of the National Ministry of Agriculture, echoed Castro's sentiments, asserting flatly that large estates should be abolished because they "retard progress."[31] One example of the impediment of progress by an "opulent" absentee owner came to light in 1905. Deputy Guillermo A. Martínez unsuccessfully proposed the expropriation of land held by the heirs of Leonardo Pereyra. The rich but fallow holdings lay between the town of Florencio Varela and the provincial capital of La Plata. The unused lands allegedly impeded population and economic growth in a region where both farming and livestock raising represented important economic activities, and latifundism imposed insecurity and nomadism upon the many who rented land. In a letter of November 1904, William Walker instructed his ranch manager to "get rid of all the old arrendatarios [renters] as soon as possible as they will give you any amount of trouble and worry."[32] Rather than contending with added demands pressed by long-term renters, proprietors turned them out after a brief two- to five-year contract, raised the rent, and replaced them with new, more tractable tenant farmers or puesteros. The social and economic dislocations occasioned by such impermanency and forced migration can readily be imagined.

In its centennial edition celebrating national independence on May 25, 1910, the prestigious daily *La prensa* voiced unwarranted optimism concerning the nation's land tenure system: "The great enemy" of agricultural progress, it noted, "was and still is latifundism, but fortunately the subdivision of property has begun." Although the number of property owners did increase in the early twentieth century, the proportion of land held by small owners remained slight.

Latifundists retained control of the bulk of the pampa. The third national census of 1914 confirmed the extent of land monopoly and absentee ownership. In Buenos Aires province, renters occupied half of all livestock ranches, and salaried managers administered another 9 percent. Owners personally operated only four in ten ranches. Of the more than eleven thousand livestock renters, 44 percent labored under contracts of fewer than three years, 19 percent held three-year contracts, and 15 percent had four-year agreements. Only about one in five renters enjoyed contracts of five or more years. Tenant farmers fared even worse: 55 percent held contracts of fewer than three years; 30 percent had three- or four-year commitments; and only 16 percent enjoyed contracts of five years or more.[33]

The establishment and tenacious perseverance of latifundia lay rooted in the Spanish colonial heritage and in the Argentine political culture. Given the sparse colonial population, weak means of communication, and ecological peculiarities of the pampa, large holdings represented logical attempts to extend control over and utilize productively the extensive frontier. To cover chronic fiscal deficits, successive governments sold off the national patrimony for needed cash. With weak control and administration in frontier regions, land questions devolved to local officials, who responded to the desires of the most powerful. Legislation, however well-intentioned, usually suffered from inefficient or corrupt political administration. A built-in multiplier effect facilitated further land concentration by latifundists and speculators who wielded great political and economic influence throughout the nineteenth century.[34]

Latifundism formed the bulk of rural society into two groups of nomadic, economically insecure workers: the landless gaucho, who roamed in search of seasonal ranch employment, and the immigrant farmer, who shifted from one short-term tenancy to another. The extensive and seasonal nature of rural economic production prevented many from finding full-time employment, thereby forcing workers to migrate from the countryside to towns and cities. In political terms, latifundism inhibited the formation of a substantial rural middle class, which would have been a conservative and stabilizing influence. Sheep ranchers, who usually rented their lands, most nearly qualified as middle-class, but they remained numerically insignificant and politically powerless compared to the well-organized, influential cattle ranchers. This contributed further to the consolidation of political power among the rural and urban elites of a seriously truncated political spectrum.

Best epitomized by the Generation of 'Eighty, which controlled national politics from 1880 to 1910, elite political rule exacerbated already marked class inequities by totally excluding entire sectors of society from the benefits accruing from the great export boom economy. Economic favoritism, electoral fraud, corruption, and chicanery kept major social sectors marginal and unintegrated and generated a polarized political culture that continues to haunt the nation today. Martín Fierro captured the gaucho's attitude toward the exploitation of successive modernizing elite governments:

> They turn everything into schemes
> for railways and settlements,
> and chucking money away
> in thousands, on hiring gringos—
> while as for the poor soldier,
> they strip him bare, the swine.[35]

7
Estanciero
versus Gaucho:
Legal Restrictions

Conflict and violence characterized the rural society of Buenos Aires province in the nineteenth century. The interests of large landowners, desiring servile, sedentary, low-wage laborers to tend their vast herds, and of gauchos, whose traditional lifestyle and economic welfare depended upon geographical mobility, clashed head-on. "Criminality" on the pampa often reflected the socioeconomic conflict between gauchos and terratenientes, whose political power permitted them to enforce their class interests through such local officials as *jueces de paz* and alcaldes. National and provincial leaders often sought to conscript the skilled horsemen of the plains into army and militia cavalry units. Officials and ranchers adeptly utilized the law and the prevalent broad definitions of criminality to exert social and labor control over the rural population.

Criminality is not always the simple manifestation of antisocial behavior by pathological or inadequately socialized individuals unwilling or unable to act in an acceptable manner. In some instances, crime reflects not biological, psychological, or even behavioral phenomena, but, rather, a social and legal condition determined by how a person is perceived by police and judicial authorities. Those groups in society capable of controlling the legal and political machinery frequently determine what is legal and what is criminal. In short, political power may define legality. These premises underpin the conflict perspective on criminality, a viewpoint that differs markedly from the functionalist position and one that offers a useful tool for analyzing pampean society. According to functionalists, society charges the state with the duty of restraining those who do not act in accordance with shared fundamental values that are codified into law. A consensus of commonly held interests and customs determines what is legal, and the state protects society from those who are inadequately or criminally socialized.[1]

Drawing upon but not confined to Marxist thought, the conflict viewpoint rejects functionalism's consensual vision of society and focuses on class relations. Conflict between competing social groups becomes institutionalized and codified into law. Under some circumstances, law may become a principal means by which a ruling elite perpetuates its power. Criminality represents socially created categories of behaviors and characteristics that conflict with the interests of the most politically powerful segments of society. Socially marginal groups, which take little or no part in formulating definitions of criminality, clearly stand the best chance of being classified as criminals. Gauchos are a case in point.[2]

Beyond protecting the interests of a ruling elite, law exists, as E. P. Thompson has noted, as an ideology that not only serves but also legitimizes class power. This ideology powerfully shapes that which a society deems acceptable or legal and serves to justify class dominance. According to Douglas Hay, law may operate as one of the major ideological instruments to protect the interests of the propertied; once endowed with ideological significance, property may "become the measure of all things," including legality. Criminality, then, is mutable, and it changes constantly as different groups come to power and redefine it. Social change produces legal change and new definitions of criminality. Conversely, consistency in law over time reflects a continuity of social structures that perpetuate the same class in power.[3]

This was the case in Buenos Aires province, where a ranching and commercial elite maintained and strengthened its legal control over rural society and retained its influence and ability to shape law throughout the nineteenth century. The manner of defining and prosecuting vagrants, deserters, rustlers, and other rural criminals reflected salient class economic interests. The need for tractable ranch workers on the labor-short pampa prompted ranchers to push hard for the enactment of many legal labor controls. The military and political interests of the national and provincial governments coincided and gave final form to numerous vagrancy and conscription statutes that culminated in a comprehensive rural code in 1865. The code gave ranchers control over the rural labor force and provided a bountiful harvest of conscripted "criminals" to fill the ranks of the army and frontier militia. It also presented a clear ideological statement of the goals and values of the landed elite and porteño politicians, whose control of law made de facto criminals out of most of the adult rural male population.

As E. Bradford Burns has noted, the goals, values, and culture of European-oriented elites conflicted with those of the "folk," the rural masses, throughout nineteenth-century Latin America. On the Argentine pampa, the landowners' imposition of law brought them into direct conflict with long-established customs of a gaucho subculture. Colonial officials defined those licensed to kill cattle as peons and those who did so on a free-lance, contraband basis as criminals—changadores, gauderios, and later gauchos. The natural abundance of cattle, horses, ostriches, and other wild game on the pampa meant that a skilled horseman and hunter could live without permanent employment by selling hides, feathers, and pelts and eating free beef. The customs and way of life that gauchos developed placed them in diametric opposition to the legal constraints imposed by rancher-dominated governments.[4]

Pampean ranchers, often faced with serious labor shortages, pushed the enactment of a series of statutes limiting the geographic mobility and economic options of the gaucho. Vagrancy and conscription laws and internal passports proved successful enough that other types of labor controls, like debt peonage, were unnecessary. Argentine vagrancy laws found precedents in the medieval legislation of Spain, England, and other European countries, where such laws had served as means of labor, criminal, and social control. The Black Death that decimated the European labor force in the mid-fourteenth century motivated English gentry to impose that region's first vagrancy law in 1349 and to strengthen it three years later. The statutes persisted even after the precipitating factor, labor scarcity, had disappeared. By the 1530s the flexible acts had become weapons of criminal rather than labor control. During the mid-sixteenth century, the final phase of vagrancy law expansion extended the intent from merely criminal to broader types of social control, and these laws served this function through the mid-eighteenth century. Officials used branding, physical disfigurement, and the death penalty to prosecute the so-called "dangerous classes": the poor. The definition of vagrancy expanded to encompass "rogues," "vagabonds," and most of the rural and urban poor—the same process that made gaucho synonymous with criminal on the pampa.[5]

Seventeenth-century statutes in Valladolid, Spain, dealt harshly with the unemployed, whom authorities feared as socially dangerous. The lash, the galley, and the branding iron awaited the convicted vagrant. A law of 1692 set military service as the penalty for vagrancy, fixing a pattern that was also followed in Argentina. Spanish authorities, like the English, came to view "paupers, vagrants, rogues, and felons" as a single dangerous class. In effect, poverty became a crime. The hostile attitude toward the poor and the broad application of vagrancy laws carried over into colonial legislation in the Americas, where the unpropertied suffered from the social attitudes and political power of the landed.[6]

In the Río de la Plata region, vagrancy laws fulfilled the same diverse functions of labor, criminal, and social control that similar statutes had performed in Europe. As in England, labor shortages prompted official action on behalf of the landed. Authorities in mid-eighteenth-century Buenos Aires ordered all "vagrants and idlers" out of the city to aid with the wheat harvest. In addition to applying vagrancy laws, colonial officials required rural laborers to carry a working paper, or *papel de conchavo*. Viceroy Rafael de Sobremonte in 1804 ordered peons to carry a document signed by a patrón that attested to their employed status. The document was renewable every two months, and workers could be declared vagrants without it; two months of labor without pay on public works awaited the unfortunate person caught without this paper. The relatively light sentence, compared with subsequent punishments, clearly indicates that the intent of the legislation at that time did not extend beyond labor regulation to more generalized social control. Sobremonte also required a second type of document, a *certificación,* or *papeleta de fuero o alistamiento*, which affirmed the bearer's military status and served as a model for military enrollment papers demanded during the national period. The burden of military service weighed heavily on ranch workers because of the sparseness of the rural population and because the gaucho's superb horsemanship and skills with lance, facón, and bolas made him a highly desirable recruit. The gaucho's deep-seated independence, heightened by rampant official abuses of power, provoked a generalized disdain and hatred for law among rural dwellers, whose livelihood depended on unfettered mobility to seek employment and to stalk game anywhere on the pampa. In attempting to present a more favorable image of pampean society, Jonathan Brown theorizes that the "harsh rural labor laws" were only occasionally

enforced, and that such laws indicated "the desperation of the
landowners—not the workers." Unfortunately, Brown failed to
examine the crucial *juez de paz* and police archives at the county or
provincial level. Therein resides the damning evidence showing that
the harsh laws were indeed stringently applied against thousands of
hapless gauchos.[7]

During and after the independence struggles of 1810 to 1816,
Argentine leaders further developed and refined the legal labyrinth that
entangled the gaucho. An increased demand for soldiers prompted a
series of conscription laws beginning in May 1810, when all males
aged eighteen to forty became subject to active militia service. Laws of
March 23, 1812, February 11, 1814, and May 30, 1815, imposed
additional military obligations. The 1814 law required males to carry a
billete impreso, an official form attesting to military service. Rural
workers also faced continued requirements for working papers. Manuel
Luis de Oliden, governor of the province, decreed on August 30, 1815,
that workers must carry a document signed by both an employing
rancher and the county *juez de paz*. Those who did not renew the paper
every three months could be classified summarily as servants or
vagrants and assessed attendant obligations or punished.[8]

Minister of Government Rivadavia gave Argentine vagrancy
statutes their enduring force and form during the 1820s. A decree of
July 17, 1823, forbade workers to leave an employer's ranch without
his written permission. Further decrees enacted from 1822 through
1824 broadened and strengthened the classification of *vagos y mal
entretenidos* (vagrants and ne'er-do-wells) to include, at a justice's
whim, virtually any rural male. With nothing more than verbal
testimony by a justice, a man could be sentenced to several years of
military service as a vagrant. Two years of military service or, less
commonly, of public works, chastened the ranch worker who lacked a
job or proper document. By the 1820s, the intent of rural vagrancy and
labor legislation clearly extended beyond simple labor control to the
broader realm of social control. The European-oriented Unitarian
government consciously sought to reduce the gaucho's options to those
of an obedient ranch peon or a servile soldier. Then, a third type of
document, an internal passport for travel between *partidos* or outside
the province, sealed the gaucho's fate: a decree of February 22, 1822,
imposed the passport on pain of military service, thereby drastically
curtailing the mobility of the rural population. Violations of the

passport requirement became the most common crime on the pampa, and countless men served extended terms of military service for not possessing a document they could not even read.[9]

The welter of legislation passed in the 1820s laid the judicial foundation for the subjugation of the gaucho. The political, military, and legal constraints solidified at that time persisted throughout the century. Governments, whether Unitarian or Federalist, liberal or conservative, bolstered and extended the power of the landowning elite over rural society. Far from breaking with the unitario legislation developed by Rivadavia, the porteño federalist Rosas vigorously enforced it. This Restorer of the Laws redoubled the prosecution of vagrants and exhorted his officials to enforce passport and conscription laws with energy. From his early days as a ranch administrator and estanciero, Rosas proclaimed and championed the rights of the propertied and sought the subordination (a favorite term of his) of the rural masses. In 1817 he complained that "lazy ne'er-do-wells abound everywhere" and railed against the "multitudes of vagrants" that plagued the county of Monte, where his ranch was located. He blamed the backwardness of the pampa on the "throng of idlers, vagrants, and delinquents" that afflicted the countryside—a view, ironically, no different from that of his arch-enemy in future days, Domingo Sarmiento. Rosas expended much administrative energy on converting those he considered idlers into sedentary contractual peons or into cavalrymen for his army.[10]

Capricious application of the law under Rosas made the judicial system even more oppressive to the rural population. Officials often adjusted sentences according to the victim's age so that he would face military service until age forty-five or fifty. Thus, for the sole crime of traveling without a passport, Florencio Almoras, age forty, received a ten-year sentence; and Manuel Aguirre, age thirty-five, faced fifteen years; so both would serve to age fifty. Additional examples abound. Rosas himself, exhibiting a marked obsession with rural crime, frequently intervened directly in the judicial process, acting alone as judge and jury. On matters of political security and rural order, he often dispensed summary "justice" according to his own whims. Cases end with his terse notations of "shoot him," "imprison him," or "to the army."[11]

In mid-1839, authorities in Ranchos arrested Francisco Solano Rocha for not having a passport or patrón. His employer at "Los

Cerritos," Juan José Díaz, had given him a month's leave to journey to Tapalqúe. Though Solano Rocha was termed a good peon by Díaz, and though he had already served three years in the military, the lack of proper documents condemned him to further service. The description of Bartolo Díaz, a native of Santiago del Estero who was arrested in 1846, is typical of many of the pampa's "criminals" during Rosas' rule: twenty-eight years old, single, illiterate, healthy, of the peón del campo class, dressed in a typical chiripá, barefoot, no passport.[12] Being a migrant ranch worker had virtually become a crime—given the myriad legal requirements, the government's constant, heavy demand for troops, and the estanciero determination to subjugate and domesticate the gaucho.

The fall of the Rosista dictatorship on February 3, 1852, afforded rural society only a brief respite from restrictive legislation. On February 15 the new provincial government repealed the statute requiring internal passports, and rural citizens enjoyed "absolute liberty" of travel for the first time in several decades. Less than six months later, the victorious General Urquiza reinstated the passport requirement toward more effective control of crime. A prominent rancher and saladerista in his native Entre Ríos province, Urquiza shared the viewpoint and values of the class that had also supported Rosas—the terratenientes. Responding to complaints of widespread abuses by local officials, he did abolish in 1853 the previously required fee and use of stamped paper for passports.[13]

As *La tribuna* of Buenos Aires noted on January 11, 1854, Rosas had bequeathed to the province a "legislative labyrinth" of decrees that remained in force long after his ouster. Legal inertia, the continuity of rural officials, and the sustained power of the ranching elite kept the restrictions in force even though their legitimacy had rested upon nothing more than the personal power and prestige of Rosas. The newspaper urged a substantial revision and codification of provincial law, a task that was in fact undertaken later in the decade.

Continued labor shortages generated support among ranchers and their spokesmen for strict enforcement of vagrancy laws. On July 6, 1854, *La tribuna* called for strong measures to force idle but "robust men" out of pampean towns and into the labor-short countryside. The editor incredulously questioned why men would settle for two or four pesos per day as street vendors when the lowest rural peon earned fifteen. Those calling for stringent prosecution of vagrants overlooked the possibility that strict enforcement of the various laws could exacerbate rather than alleviate the rural labor shortage. In November 1853 Justice of the Peace José C. Ruíz reported from Federación, near the Santa Fe border, that countless able-bodied men had fled the county to escape the oppressive laws. Active prosecution of so-called "vagrants and undesirables" was depopulating the countryside—the last thing that a sparsely settled region threatened by Indian raids needed. Ruíz accurately diagnosed the problem as a "head-on clash" between the gaucho's traditional customs, especially the desire and need for free transit, and the government's determination to control the rural population. Most workers opted for forced migration north to Santa Fe or westward to the uncertain Indian frontier rather than accept the burden of indefinite military service. The justice proposed, and Minister of War Manuel de Escalada concurred, that only the most serious and violent crimes should be punished with military service. In 1856 Mariano Gainza, an estanciero, voiced similar thoughts. Offering suggestions for a proposed rural code, Gainza questioned the unduly broad definition given the classification of vagrant. Is a man who owns ten or fifteen horses, who works four or five days per month, and who earns 150–200 pesos per year to be classified as a vagrant? If so, opined the rancher, then half the rural adult male population qualified. Gainza foresaw more negative than ameliorative effects in a sweeping, arbitrary definition of vagrancy that ignored rural customs and economic conditions.[14]

The reservations expressed by Gainza, Escalada, and Ruíz went largely unheeded, and most commentators demanded vigorous enforcement of the vagrancy statutes. Rural justices during the 1850s zealously prosecuted and condemned to military service many gauchos who traveled without a passport or national guard enrollment paper. Juan Dillon, justice for Morón, advocated strict application of the passport requirement as one of the few measures available to aid "our poor rural police" in crime control. Though an acknowledged imposition on the honest, the passport provided a means of social control on the vast pampa, where a well-mounted criminal with spare horses could escape over 250 kilometers in half a day. The great distances and isolation also prevented some crimes from being reported for days. Dillon proposed fines of up to 1,000 pesos in addition to military service for passport infractions. The provincial government responded to the sentiments expressed by Dillon and others on October

31, 1858, with a strengthened vagrancy law. Two to four years of military service awaited "those who on workdays habituate gambling houses and taverns, those who use a knife or firearms in the capital or country towns," those wounding another person, and those found to be "vagrants and ne'er-do-wells." Men failing to register for the national guard or detained with out-of-date papers could be sentenced to two years of service. Verbal testimony of a justice sufficed for conviction; and no appeals would be heard.[15]

Realizing the need for a comprehensive rural code on the rapidly changing pampa, the provincial government began soliciting suggestions from prominent ranchers in 1856. Large landowners, including the powerful Ramos Mejía, Lynch, Elia, and Martínez de Hoz families, offered their views. In late 1862, Valentín Alsina began compiling the information gathered, and in mid-1865 he submitted a proposed code. The legislation that resulted, passed in November 1865, proved even more restrictive to the rural population than Alsina's original proposal, fashioned by the ranchers. The code's broadly construed vagrancy clause utterly nullified for rural citizens those civil rights granted under the national constitution of 1853. The Rural Society scrutinized the code in thirty-eight sessions and offered no substantial modifications. The terratenientes had what they wanted and more.[16]

The rural code of 1865, consisting of 319 articles in five sections, covered the major legal questions central to the ranching economy: property and water rights, registration and protection of brands, livestock transit, duties of rural officials, and rural crime. The third section, articles 222 through 242, set out the boundaries of the gaucho's shrinking world. The code demanded written work contracts stipulating wages and terms for all rural workers except day laborers (articles 224–225). Workers enjoyed Sundays free except during busy harvest and shearing seasons but had to work beyond contractual conditions when unexpected conditions arose (articles 226 and 229). Under article 232, a peon who wished to work outside his county of residence had to secure a permit from the local justice specifying the place and duration of employment. Justices arbitrated all worker-rancher disputes without appeal. A rancher could fire a "disobedient, lazy, or vice-ridden peon," but could be held responsible if his orders resulted in crimes or injury (articles 237–39). The code also severely curtailed the gaucho's hunting activities, his important source of additional income. Unlawful

Balling Ostriches. This and the following two illustrations are taken from Emeric Essex Vidal's *Picturesque Illustrations of Buenos Ayres and Montevideo* (London, 1820), courtesy of the Edward E. Ayer Collection, the Newberry Library, Chicago.

South Matadero (Public Butchery)

A Horse Race

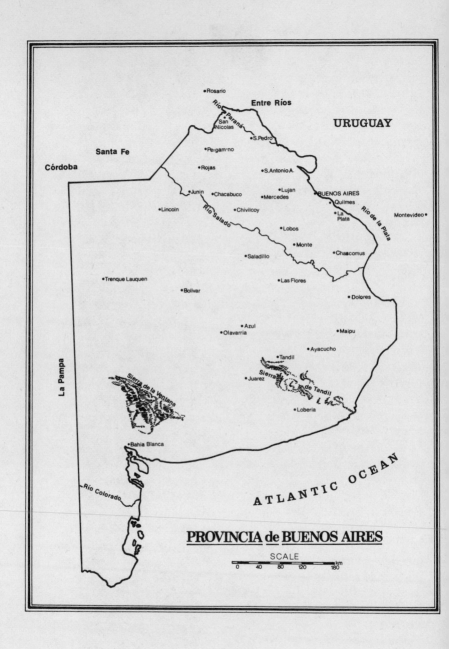

PROVINCIA de BUENOS AIRES

SCALE

0 40 80 120 180 km

hunting could result in a 500-peso fine or forced labor on public works (articles 259–66). Predictably, vagrants met with harsh punishment. Section four specified penalties ranging up to three years of military service or one year of labor on public works for vagrancy (article 292). Article 289 stated that "all those lacking a permanent residence or known means of support, who prejudice the public good because of bad conduct or habitual vices, shall be declared vagrants." This sweeping classification, subject to interpretation by local officials, marked the culmination of more than a century of Argentine vagrancy legislation. The close relations between prominent ranchers and local officials assured enforcement on the landowners' terms. As Donna Guy has shown, similar legal repression afflicted peons in the interior province of Tucumán.[17]

In functional terms, the code served to tie laborers to a given geographical region by means of the vagrancy articles, the written work contract, and the still required internal passport. In curtailing worker mobility, it functioned much as had the tribute and labor systems of *encomienda* and *yanaconaje* in controlling Indians in colonial Peru and Mexico. The flexible vagrancy classification also gave rural justices an efficient means of filling draft quotas. In July 1869 Melchor Hanabal, justice for Carmen de Areco, arrested Pedro Nolasco Rodríguez on suspicion of horse theft. The accused, lacking both national guard papeleta and passport, was sentenced to military service under article 289.[18] Regardless of the type of criminal sought by rural officials, they could almost always "create" a vagrant and send him off to fill the county's conscription quota.

On January 18, 1873, the province abolished the internal passport and granted residents freedom of transit between partidos. The action drew varied responses. *El monitor de la campaña* of Exaltación de la Cruz opposed abolition of the document because this would supposedly increase livestock thefts by permitting criminals to move unchallenged about the province. *La voz de Saladillo* countered that passports had never deterred rustlers in the past but had decreed "slavery for the gaucho." Rural Society president José María Jurado deemed the passport an absolute necessity in controlling rural crime. Although he readily admitted that national guard service had proved injurious to family stability and work habits, he insisted upon retention of the passport and the military service penalty. Urban standards of criminality and rights could not be applied to the pampa, he claimed, because of the "semi-migratory" nature of the rural population and the great mobility of the mounted criminal. In the absence of the passport requirement after 1873, the elastic vagrancy articles of the rural code and the unchecked authority of rural officials grew in importance. The goal of the liberal pro-European elite, to civilize the barbarous gaucho—and that of the ranching interests, to subjugate and domesticate the free-spirited gaucho—coincided in the realm of social control. Vagrancy statutes served well the needs of the urban and rural elites.[19]

A vagrant conscripted into the military often quickly became a deserter, a second large class of criminals on the pampa. Gauchos made it abundantly clear through massive flights from conscripting officials and high desertion rates that they felt little compulsion to serve the province or the nation militarily. While the wealthy could hire substitutes, and urban workers enjoyed draft exemptions, rural workers faced only two alternatives: extended service or evasion. Intimately tied to the Draconian vagrancy laws, forced military service remained the most common form of punishment for vagrants and other "criminals" until late in the century.[20]

To combat desertion, the government offered rewards in 1815, 1827, and 1855 to persons who turned in deserters. Alternating carrot and stick, other laws provided amnesty to deserters in December 1813, September 1815, and September 1821 and the death penalty in March 1813 and November 1854. But in most cases, captured deserters faced the bite of the lash and more long years of servitude. Early in the war with Brazil (1825–28), Francis Bond Head encountered some three hundred forced recruits in San Luis province, ill-fed and clothed in tattered ponchos, awaiting shipment in chains to Buenos Aires. The night before they had assaulted their guards in an unsuccessful escape attempt. A French visitor, Alcides d'Orbigny, cited cruel corporal punishment as the cause of high Argentine desertion rates.[21]

The many civil conflicts, blockades, and threats of foreign invasion during the Rosas era raised troop demands to an even higher level. Deserters and draft evaders ranged the countryside, especially in remote partidos such as Pilá and Lobería. Often unable to work for lack of proper documentation and fear of apprehension, deserters and vagrants resorted to rustling and theft for survival. At times, however, the great scarcity of rural peons worked to the deserters' advantage. A 50-peso bounty for deserters notwithstanding, Paulino Gómez, a deserter, was able to work on various ranches for five months in 1845 before being captured in Lobería. Rosas issued repeated circulars exhorting rural officials to capture and return deserters to his head-quarters at Santos Lugares for punishment and further service; but the task proved formidable, as hundreds deserted his forces in Tandil alone during 1851. Nevertheless, the constant demand for Rosista troops brooked no exceptions and tolerated no evasion willingly. In late 1847 officials in Chivilcoy arrested Feliciano Pereyra, a nine-year-old lad who played fife in the army. Convicted of desertion, the youth received an additional eight years of military service as punishment, though authorities did spare him the two or three hundred lashes customarily accorded deserters, and his captor collected a 50-peso reward. Another young offender was less fortunate. In 1846 John Anthony King, an adventurer from the United States who became a colonel in the Argentine Army, reported that a twelve-year-old boy had been shot as a spy "by Rosas' order."[22]

After Rosas' fall, gauchos continued to form the main body of Argentine troops. Many deserted because they had been impressed unjustly at the outset. Others tired of miserable provisions, late or nonexistent pay, and ill-treatment. The chargé d'affaires for the United States, John S. Pendleton, described the sorry plight of the common soldier in 1852. Caudillos, he noted, exhibited "total indifference to the comfort and rights of their soldiers." Thomas W. Hinchliff, a British traveler, readily grasped the untenable position of the gaucho-soldier. "The poor devils may well be excused" for deserting, he noted, "when we remember that they have everything to lose and nothing to gain among the miseries of civil war." The Englishman empathized with the conscript's frequent and logical response—to mount his best horse and flee across the plains.[23]

Minor infractions of military etiquette called forth violent punish-ment. Robert Crawford, an Englishman surveying railway routes across the pampa in the early 1870s, observed the common practice of "staking out." The victim, face down, was lashed at the ankles and wrists with wet rawhide thongs. As the leather dried, the limbs were stretched in a manner that "must have been exceedingly uncomfort-able." Provincial governor Carlos D'Amico acknowledged the wide-spread use of the *cepo*, or stocks, throughout the countryside. *El eco de Tandil* reported in 1886 that the police commissioner of Navarro had placed a fifteen-year-old boy in the stocks to extract testimony against the lad's father.[24]

Deserters frequently lived in remote areas, banding together for mutual protection and survival. Others joined Indian raiders in attacking pampean estancias. Richard A. Seymour, a North American rancher who settled in southern Santa Fe province in the 1860s, lost his horses to an Indian band accompanied by a gaucho interpreter. In another foray, gauchos interceded to save the lives of a native peon and a boy but acquiesced to the murder of three Englishmen—harsh evidence of gaucho xenophobia. In late 1872, Francisco Borges reported to Minister of War Gainza that a band of "fifteen or twenty Indians or Christians" believed to be gauchos were stealing horses in the partido of Rojas.[25]

In addition to deserters, other criminals, including murderers, ranged along the Indian frontier beyond the reach of white civilization and law. To the pampean ranch worker, being without a facón was as unthinkable as being without a horse, and he continued to favor the weapon even after Remington and Winchester rifles appeared on the pampa. According to gaucho proverb, "he who has no knife does not eat." Not surprisingly, the knife played a central role in most pampean murders. The pulpería served as the arena for many homicides because the volatile mixture of liquor, gambling, and ready knives often proved fatal. As Caldcleugh noted in 1819, "numberless are the crosses about the doors of the pulperias." Gauchos customarily stuck their knives into the pulperia counter when gambling as a sign of goodwill. Sufficiently provoked, however, a patron would quickly grab his facón, wrap his poncho about one arm as a shield, and commence dueling.[26]

A gaucho who killed another, even in a fair fight, became in the eyes of the law a *matrero*, a murderer and an outlaw. To the people of the countryside, however, he was the victim of a *desgracia*, or misfortune, not a criminal. Knife fighters usually attempted only to mark and scar an opponent, not to kill him. The gaucho who killed a man in a duel became the most storied of all rural criminals. He passed into the literary and popular imagination in the personages of Juan Moreira and Martín Fierro. Figures like Moreira and Fierro, murderers to the state, became folk heroes and champions against oppressive authority to the rural masses. Like the social bandit described by Eric J. Hobsbawm, the matrero stood as a man to be aided, supported, and even admired.[27]

As in the American west, with its legendary gunslingers, the frequency of murders on the pampa may have been distorted and sensationalized. Police records show many deaths from knife wounds, but Arthur E. Shaw, a British immigrant, recalled seeing only one fatal stabbing in a full decade of rural life. By the twentieth century, firearms played a significant role in rural violence, but the knife still figured prominently. Of 3,735 woundings in 1909 in Buenos Aires province, knives accounted for 40 percent and firearms 18. Of 443 murders, however, 48 percent resulted from firearms and 44 percent from knifings.[28] The blade retained its popularity.

Less renowned than the matreros but more important in reality were *cuatreros*, or rustlers. Like the crimes of vagrancy and desertion, livestock theft stemmed more from economic hardship created by latifundia and the integration of the pampa into the European market system than from premeditated criminality on the part of the gaucho. The established customs of the colonial and early national periods conflicted sharply with newer concepts of private property inherent in Argentina's booming export capitalism. Earlier, when hides alone had held commercial value, stray or branded cattle could be slaughtered for meat as long as the hide was staked out and delivered to the owner. Property boundaries, vague and flexible on the unfenced pampa, rendered null the concept of trespass. With a lasso and a tropilla of extra mounts, a gaucho could acquire all the wealth he needed in cattle, for the pampean grasses belonged to everyone. A philosophical anarchist, the gaucho maintained his custom of free grazing on the open range even after terratenientes gained title to most of the better lands. To the gaucho rustling may have become an act of rebellion against authority and against a new pampa of foreigners and foreign ideas. Denied the opportunity to earn a living as ranch hands, some gauchos returned to the labor of their colonial predecessors—dealing in illicit hides.[29]

As selective breeding increased the value per head of livestock, ranchers became more concerned about animal thefts. In mid-1871 Deogracias García, justice for Saladillo, relayed grievances from estancieros about the ''considerable number'' of cattle killed illicitly for their hides. He reported to provincial police chief Enrique O'Gorman that the hides found a ready market in the town of Saladillo despite the absence of proper proof of ownership. Jurado expressed the Rural Society's concern over the illegal slaughter of animals in 1873. Although the roots of the practice extended well back into colonial times, he criticized Rosas for permitting animals to be killed for consumption on condition that the hides were delivered to the owner. The society met in extraordinary session in September 1873 to formulate plans for countering the rustling epidemic. Society president Olivera termed rustling a more important problem than the bloody massacre of seventeen foreigners by gauchos in Tandil the previous year because far more people were affected adversely.[30]

In addition to the solitary poacher, felling an occasional beef for sustenance, bands of cuatreros operated in many areas of the pampa. A circular of 1878 from the minister of government solicited information about "organized gangs of thieves" suspected of numerous crimes throughout the countryside. The minister urged rural officials to detain and question unknown or suspicious persons entering their partidos. In 1880 the *Revista de ganadería*, a rural journal, railed against the thefts, assaults, and "crimes in the countryside" that had grown to "alarming proportions." Marauding bands attempted to perpetuate the tradition-al, free-spirited life of the frontier past; but by the 1880s, most found that the old pastimes of ostrich hunting and living on "free air and fat meat" had been largely curtailed.[31]

Rustlers could not operate alone; they required market outlets for illicit hides and wool. Ostensibly reputable merchants, ranchers, and officials often facilitated the disposal of illegally procured goods. Marion Mulhall, wife of English publisher Michael G. Mulhall, recounted a delightful anecdote of rustling that also illustrates gaucho humor. The justice of the peace of Azul, so the story goes, offered to purchase hides, no questions asked, from a gaucho called El Cuervo. The gaucho was to throw the hides over the wall surrounding the justice's house, and he would receive payment accordingly. Soon thereafter, one of the official's peons discovered his employer's own brand on the hides. When confronted by the justice, enraged at buying his own hides, El Cuervo asked in cunning innocence, "Master! Whose cattle did you want me to kill unless your own?"[32]

On a more factual level, in 1873 several members of the Rural Society candidly admitted the complicity of "rich ranchers" in the illicit hide traffic. The society also suspected collusion between some local justices and rustlers and asked that rural police forces be made "completely independent" from the justices. On September 10, 1882, *El eco de Tandil* reported the apprehension of five men with a large quantity of stolen hides and wool. One confessed, implicating the others, but he also connected several "persons of influence and position" to the ring. In 1900, several ranchers with considerable

holdings figured among a group arrested in Córdoba, further evidence
of the illicit involvement of influential people. Newspapers in La Plata
and Dolores charged that police at best tolerated and at worst
cooperated with cuatreros. In 1909 *La patria* of Dolores summarized
cogently a major problem of livestock thefts: "The rustler would not
exist were he not well protected" by his *padrino*, the buyer behind the
operation. Thus the highest and humblest elements of rural society
cooperated in stealing cattle and sheep. Typically, however, the
corrupt official or contrabanding estanciero escaped prosecution,
whereas the hapless peon suffered the full weight of the law.[33]

Livestock thefts showed no appreciable decline until about a
decade after the turn of the century. On June 20, 1909, *El municipio* of
Buenos Aires reported that provincial animal thefts had finally dipped
to fewer than 600 during the month of May—an average of less than 6
animals lost per county. The paper attributed the decline to increased
vigilance by rural police. The actual incidence of animals stolen in the
province is difficult to evaluate. In a 1910 report, Diógenes Muñiz and
other provincial police officials estimated the total numbers of animals
stolen from 1880 to 1909 to have been about 44,000 cattle, 73,000
horses, and 286,000 sheep.[34] For those three decades, thefts averaged
only about 1,500 cattle, 2,500 horses, and 10,000 sheep lost per
annum. These figures pale in significance when compared with the
millions of animals killed by disease, drought, flood, frost, and other
natural disasters. Although rustling gained notoriety and drew sharp
criticism, it actually ranked low among the many problems faced by
pampean ranchers.

Commentators offered varied interpretations of the motives for
rustling. Some provincial newspapers attributed the "continual robberies" in the countryside to habit, not necessity, because thieves
frequently took only hides and left the meat. On March 26, 1873, *El
centinela del norte* in San Nicolás blamed lack of rural police protection
and demanded an increase in the county's forces. The paper insisted
that each partido needed at least 50 rural police to deter thieves. *El
progreso de Quilmes* on March 15, 1874, also backed the expansion of
rural security forces to protect the rancher and his property. Toward the
end of the century, Antonio G. Gil, of the provincial Agrarian League,
criticized the government for providing only two policemen per 27,000
hectares (66,717 acres) in rural areas, or about 2,700 men for the entire
province.[35]

Other observers looked to the character of the rural population rather than to weak enforcement in explaining rural criminality. Eduardo Rosales, commenting on livestock thefts in *Revista de policía* in 1901, blamed what he termed the "cult of laziness": the rural native preferred stealing to working. Naturally lazy, indifferent to misery, homeless, addicted to long siestas, and living far from civilization, paisanos developed into barbarous idlers and thieves. Children, growing up in the "bleak solitude" of the great, primitive plain, inherited the same roguish character from their shiftless fathers.[36] Other racial interpretations of Argentine socioeconomic problems abound. Such facile explanations, grounded in the popular strains of Spencerian and positivistic thought, fall woefully short of illuminating the nature of rural criminality.

Some nineteenth-century commentators exhibited a better grasp of the social roots of gaucho criminality. On October 8, 1882, *El eco de Tandil* remarked the unhappy irony of punishing "forced vagrants" for living in conditions created by provincial juridical and economic structures. The unlimited powers of local authorities and the potent threat of frontier militia service forced the "unfortunate gaucho" to live outside the law. Administrative machinery operated as a "vagrant factory," legally making vagrants out of honest ranch workers. The Tandil daily exhorted provincial leaders to organize agricultural and livestock-raising colonies, and to provide public education for the rural population. *El pueblo* of Azul for January 28, 1900, presented a similar vision of rural society. Pampean crime resulted from the exclusion of a vast proportion of the rural population from access to permanent employment. "Our gaucho is not a thief by profession or nature," asserted the editor, but rather out of necessity. The paper advocated filling provincial schools rather than jails to help raise paisanos from their miserable status as the "Bohemians of our countryside."

Successive administrations responded not with schools, jobs, and land, but with conscription and vagrancy laws, the stocks and the lash, and the autocratic justice of the peace. This juez de paz, the personification of arbitrary, repressive authority, best embodies the Argentine response to the social roots of rural crime in the nineteenth century. Justices, especially in frontier regions, exercised broad administrative, economic, police, military, and judicial functions. Such administrative changes as the formation of municipalities after 1854 and the appointment of separate police commissioners after 1857 did little to reduce the justices' power. Rosas and subsequent provincial governors often placed influential ranchers in the position and lesser ranchers in the lower alcalde positions, thereby giving the landed interests direct control. Not until 1884 did the justices' functions devolve to strictly judicial matters, but even then wider, if more subtle, political and electoral influences remained.[37]

Contemporaries criticized local justices and other officials as uneducated, illiterate, and ill-qualified for public service. United States diplomat Francis Baylies described Argentine politicians and officials in 1832 in unflattering terms and compared the nation unfavorably to a tribe of Indians. Because·of endemic political corruption, especially bribery, Darwin forecast that "before many years, [this country] will be trembling under the iron hand of some Dictator"; but he did not suspect that the dictator would be a man he met on the southern pampa fighting Indians, Juan Manuel de Rosas. Toward the end of Rosas' rule, Xavier Marmier described rural military and civilian officials as "men more fearsome than outlaw gauchos and who cause more harm without having to flee from justice, because they themselves represent the legal authority and justice." Even taking into account the foreign bias of these observers, the appraisals are negative enough on the whole to lend them some credence. As John Lynch has noted, official delinquency under Rosas was "just as bloodthirsty as gaucho delinquency."[38]

Following the end of Rosista censorship, the unmuzzled press loosed a vituperative chorus of criticism against rural officials. On February 15, 1855, *La tribuna* condemned justices as "absolute governors" whose "arbitrary conduct" demanded rectification; it suggested clarifying and codifying the diffuse, inordinate powers exercised by the rural justices. The porteño English-language *Standard*, published by the Mulhall brothers, aired complaints of official abuses in Ranchos in its edition of January 18, 1865 and branded local officials as a "class most disreputable" and one of the "principal causes of all the crimes committed in the camps" (meaning countryside, from *campo*). On October 25, 1876, the companion English-language *Herald* denounced the entire rural legal system by which the gaucho, an "unfortunate victim," was "deprived of everything he holds dear." Written complaints against rural officials reached such volume that in 1867 the government refused to continue receiving them. A circular in 1869 from the provincial government cautioned officials to remit only convicted vagrants for military service. Justices had "repeatedly sent" men who had not been judged by a jury and who had committed no crime. José Ortubia, held for several months in 1872 on suspicion alone, put the matter succinctly: "For the poor, like me, constitutional guarantees are dead letters."[39]

The barrage of condemnation heaped upon the justices spurred some ineffectual calls for reform. The 25 de Mayo Club of provincial reformers urged limiting the powers of justices. Its manifesto of January 1870 recommended popular election of justices and reduction of their powers to solely judicial matters. Like most reformers' proposals, these went unrealized.[40]

Part of the justices' immunity to reform stemmed from their considerable political roles. Throughout the century, they acted as rural electoral agents who insured victory for official candidates, with fraud and force when necessary. Sarmiento informed a friend in a letter of 1857 that "gauchos who resist voting for government candidates were jailed, put in the stocks," or shipped off to the frontier for military service. On March 5, 1863, the *Standard* described a rural election with justices driving gauchos, "with little bits of colored paper in their hands," to the polls. (The colored ballots helped officials to monitor voting.) On March 19, 1874, *El amigo del pueblo* in Carmen de las Flores reported that the threat of conscription was being used against the opponents of Adolfo Alsina in his bid for the governorship. An electoral appeal by supporters of Col. Benito Machado in 1886 bespoke the realities of pampean politics: "To our countrymen: to our rural friends, to the men of poncho and chiripá, *eternal victims of the bosses*."[41]

Despite the considerable political infighting between factions seeking control of provincial and national administrative machinery, the class interests represented did not change. Regardless of banner or slogan, politicians and local officials protected and promoted the interests of the landed, and they often came from the ranks of the ranching elite. Victimized economically and politically, the gaucho found recourse only outside the political system and the law. A simple dichotomous view of good officials, defending widely shared social values, and bad outlaws, tearing at the social fabric, clearly fails to capture the complexities and contradictions of pampean society. Like social bandits in other cultures, the gaucho was often forced to live marginally. Policy makers did not attempt to integrate ranch workers into modern rural society on other than repressive terms, and the gaucho's heartfelt independence and individualism kept him from submitting willingly. In one peasant phrase, quoted by Eric J. Hobsbawm, gauchos were among those "men who make themselves respected" by resisting oppression.[42]

As social criminals, that is, criminals created by changing definitions of legality and changing social conditions, gauchos represented a rebellious and potentially revolutionary class to the ruling elite. Politicians from Sarmiento onward believed that gauchos—the mass military support for caudillos such as Facundo Quiroga and Rosas—had to be eliminated to bring about political stability in Argentina. But in their own eyes gauchos simply attempted to maintain a way of life to which they remained deeply committed—a normal, natural existence in harmony with the great grassy plains and the abundance of livestock enjoyed by the Río de la Plata region.[43]

The so-called criminality of the pampa also provides evidence of the illegitimacy of the Argentine judicial-political system. The law promoted rancher interests at the expense of the gaucho masses, and gauchos chose to disobey the many laws they found oppressive and unjust. Through corruption, abuses, and arbitrariness, the government forfeited its right to rule in the eyes of gauchos, who chose instead to live according to their own customs. A mass of behavioral evidence documents the gaucho's determination to maintain his traditional folk culture and activities despite repeated prohibitions by elite governments. The large number of arrests recorded in police and judicial archives at all levels amply illustrates both the gaucho's prolonged attempts to remain unfettered and the equally determined and ultimately successful efforts of the elite to subordinate and domesticate him.

8
Forced Military Service

Before I left with the army draft,
I had cattle and home and wife;
But when from the frontier I came back,
All I could find was my ruined shack;
God knows my friends, when we'll see the end
Of all this sorrow and strife.[1]

Argentina suffered perpetual warfare from its struggle for independence through the federalization of Buenos Aires in 1880. The Argentine past, noted the eminent historian Ricardo Levene, is "one of continuous revolutions, of violent governmental crises, of the transformation of political parties with principles into personal parties." Civil wars, continual battles against fierce pampean Indian tribes, and conflicts with Spain, Brazil, Paraguay, France, England, and José Artigas in the Banda Oriental, took an immense human and economic toll. In addition to the many battlefield deaths, the ceaseless strife left the frontier vulnerable to Indian attack, intermittently depopulated the countryside, disrupted the rural economy and work habits, precluded stable rural family life for the masses, and impeded the formulation of coherent national policies. Martín Fierro, hero of the popular epic poem of José Hernández, put the matter simply:

I must tell you there's scarcely a gaucho left
All round my native parts;
Some are under the grass, and some have fled,
And some in the frontier wars are dead;
For as soon, in this land, as one war is done,
Some other rumpus starts.[2]

For the most part, the gaucho felt no pressing ideological or patriotic urge to sacrifice himself in battle for a distant and oppressive government. As Esteban Echeverría, the romantic writer and philosopher, observed in his *Dogma socialista*, localism dominated Argentina. "The fatherland, for the *correntino*, is Corrientes; for the *cordobés*, Córdoba; for the *tucumano*, Tucumán; for the porteño, Buenos Aires; for the gaucho, the *pago* where he was born"; larger national interests stood as an "incomprehensible abstraction for them." In nineteenth-century official documents, especially during the Rosas era, the term *patria* refers to a citizen's native province, not to the Argentine nation. Hudson also commented on the gaucho's lack of national fervor. "The gaucho is, or was, absolutely devoid of any sentiment of patriotism and regarded all rulers, all in authority from the highest to the lowest, as his chief enemies, and the worst kind of robbers, since they robbed him not only of his goods but of his liberty." Walter Larden recalled that when military recruiters visited ranches some peons would run away, and workers fleeing the draft from other counties would appear. Gauchos did not seek military glory.[3]

Given the gaucho's aversion to military service, draft quotas precipitated serious rural labor shortages as thousands fled to the frontier or to neighboring provinces to avoid conscription. This forced migration hurt the rural economy, already short of labor, even more. In 1810, a conscription call temporarily depopulated the countryside to the point of threatening the wheat harvest; a government circular in November promised draft exemption and freedom of movement to all peons engaged in the harvest. Argentines in rural areas fled the draft in large numbers to avoid serving in the war with Brazil during the mid-1820s. D'Orbigny noted a serious labor shortage for the wheat harvest in San José de las Flores. Residents fled the county, and workers from the interior, principally Santiago del Estero, refused to sign work contracts for fear of conscription. Harsh corporal punishments and the low moral tone of army life fostered high desertion rates, which in turn necessitated higher draft quotas. In the northern county of Pergamino in 1827, ranchers complained to the justice of the peace of a war-induced shortage of workers; peons from the interior were returning to their native provinces or to neighboring Santa Fe to avoid enrollment. Manuel Dorrego, who became provincial governor in 1828, condemned the levas, or draft quotas, as an evil that "demoralizes and humiliates the people."[4]

The assassination of Dorrego in late 1828 left a power vacuum quickly filled by Rosas, who assumed leadership with the support of the rancher elite and the force of his gaucho militia, the Red Rangers. To maintain his large military force, estimated variously at 10,000 to 36,000 strong, he issued decrees in 1830, 1837, and 1842 condemning vagrants and other criminals and unfortunates to armed service. As an Irish visitor noted in 1838, because of the incessant interprovincial and Indian wars, the gaucho was "always a soldier." Massive draft evasion continued to create labor shortages that affected even Rosas' ranches. In mid-1839 Basilio Páez complained of losing many workers at "Rincón del Rosario." When their contracts expired, peons departed to other provinces, "where they are free from the service." The revolución de los Libres del Sur, an anti-Rosas uprising in several southern partidos late that year, further increased the drain of the ranch labor force. In December, Páez informed his employer that only five peons remained on the ranch because all black workers had been drafted; with such a reduced labor force, Páez could care only for the orchards and fields around the ranch house. The conscripted men had still not returned by February 1840, so the manager continued to assign only the most essential tasks to his few peons. In September 1841 Páez again complained that "many times the few men I have have been occupied by the justice of the peace in the service of the State." On a moment's notice, even employees of the provincial governor could be pressed into military service. Labor shortages and economic dislocations persisted throughout Rosas' regime. In March 1846 a porteño merchant, José Braulio Haedo, could not fill a contract for hides because of the suspension of work on most estancias: an Anglo-French blockade had closed off market outlets for ranch products, and troop demands had again absorbed large numbers of peons. Throughout the province, Haedo noted, "instead of peons one sees only soldiers."[5]

The perpetual strife created other shortages that also adversely affected ranching. In 1842 Samuel Morton, an English rancher in Chascomús, protested the grave lack of horses resulting from the high demand for cavalry mounts. The government had requisitioned all horses, both to fill its needs and to prevent them from falling into enemy hands. MacCann commented in 1848 that the government's heavy exaction of horses and cattle paralyzed ranching. Even worse, however, military commanders could "take as many men as they desire for their employments" and impress them into the army. Rosas zealously sought gauchos who could tame wild horses for his cavalry units. In 1843 Manuel Donato killed a man and stole his herd of horses. Because of his traditional dress (chiripá and poncho) and horsemanship, Rosas deemed him "good for a cavalryman" and imposed five years of military service. Rosas' fall brought little change in legal or military status for the gaucho, except for a short-lived reprieve from travel restrictions from February through August 1852. In place of the defunct provincial militia, on March 8, 1852, the new government established national guard units for each county, mostly to protect against Indian incursions. Despite the new name, the harsh reality of conscription and service remained unchanged. The law of December 17, 1823, requiring army service of all adult male citizens, also remained in force.[6]

Many continued to attack the abuses and injustices of the military recruitment system after Rosas. In May 1852 Francisco Llobert protested the plight of residents of San Nicolás de los Arroyos, where military officers hunted rural workers "like savages" and impressed them into the national guard or army. In Tandil, to the south, the same sad spectacle existed. Colonel Agustín Acosta recruited as many volunteers as possible to form a new regiment, the Hussars of La Plata. Finding the quota yet unfilled, he deemed it "necessary to proceed with the capture of twenty-five individuals" to complete the unit. The emptiness of official promises again impressed itself on the gaucho, who remembered that "Urquiza said we were free!" The liberating Urquiza issued an order in August 1852 that the great numbers of vagrants and "suspicious persons" be placed immediately at the disposal of military commanders. To meet rising troop demands more efficiently, a decree of January 1853 empowered national guard commanders to enter homes and draft for two years those males not enrolled in a local unit. Even the previously required ceremonial trial before a justice of the peace became superfluous.[7]

Rural officials sought to meet draft quotas by any means possible. In September 1855 the justice for Matanza requested an eight-day extension to fill a quota of twenty-five because "very few vagrants" could be found. In October he petitioned for the release of two men who had been sent with the county's contingent, explaining that the two, both "honorable and hard-working residents," had been sent merely to meet the quota by the specified date. Neither man was a vagrant nor under any legal obligation for service. The justice of San José de las Flores also failed to meet his quota of thirty men. Recruitment had proved difficult, he explained, because "the workers hid." Unable to meet military manpower needs even with sweeping legislation, the Argentine government recruited volunteers from Europe. Throughout 1854 *La tribuna* and other porteño newspapers carried advertisements offering *enganchados* who enlisted a 1,000-peso bonus for two or three years of frontier service. The men received half of this amount upon enlistment and the other half upon completion of a tour of duty. They collected a regular salary as well.[8]

Native Argentines refused to join voluntarily, so foreigners constituted the bulk of the enlistees. Few of the immigrants could ride a horse, so they could not serve in cavalry units, the backbone of frontier defense. Mounted troops continued to be made up of *destinados*, usually gauchos impressed by force or for crimes, but infantry and some artillery units included a high proportion of foreigners. In 1855 enganchados constituted 62 percent of the infantry company of the line at Fort Argentina, in Bahía Blanca. Except for two volunteers, the remainder of the company were destinados. Enganchados constituted 44 percent of the line company of the Fifteenth National Guard Regiment at the same fort. Because of their poor horsemanship, however, one porteño paper, *El industrial*, termed immigrants a "nuisance" on the frontier.[9]

As in the time of Rosas, conscription weighed most heavily upon the rural laboring population. Gauchos between the ages of 17 and 44 made up the bulk of national guard troops on active duty. In March 1855 the justice at Canuelas, Juan de Olivares, reported on the status of the Eighth Infantry. Single rural males outnumbered married men in the active unit, but more married men, probably ranchers or foremen, served safely as inactive or passive troops. Many in the urban population received exemptions from service, including doctors, lawyers, students, scribes, and pharmacists. Wealthier rural males, ranch foremen, and managers with capital exceeding 4,000 pesos also enjoyed exemption. A poor man could be spared only if he could prove that he was a sole surviving son. James A. Peden, United States minister to Argentina, observed the identity between gaucho and soldier in 1856, describing "the wild restless life of the 'Gaucho' (peasant), generally without a fixed habitation, and family ties, as easily sundered, as contracted—passionately fond of excitement of all kinds,—always mounted—a change from peasant to—soldier is only a change of names." William Hadfield lamented the "demoralization and recklessness'' that resulted from the gauchos, ''naturally a good-natured, hardy, and courageous race ... being forcibly taken from useful and peaceful occupations to swell the ranks of some ambitious 'caudillo.' ''[10]

Whereas the demand for army troops rose and fell according to the level of civil and international strife, frontier garrisons required a continual supply of men to fight marauding Indians. Colonial authorities established a series of forts at Luján, Salto, and Zanjón and formed units of *blandengues* (gaucho cavalrymen) in 1751 to protect the long frontier line. The outposts, or *fortínes*, hardly more than feeble stockades, gradually radiated outward further from Buenos Aires for the next century. The fierce pampean tribes, skilled cavalry tacticians who proved deadly with their long cane lances, cudgels, and bolas, resisted strongly until Julio A. Roca's definitive conquest of the desert in 1879.[11]

Rosas had maintained generally amicable relations with the tribes through tributes of cattle, sheep, horses (Indians favored mare's meat), and other supplies. His ouster disrupted the customary flow of goods and touched off a wave of ferocious attacks that rolled back the frontier line from Tandil and Azul to a position of several decades earlier. In late 1855 the cacique Calfucurá swept into Tandil and forced residents to flee northeast as far as Dolores. Troops arrived belatedly from neighboring Fort Azul, but, according to Danish settler Juan Fugl, the soldiers looted as much from the abandoned houses as had the Indians. Tandil's urban population, about 600 in 1854, did not recover until 1862, when it reached 745. To the northwest the county of 25 de Mayo suffered similar devastation, as its population of more than 5,000 inhabitants in late 1855 dropped to a mere 600 by March 1857 after raids led by the caciques Catriel and Cachul. The raiding Indians ran off thousands of head of livestock and abducted many women and children.[12]

Aside from the considerable dangers of battle, frontier service also entailed serious deprivations for the soldier. Troops went without pay for extended periods. In March 1852 Manuel Viera de Andrade filed for military back wages due him since May 1841, nearly eleven years. In this exceptional case the petition met with success, and Viera received his pay. In late 1855 Juan del Campillo informed General Urquiza that frontier soldiers and officials were receiving wages at least nine months late. A year later, Minister of War José M. Galán reported wages paid six months late.[13] The Argentine soldiers also served underfed. According to John S. Pendleton, reporting to United States Secretary of State Daniel Webster in 1852, Argentine troops received only a ration of beef, plus the promise of 20 paper pesos (1 hard peso) per month ''that is very rarely paid.'' Armies were ''composed of men impress'd into the service, and kept there against their will.'' During Calfucurá's uprising in 1855, Minister of War Bartolomé Mitre reported to provincial Governor Pastor Obligado on the privations suffered by the garrison at Fort Azul. The cacique and more than one thousand braves surrounded the seven-hundred-man contingent, cutting them off from water and supplies. Reduced to eating horsemeat and without water, the garrison finally drove off the Indians. Troops on patrol away from the forts subsisted on beef and mate only.[14]

Critics demanded changes in the meager military diet for a variety of reasons ranging from humanitarianism to progressivism. *La tribuna* of Buenos Aires in 1855 termed fresh meat on the frontier a wasteful extravagance and recommended jerked beef as a more portable and less costly alternative. The paper further urged that vegetables rather than meat be made the basis of the soldier's diet so that the gaucho would learn to eat and eventually grow them.[15]

Meager rations, late pay, and harsh conditions continued to drive many gauchos to desert from frontier units. Others fled because of the arbitrary manner in which they had been impressed. *El industrial* of Buenos Aires accurately assessed the motives for flight in an editorial of January 18, 1856. ''The gaucho who is classified as a vagrant knows perfectly well that he is the victim of an unjust act.'' The ''extraordinary delegation of power'' to justices permitted them to classify anyone as a vagrant and order him to the frontier, where insubordination and desertion logically resulted. A government report in 1858 also cited the ''corrupt recruitment system'' as the principal motive for many desertions.[16]

Manuel Viliarino, a Chivilcoy rancher, recognized the social ills that resulted from forced military service. National guard service exposed the young gaucho to a vice-ridden life of wanderlust and excessive independence. He suggested increasing taxes to support an adequate rural police force to replace the unwilling guardsmen. Juan Dillon, justice of the peace for Morón, agreed that military service bred bad habits among the troops. But repression, not reform, characterized the government's response to problems of recruitment and desertion. In

1857, when a colonel's aide in Pergamino beat a man senseless for no apparent reason and left him face down in the stocks, indignant townspeople released the hapless victim and saved his life. Nicolás Calvo, editor of *La reforma pacífica* of Buenos Aires, received letters from throughout the province decrying similar abuses by rural military and civilian authorities. In 1859, a Captain Quirós fatally stabbed a drunken sergeant in Bragado while beating him with his saber. Provincial Governor Adolfo Alsina reported numerous complaints of "cruel treatment" of soldiers that resulted in a "great desertion."[17]

The Paraguayan War (War of the Triple Alliance), which broke out in 1865, added new troop demands, and the gaucho again became the principal victim. Like past conflicts, the war temporarily retarded rural economic growth, exacerbated the rural labor shortage, and exposed the southern frontier to Indian attacks. As President Mitre noted with great understatement, this "sorrowful" war "was never really popular." Juan Bautista Alberdi, José Hernández, and many other political leaders wrote and spoke in opposition to the porteño attempt to subjugate Paraguay. Henri Armaignac observed the inequities and suffering that it brought on. The wealthy hired substitutes and thus avoided conscription altogether; but the troops, often unpaid for years at a time, were forced to serve two or three times longer than their stipulated terms. Despite the threat of a death sentence, many deserted and returned to their families.[18] In late 1865 Luis Giles, justice at Ranchos (today General Paz), gloomily detailed the impact of the war upon his county to Minister of Government Nicolás Avellaneda. The knowledge of certain impressment into the army demoralized the rural population and destroyed all incentive to work. Farmers realized that they would be called away before the harvest, so planting seemed futile. Many workers fled west across the Río Salado, preferring an uncertain, errant existence on the frontier to army life in Paraguay. Giles could not even raise twenty men for national guard service because most of the able-bodied had departed. Some men even took their families to the dangerous frontier. In the southern county of Azul, officials railed against the "defective and inequitable" recruitment system that depopulated the countryside and crippled the ranching economy.[19]

In decreeing another three-year enrollment period for the national guard in 1866, Avellaneda termed the disruption of rural work and the limitations on travel "necessary evils." In the official view, the frontier inhabitant was de facto the frontier soldier, so that even private life had to be controlled by a "truly military regimen." Less sanguine about rural economic dislocations occasioned by military service, the Rural Society bitterly attacked draft quotas. Speaking for the group, Eduardo Olivera urged better treatment of the "poor paisano, only rural laborer of the time." Conscripts had to leave their families to "perish in misery" and abandon their employers. Juan Angel Molina, another estanciero, agreed that the "unfortunate paisano" should not have to foresake family and livelihood to serve on the frontier. Troop contingents ordered to the fortínes were forced to remain well beyond their terms, yet more recruits were called to replace them. A serious labor shortage for the wheat harvest at Chivilcoy in 1867 forced farmers to pay excessive wages to the few peons they could locate. But even the protests of powerful ranchers did not dull the government's voracious appetite for gaucho cavalrymen, and forced recruitment continued.[20]

As the Paraguayan War wound down in 1868 and attention shifted back to domestic events, frontier military service came under even greater attack. Colonel Alvaro Barros, commanding troops on the southern frontier, harshly critized military conduct there. In a letter in 1869 to Minister of War Martín de Gainza, Barros termed many commanders "rogues" who used their troops for "private service." While soldiers tended livestock on the estancias of some commanders, Barros faced the formidable task of defending the vast frontier line at Olavarría with too few troops. In addition to the shortage of troops, frontier commanders faced the problem of unsuitable recruits. Writing to Colonel Rufino Victoria in May 1870, Julio Campos, commander at Fort Belgrano, complained of the ineptitude on horseback of foreign enganchados. He stressed the centrality of the cavalry in fighting Indians and emphasized the need for troops with equestrian skills; but he acknowledged the immigrant's usefulness as an infantryman and for such other footwork as building and maintaining forts, tasks shunned by natives. The first national census in 1869 clearly revealed the division of native and foreign soldiers according to mounted and unmounted units. On the northern frontier of Junín, only five foreigners (three from Uruguay) appeared among more than two hundred cavalrymen.[21]

Despite the usefulness of the immigrant in some mechanical areas, most frontier commandants bitterly protested when the gringos arrived to serve in their units. In a letter of April 20, 1872, General Rivas informed Gainza that a contingent of newly arrived Italians was "completely worthless for frontier service." Exasperated by their lack of horsemanship and physical debility, Rivas declared them more "prejudicial" than beneficial to the defense effort. Barros agreed that immigrants were "absolutely worthless" for frontier service, and Hernández voiced the same attitude through Fierro:

> I'd like to know why the government
> Enlists that gringo crew,
> And what they think they're good for here?
> They can't mount a horse or rope a steer,
> And somebody's got to help them out
> In everything they do.[22]

Frontier troops, foreign and native, suffered from difficult living conditions and inadequate supplies. Both Governor Emilio Castro and Minister of War Gainza acknowledged the sorry plight of frontier garrisons but offered nothing beyond sympathetic words. Gainza opined that, once freed from the abuses and injustices of conscription, the native could enjoy a stable home life, the rights of a citizen, and a brighter future grounded in honorable work. In 1871 Castro termed military conditions "a scandal" and urged adequate rations and clothing for the "unfortunates serving on the frontier." No changes resulted. Writing in *La república* in December 1871, José M. Morales sharply attacked Gainza for tolerating numerous and varied abuses suffered at the fortines. He repeated the litany of grievances: lack of adequate food and clothing, late or nonexistent pay and replacements, corruption among commanders. Barros corroborated the charges in a series of articles published in the journal *Revista del Río de la Plata* in 1871 and 1872. The untenable conditions forced guardsmen to desert by the thousands.[23]

Hernández also wrote a vitriolic criticism of governmental military policies. In the newspaper *El Río de lat Plata* in 1869, he attacked the "arbitrariness" and "despotism" of frontier service and pointed out that, though urban residents enjoyed the full protection of the law, the gaucho had lost his home and been denied a productive social role. Hernández proposed the formation of settlements on the frontier populated by native Argentines, because, if provided with tools and land as well as arms, gauchos would willingly defend their own interests. Significantly, this poet-politician devoted nearly one-fourth of *Martín Fierro*, some seventeen hundred lines, to frontier service and battles with the Indians.[24]

Even as Hernández published the first part of his epic in 1872, others joined him in criticizing injustices against the gaucho. José María Jurado addressed the provincial legislature on August 23, 1872. "It is a known fact, Mr. President," he observed, "that frontier service has caused the greatest ills to our province. . . . It makes a normal life impossible for the inhabitants of the countryside." The Rural Society addressed letters to Governor Castro expressing alarm that "some of the exterior forts totally lack arms." The ranchers solicited horses to send to frontier garrisons in hopes of bolstering the defense of their estancias.[25]

A call in 1873 for eighteen hundred provincial guardsmen touched off renewed protests. *La Redención* of Buenos Aires decried the misuse of frontier troops utilized to care for livestock rather than to fight Indians. Soldiers did not even know who owned the animals they tended. According to the journal, "education and colonization" rather than forced service would solve the frontier problem. In San José de las Flores, *El progreso de Flores* seconded the sentiments of its porteño colleague: Carlos Mathón, the editor, could conceive of "nothing more hateful" than the "unconstitutional service" demanded of the "poor gaucho." Mathón particularly objected to the government's order that provincial guardsmen must fight in a civil war in Entre Ríos. José Antonio Wilde, owner and editor of the Quilmes newspaper, *El progreso de Quilmes*, led a movement to hire substitutes for local guardsmen called to active military duty. Through a land auction and donations, the town raised 4,280 pesos for the cause. Like many critics, Wilde recognized the need for frontier defense but objected to the "abusive system" of recruitment, so "demoralizing to the masses."[26]

Commander Manuel Prado's lively memoirs of service on the western frontier provide a vivid portrait of the hardships and penuries of military life. At Fort Timaté in Trenque Lauquén, soldiers slept in cave-like shacks and lived on horsemeat, ostriches, pampean tea, and "goodwill." In true gaucho fashion, men wore long hair and beards and dressed in traditional chiripá and botas de potro. Soldiers relied upon greatly discounted scrip issued by the local pulpero because pay arrived so infrequently. Their monthly wage of 140 pesos disappeared quickly on mate at 20 pesos per pound, cigarettes at 5, and other expensive goods. Deserters met the same capricious but implacable "justice" everywhere on the pampa. Three captured deserters protested that their terms of service had long since expired and that they wished to return to their homes. A lottery determined the sentences: prison for two; death for the third.[27]

Alfredo Ebelot found little to admire in frontier policies or official conduct. Through the "worst recruitment possible," the government threw together murderers and other felons with honest rural laborers impressed from provincial ranches. In this Frenchman's opinion, the destructive social climate encouraged law breaking and instability and hindered the transformation of the gaucho from a free-living vagabond into a dependable, sedentary worker. After long enduring the lash and other forms of "cruel and even brutal" discipline with "fatalistic resignation," the soldier finally deserted. Some found succor among labor-short ranchers who welcomed any peon, regardless of status. Others fled to the Indian frontier and adopted "semi-barbaric customs." Ebelot acutely diagnosed the link between the oppressive, arbitrary demands on the gaucho and the many social ills of Argentina's richest province.[28]

The project on which Ebelot was occupied, a long, deep ditch across the pampa, failed to halt Indian incursions, which continued despite the proliferation of garrisons and increasingly sophisticated telegraph and rail connections. In December 1875, cacique Juan José Catriel led five thousand braves in an attack on settlements in Azul, Olavarría, Tandil, Tapalqué, Tres Arroyos, and Alvear. Government forces finally defeated Catriel and ended the Great Invasion in March 1876, but not before the raiders had killed three or four hundred persons, burned forty houses, captured five hundred hostages, and stolen three hundred thousand head of livestock. Chief Pincén invaded Junín in late 1876, stole cattle, and returned to his frontier village, or toldería. In 1878 Colonel Enrique Spika and a force of thirty men defeated the last group of Indian raiders to enter Azul. Residents of the port city, comfortably distant from the horrors of frontier fighting and service, could reflect humorously upon the remote situation. *El fraile*, a satirical porteño paper, ran an advertisement titled "Frontier Theater" in its entertainment section in October 1876. The announcement promised a "great invasion of Indian actors any day," starring the caciques Catriel and Namuncurá and Minister of War Adolfo Alsina. The price of admission: "all that you own plus your skin."[29]

Minister of War Julio A. Roca's conquest of the desert in 1878 and 1879, the last of the great Indian campaigns, brought suffering with its military successes. One soldier recalled long forced marches during which roots, birds, and horsemeat sustained the troops. Lacking water, men drank horse urine or placed metal in their mouths to induce salivation. Such sacrifices hastened the conquest, however, and Roca added 54 million hectares (133 million acres) of rich grasslands to the national patrimony. The Rural Society, which had called for a radical change in frontier policy as early as 1870, found a windfall of new provincial lands available to its members. The vast areas opened by Roca went to speculators and terratenientes, as had all previous land. Like his military predecessor Rosas, who had opened the south pampa to purchase by large landholding supporters, Roca facilitated the continued consolidation of landownership and political power by the ranching elite. Later, as leader of the "peace and administration" government of the modernizing Generation of 'Eighty, he brought the landed elites from the provinces of the interior into the coalition. His presidencies (1880–86 and 1898–1904) marked the successful political institutionalization of the ranching/export elites of the interior and littoral in the Partido Autonomista Nacional.[30]

Although Roca's triumphant sweep to the Río Negro established white dominion over the entire province, sporadic raids continued into the 1880s. Chief Pincén and fifty braves attacked several German ranches in Trenque Lauquén in 1883. They killed eight, wounded fifteen, and drove off some three thousand cattle and hundreds of horses. According to *La campaña* of Buenos Aires, gauchos, probably deserters, accompanied the raiding party.[31]

The passing of the Indian threat during the 1880s did not eliminate the burden of military service for the rural population. Political crises continued to stir troop demands. The number of vagrants sentenced to three years of military service in Chacabuco rose sharply in late 1879 and 1880, as the government armed for political conflict. Even though the frontier draft ended in 1880, justices continued to remit gauchos for service without even a thin veneer of legality. Government mobilization of the national guard in 1880 prompted many workers to flee to remote counties such as Vecino, Mar Chiquita, and Tuyú. Servando García, a local official in Dolores, complained that the combination of threatened military mobilization and "poverty and hard times" had driven many men away from the county. Some migrated westward as far as Juárez, Azul, and Lobería in the hope of earning a living, unmolested by military obligations.[32]

Many progressive Argentine leaders viewed the political use of the military as yet another aspect of the nation's backwardness. Civilian and military leaders from the 1860s onward began moving the armed forces toward a more professional posture. In 1864 the first young officers departed to study at European military institutes. Under Sarmiento's leadership, and spurred by the army's uneven performance during the Paraguayan War, the professionalization of the military moved forward substantially. In 1869, the first year of his presidency, Sarmiento, a staunch advocate of education, created the Colegio Militar to train the nation's officer cadre. During his first term as president in 1884, Roca opened the Academia Militar to provide remedial training for older officers who had not studied at the Colegio. Hungarian-born Colonel Juan F. Czetz directed both the Colegio and the Academia, thereby providing continuity in officer training. The apex of the military educational system, the Escuela Superior de Guerra (Higher war college), opened in 1900 under Minister of War General Luis María Campos to offer advanced classes to senior officers.[33]

In addition to upgrading the officer ranks, leaders also sought to improve the faulty recruitment system for enlisted personnel. High desertion rates, lax discipline, and poor performance made reform imperative. The centralizing Generation of 'Eighty also wished to monopolize military power by strengthening the national army and debilitating provincial national guard units. Universal obligatory military service became the vehicle for this centralizing reform effort, but many years of debate preceded the consummation of this goal in 1902. In early 1888, *La opinión pública* of Bahía Blanca criticized the old draft quotas that had uprooted the ''disinherited gaucho'' from his peaceful, pastoral livelihood and thrust him into uniform. However, the writer opposed obligatory service as premature and warned of the negative social consequences of six years of required service. In March 1888, a lottery replaced the old quotas. The wealthy could still hire substitutes for 248 pesos, well beyond the reach of rural peons, who earned 20 pesos monthly. The poor continued to bear the burden of national defense, but the lottery moved recruitment one step further toward universal service.[34]

The mistreatment and misuse of national guard trainees prompted some observers to oppose obligatory service. Near the close of the

1890s, *La vanguardia* of Buenos Aires and *La patria* of Olavarría detailed the abuses suffered by guardsmen in training. Poorly clothed and underfed, kept beyond their stipulated terms, and harshly worked, the recruits "inspired compassion" when they finally returned home. In 1900, *La palabra libre* of Rojas criticized such mistreatment and expressed the fear that obligatory service would perpetuate it. According to this provincial journal, trainees labored with pick and shovel as peons and received no military instruction. Such misuse of the twenty-year-old recruits was unjust and added nothing to the nation's military preparedness, complained the paper.[35]

In 1902, during Roca's second administration, Argentina instituted universal obligatory military service. Both the president and the minister of war, Colonel Pablo Ricchieri, deemed the move necessary to the further professionalization of the armed forces. Universal service was also viewed as a means of inculcating patriotic values and of speeding the cultural assimilation of immigrant masses. The new system reduced some inequities and abuses in service, but it proved no more popular than had earlier conscription. Only 47 percent of the 5,691 young men called to service in 1909 appeared.[36]

Regularized obligatory service ended a century of arbitrary military impressment for the rural population. Throughout the century, gauchos, victims of relentless vagrancy and passport laws, had borne the burden of forced service more heavily than any other social group. The Uruguayan poet Juan Zorilla de San Martín aptly summarized the gaucho's plight in a speech given in 1888: "If he hasn't learned to work much, it is because he had to fight much . . . [He is] not very used to watering the land with the sweat of his brow because he has had to water it for a long time with the blood of his veins."[37]

9
Sheep,
Fences,
and Farming

The legal strictures and social structure of Buenos Aires province changed little during the nineteenth century, but the rural economy underwent profound alterations that irrevocably erased the traditional life of the gaucho. From the 1820s onward, sheep began to compete with cattle as the principal source of livestock wealth. Sheep required different care and facilities, so that ranch workers had to either adapt or migrate to regions where cattle still predominated. By the 1870s sheep had effectively displaced cattle from much of the improved pasturage near Buenos Aires. Gauchos participated in the sheep cycle, shearing, marking, castrating, and herding on horseback. But the old pampa gaucha of wild creole cattle slain for hides and tallow alone had long passed away.

Of the many changes from traditional to modern ranching, fencing perhaps altered the gaucho's life to the greatest extent. The thousands of miles of smooth wire, and later barbed wire, that stretched across the plains during the last half of the century severed the gaucho from his accustomed way of life, further segregated him from the mainstream of the nation, and facilitated land consolidation. With fencing came farming. Agriculture, even more than sheep raising, called forth new skills and initiated drastic changes in the nature of the rural labor force. The native peon, for whom unmounted labor represented an unspeakable denigration, largely withdrew from farming, leaving it to the European immigrant, who tilled the soil willingly. In 1904 agricultural goods exceeded livestock produce in export value for the first time. As in the case of sheep, farm crops including wheat, corn, flax, and other cereals displaced cattle and forced cowhands to migrate.[1]

During the 1820s and 1830s sheep began to compete with cattle for lush grazing lands near the port. Within a few decades, wool had become the nation's leading export, supplying mills in England, Germany, France, and the United States. In 1875 José María Jurado pronounced the rapid rise of sheep raising to be the most significant economic change in nineteenth-century ranching. Animal hides and skins, horsehair, and tallow continued to be important exports, but by 1885 wool and sheepskins accounted for 69 percent of the value of Argentina's nonmeat exports. In 1899, the first year in which total nonmeat exports exceeded one hundred million pesos in value, sheep products contributed 81 percent of the total. From 1901 to 1912, frozen mutton shipments ranged in value from five to seven million pesos per year. Sheep grazed on the finest *cabañas* (breeding ranches) in the province and ranked with purebred cattle as leading attractions at the prestigous Palermo stock exhibition sponsored by the Rural Society.[2]

Foreigners, mostly Britons, introduced merino sheep during the Rosas era to meet the booming demands of French and English textile mills. Many of them purchased rich lands for next to nothing from persecuted unitarios who had been driven from their holdings by Rosas. These lands, in the northern part of the province, developed into the nation's first major fine wool-producing region.[3]

Although cattle production for saladeros remained his prime economic activity, Rosas also raised sheep on several of his ranches. Contrary to John Lynch's assertion that Rosas was "not an improving landowner," he showed a cautious but persistent will to upgrade and diversify his ranching activities. His sheep raising, attempts to improve animal breeds, and experiments with agriculture show a cautiously progressive spirit—at least in the area of ranch management. The shearing in 1838 at "San Martín" yielded only 2,711 kg. (5,964 lb.) of wool, 45 percent of which was high-grade mestizo quality. A decade later, production rose 88 percent to 5,088 kg. (11,194 lb.). Mestizo wool accounted for 64 percent of the 1848 shearing, as Rosas, like other estancieros, improved the breed of his flocks.[4] By mid-century, sheep occupied much of the safe, rich pasturage within 150 kilometers (93 miles) of the capital. Sheep forced the hardy, creole cattle out onto coarse grasslands nearer the Indian frontier. Some ranchers, like Pedro Sheridan, owner of "Los Sajones," produced large quantities of premium wool from the favored merino breeds, Saxony elector and *negrete*. At the time of his death in 1844, Sheridan owned forty-thousand purebred and mestizo animals grazing on sixteen puestos. Rosas solicited his advice on combating sarna.[5]

Rising wool prices during the 1850s fueled the merino cycle. One observer judged sheep raising "one of the most lucrative occupations in the country." Land values near Buenos Aires jumped 250 percent between 1852 and 1860, as ranchers eagerly rented pasturage for their flocks. On the southwest frontier in Tandil, on the other hand, ranchers in 1852 registered only 4 sheep brands, compared with 131 for cattle and horses.[6] Civil war in the United States further spurred Argentine wool production by eliminating the southern Confederacy's competing cotton. A coincidental crisis in saladero cattle prices added incentive for ranchers to diversify into sheep production. A new breed, the Rambouillet—larger, hardier, and bearing thick, heavy fleece—appeared during the 1860s and quickly spread across the pampa. Emilio Delpech, a French wool buyer, observed in 1885 the predominance of the Rambouillet in the pastures of Juárez, Dolores, Maipú, Tandil, and other southern partidos as sheep-raising moved out to frontier regions.[7]

With the development of frozen meat technology, ranchers again changed breeds; Lincoln and Romney Marsh sheep, which yielded both quality wool and good mutton, gained popularity toward the end of the century. But the frigorífico boom during the 1890s increased the profit margin for high-grade beef and reversed the migration of cattle from central to peripheral pastures. Purebred and mestizo cattle reconquered the richer grasslands near the port and pushed sheep toward outlying counties. Argentina's rail network, built and run largely by the British, provided transportation for bulky pastoral and agricultural produce to Buenos Aires. The nation's rail system grew from a mere 11 km. (7 miles) in 1857 to nearly 3,700 km. (2,294 miles) by 1885, then zoomed to 33,429 km. (20,726 miles) by 1914.[8]

The national census of 1895 recorded nearly 53 million sheep in the province, 83 percent of them mestizo. Lincoln sheep had thoroughly supplanted the pioneering merino breeds. "Estanciero," writing in *El eco de Tandil* on April 27, 1905, analyzed the changing breeds. The Rambouillet, with its "fine, long, and silky" fleece, ideally met strong early textile demands. Lincoln sheep, on the other hand, grew rapidly to greater size, better resisted cold weather, and yielded good mutton in addition to wool (albeit of lower quality). "Estanciero" counseled ranchers to raise both breeds in order to avoid disastrous losses from sudden market fluctuations.[9]

The rapidly changing sheep industry forced significant adjustments upon the rural labor force. As cattle and sheep migrated to different areas of the pampa, workers seeking employment on either cattle or sheep ranches also had to move. Labor requirements for sheep ranching rose and fell seasonally, as did those for cattle. In place of cattle roundups and branding, every fall sheepmen notched the animals' ears for identification, cut off the ewes' tails to facilitate breeding, and castrated young rams. Older creole sheep, increasingly rare in the province, required occasional hoof trimming. The busiest time on the sheep estancia was during the esquila, or spring shearing, when ranchers contracted gangs of twenty to forty shearers, working under a foreman. Two or three mounted peons first herded the animals into corrals. After shearing, a "doctor," generally a boy or old man, treated cuts inflicted by the shears to reduce the danger of infection. One worker sharpened shears to insure clean, rapid cutting; others bundled wool into bales for shipment to Buenos Aires. Ranchers issued latas imprinted with the name or brand of the ranch, which frequently circulated as specie at pulperías on the coin-short pampa. Workers collected wages at the end of the month-long operation and then moved on, seeking employment at another estancia.[10]

Shearing competed with wheat sowing for scarce rural labor, so wages for the brief season usually ran high. The long-term trend from the 1840s through the 1870s shows generally increasing wages, with considerable fluctuations from year to year because of varying political and economic conditions. Wages on Rosas' estancias stood at 8 pesos per 100 sheep in 1838 and rose to 11 in 1840. A serious labor shortage prompted by high draft quotas in 1843 drove wages up to 25 pesos, but the level dropped back to 20 in 1845. By 1868 shearers earned 40 pesos, and the wage remained at 40 or 45 throughout the following decades.[11]

Native workers, including women, who earned equal wages and did equal work, clipped an average of 35 to 50 animals per day. The level of native worker involvement is made clear in correspondence between Enrique Bird and his uncle William Walker, both Scottish ranchers. Bird complained to Walker in November 1904 that he could find no men with horses to move a herd of his livestock. "All the natives with tropillas," he noted, "are busy shearing presently."[12]

Permanent labor needs ran far below the large shearing gangs required once a year but still averaged four or five times the number of workers needed on cattle ranches. The sheep cycle, which initially expanded ranch employment opportunities, was the only change to do so. On the traditional unfenced cattle estancia, one peon could handle a thousand cattle ranging over two-thousand hectares (4,942 acres). Five times as many sheep—perhaps five flocks of eight to twelve hundred animals, each requiring a resident shepherd—could graze on the same area. Consequently, four or five puesteros tended flocks in place of the lone peon who handled a large herd of cattle. Until late in the century, the increased demand for shepherds partially offset declining employment opportunities for cattle ranch workers in the Río de la Plata region.[13]

On smaller ranches near Buenos Aires in counties such as San Antonio de Areco, Mercedes, and Luján, Irish and Basque immigrants tended the flocks. According to Hutchinson, "the country part of Luján might be styled New Ireland." He found few natives working in the area except as shearers, but in outlying regions Argentine shepherds far outnumbered foreign-born. According to the 1869 census, 270 Argentines and only 65 foreigners (half of them Basque) worked on sheep estancias in Azul. Eighty-three percent of the natives hailed from Buenos Aires province, with Santiago del Estero and Córdoba adding most of the remainder. Puesteros received a modest wage but enjoyed several types of subsidies. They could kill old sheep, aged three or four, and eat the meat so long as the tallow, skin, and grease went to the estanciero. They could also collect excrement and giant thistles for fuel. Supplies, including mate, sugar, biscuits, and salt, had to be purchased from wages. In 1888, Estanislao Zeballos noted that the puestero was usually a gaucho with a family. The shepherd worked for a wage of 16 pesos per month or held a contract for a half, third, or quarter of the year's profits. He could slaughter up to six old sheep per month for food. In contrast to the migratory life of most rural workers, the puestero lived a more routine, secure, and sedentary existence.[14]

By the 1890s, however, the once relatively comfortable and favorable position of the puestero had declined sharply. In early 1891 the Federación Obrera Regional Argentina (FORA) outlined the sorry plight of the sheep puestero in a lengthy open letter to President Carlos Pellegrini that was reprinted in *La prensa*. Shepherds devoted fifteen hours a day to the landowners' interests, which left them little time to work on their own behalf. Falling rural wages and unfavorable rental contracts forced many to abandon the countryside and seek employment in cities. The volume of complaints convinced FORA that conditions for rural workers were even worse than for the urban proletariat. Because of the surplus of capable puesteros, landowners selected renters with small families in order to reduce meat consumption. They also forbade puesteros to keep milk cows or extra horses beyond those needed for ranch work. Owners demanded that shepherds and their families perform additional work on the estancia whenever needed. In 1897, *La patria* of Olavarría stated that the position of puesteros was seriously disadvantaged. Their scant wage of 20–25 pesos per month did not provide adequate income to support a family.[15] The earlier possibility of rising from a tenant or sharecropper to a small sheep rancher and landowner evaporated in the face of falling wages, unfavorable rental contracts, and skyrocketing land prices.

Toward the end of the century, life for migratory shearers as well as for sedentary puesteros took a turn for the worse. New economic opportunities opened by the sheep-raising boom vanished in the face of advancing technology. Shearing machines drastically cut into the seasonal employment that had earlier required thousands of people working with hand clippers. *El eco de Tandil* reported on September 3, 1882, that two Santa Fe residents named Van Oppel and Febert had invented a mechanical shearer. An animal-driven wheel powered the machine, which, according to inventors, yielded a "uniform and even cut." A decade later the progressive rural journal *La agricultura* published descriptions and illustrations of several different shearing machines. The Newell model, powered by a man- or horse-driven wheel, first appeared at the London Agricultural Exposition. The Bariquand clipper promised greater economy and better trimming. The Wolseley shearer, incorporating the most advanced features then known, represented the state of the art during the early 1890s. In 1894 Argentina held the first national exposition of shearing machines. Manufacturers touted the multiple benefits to the purchaser or lessee of their inventions. Compared with hand shearing, a machine clipped more closely, with fewer injuries to the animals, resulting in more wool and less infection. Machines also reduced labor needs and saved time because fewer workers could complete the task more quickly. Pedro A. Vinent, writing in the *Anales* of the Rural Society, envisioned added social benefits accruing to the rancher who utilized machines: reduced labor requirements would allow elimination of the "plague of shearers" and "people of bad customs" who gambled and raced horses instead of working productively. With mechanical shearers, a trusted, dependable puestero and his family could handle the esquila without additional day laborers of questionable moral virtue and economic worth.[16]

Rented and purchased machines spread quickly throughout the Río de la Plata region. The mechanical wonders permitted the average worker to clip at least seventy and as many as one hundred animals during a 10- or 12-hour workday. Increased productivity cut labor requirements by at least 50 percent. The normal work routine also suffered transformation because the noisy clippers drowned out conversation between workers. Shearing stalls made the operation more efficient but increased the physical and social distance between laborers. Ranchers also replaced the traditional pay system of latas to curb gambling for the tokens. They held that late-night games of chance hurt worker productivity and contributed to poor clipping and more injuries to the animals.[17]

In addition to altering relations between workers and discouraging sociability on the job, technological innovation also changed the nature of employer-laborer relations on the sheep ranch. Estancieros had earlier had to adopt a tolerant, accommodating attitude toward shearers because of chronic seasonal labor shortages. Relatively high, short-term wages, Sundays and holidays free, and a grand fiesta attracted migrant workers to the same ranches year after year. Automation gave ranchers the bargaining power to reduce wages and to select from among competing laborers. Jorge MacKitchie, manager of William Walker's estancia, complained in 1912 that some of the regular seasonal shearers were getting "a little to large for there boots" (sic): in spite of three days lost to rain and festivities, the shearers refused to work on Sunday. MacKitchie marked their names in red as a reminder not to rehire them the following season. Having refused work to more than 20 men, each claiming to shear 150 animals per day, the manager could afford to hire selectively and to fire any worker who met with disfavor.[18] Technology and massive immigration had closed off new avenues of employment in sheep ranching within a few decades after they had appeared. Some early puesteros earned enough money through sharecropping contracts to purchase flocks and become ranchers, but most remained tenants who, though better off than migrant shearers, enjoyed little of the riches brought to the nation by the wool and mutton export boom. Terratenientes retained control of the pampa and reaped a substantial unearned increment in land values that contributed further to their maintenance of political power.

Like mechanical shearers, fencing reshaped rural work patterns. Ranchers of the colonial and early national periods had often utilized ditches and "live fences" of vegetation to protect crops and orchards from foraging livestock, but cattle on the range grazed unfettered, wandering far in search of grass and water. Property lines and cattle ownership depended upon the nebulous concept of the herd's "accustomed range," where the animals generally grazed, and upon the owner's ability to assert his will and claim, with force if necessary. Ranch workers spent much time rounding up and herding animals toward the *querencia*, or customary range.[19]

In 1844, the Anglo-Argentine rancher Ricardo Newton visited England and witnessed the effectiveness of wire fencing in livestock control. Returning to his Chascomús ranch laden with metal posts and wire, he constructed fences around his vegetable garden and orchards and built corrals. Fencing appeared on the pampa in 1845, the same year Sarmiento published his attack on Rosas and rural barbarism in *Facundo*. Later, in the pages of his newspaper *El nacional*, he urged ranchers to "Fence! Do not be barbarians!"[20] In 1855 Francisco Halbach, the Prussian consul to Argentina, became the first rancher to fence his entire estancia, "Los Remedios," on the Matanza River in Cañuelas. Whereas Newton's concern had been to protect plants from foraging livestock, Halbach utilized wire fencing for range control and boundary delineation—to keep animals in. The latter motive became central on the modern estancia. The consul's close friends Sarmiento and Bartolomé Mitre both supported fencing and other modern practices in ranching and farming.[21]

In the late 1850s, Thomas Hinchliff remarked the already evident social impact of fencing near Buenos Aires: "A good deal of land is enclosed by wire fence, a modern innovation which greatly annoys the thorough-bred *gauchos* who have from time immemorial been accustomed to gallop by day or night in any direction, and as far as they please." The Briton hit upon a central social effect of fencing: the further limitation of the gaucho's geographical mobility. Ostrich hunting, for example, could not be practiced on a fenced, privately owned pampa. The process of restriction, begun through legal strictures in the colonial era, came to completion with the transformation of open range into private property by the fence. Fencing also speeded the consolidation of latifundia. In a debate in 1872 over reform of the rural code, Deputy Molina, a rancher of nineteen years, complained of the inequities created by mandatory fencing. A proposed change in the code required fencing to prevent stray cattle from mixing with purebred animals. According to Molina, mandatory fencing would ruin one in six provincial ranchers, who could not afford the considerable expense. As a result the poor rancher would lose his lands to the rich. Terratenientes also extended their holdings by enclosing not only their own land but also expanses of the adjoining public domain, a simple tactic on the unsurveyed pampa.[22]

Fencing also drastically decreased the already low manpower needs of the cattle estancia. The job of actually building fences went to foreign immigrants who, unlike the native rural laborer, did not disdain foot work. An article in a ranchers' journal *Revista de ganaderia Huss y Cia.*, in 1880 acknowledged the considerable expense of enclosure but estimated that the outlay would be recouped quickly. Fencing reduced losses caused by theft and straying but, more important, it permitted reduction of the labor force, the highest fixed cost for estancieros. On the open range, twelve thousand head of cattle required fifteen peons, each earning 400 pesos monthly. Enclosure sharply lowered the number of permanent salaried employees required, thus expenditures on such provisions as meat, mate, and tobacco also dropped. It also eliminated some traditional tasks, such as the nightwatch, and some roundups. Writing in the *Anales* of the Rural Society in 1881, "R. N.," of Chascomús, summarized the benefits accruing to the fenced estancia. Subdivision of pastures into fenced paddocks economized on labor. Different breeds of livestock could be separated for selective breeding, and young animals could be kept from reproducing until the optimal age. Pastures could be held in reserve in case of drought, thereby cutting costly weight and animal losses during unseasonably dry weather. By the 1890s no rancher could ignore the many advantages of fencing, and the little remaining open range quickly disappeared. Carlos Lemée observed in 1894 that enclosure was "without any doubt the most important progress realized in Argentine livestock-raising."[23]

The porteño daily *La prensa* stressed further social and ideological effects of fencing in 1894. Enclosure definitively ended the "false communist doctrine" that the "fruits of the countryside were given by God for all," a basic precept of rural life on the open range. "Property was a myth," according to this establishment organ, until fencing forced the notion of private ownership into the "uncultured half-Indian brain of the paisano." Strands of wire cut off the gaucho from the verities and life of the past and enforced the new capitalist ethic of the modernizing elite. Integration into the world market system and technological modernization spelled displacement and poverty for the native rural masses.[24]

In contrast to *La prensa*, the Socialist *La vanguardia* criticized the social costs of fencing and other technological changes in ranching, tying increasing "misery" and "slavery principally in the country-side" to the elimination of many rural jobs. Many estancieros made their reduced labor force even more dependent upon the ranch by forbidding workers to pasture their own animals on the improved enclosed paddocks. Bereft of his own string of horses, the peon became dependent upon the landowner because he could not work without mounts. The tropilla, one of the gaucho's few possessions, became a liability because ranchers hired only workers with few or no private mounts. Only the ranch foreman and perhaps the puesteros who tended the enclosed paddocks could retain their own animals.[25]

Although it made life even more precarious for the native ranch worker, fencing opened economic opportunities for the mechanically inclined foreigner. Immigrants built most of the range fences, and their construction and maintenance became a lucrative area of employment. The new positions created for foreigners paled, however, in comparison with the number of jobs lost by native ranch workers. Fencing also generated other technological changes. Enclosed animals could not range freely in search of water, so wells had to be dug to water each pasture. Miguel Lanús constructed the first windmill in Argentina in 1880, and other estancieros quickly followed suit.[26] By protecting crops from animal depradations, enclosure also made possible the rise of large-scale agriculture on the pampa—yet another major shift in the rural economy.

Farming faced more serious obstacles than did sheep raising on the pampa. The small internal market and conflicts between ranchers and farmers hindered crop production. European demands arose for wheat, corn, oats, and linseed, but until ranchers required alfalfa pastures for purebred stock during the latter decades of the century, farming held little importance except in partidos close to Buenos Aires. Crop destruction by livestock and chronic labor shortages plagued farmers on the pampa. During the eighteenth century, the government frequently forced mulattos, Indians, and sometimes mestizos to aid in the wheat harvest, but still farmers usually lacked peons for the harvest. Compared with urban professions, which offered higher status and a genteel lifestyle, or with ranching, which yielded a generous return with minimal input of capital and energy, growing wheat for the small internal market seemed an unappealing alternative. The colonial Argentine found the easy exploitation of natural abundance in livestock far preferable to strenuous labor in agriculture. Poor transportation and the threat of rampaging Indians further discouraged prospective farmers. A census of Buenos Aires in 1774 recorded only thirty-three farmers out of ten thousand inhabitants. The city frequently imported grain because the few farmers could not meet its needs. Even Jonathan Brown, who presents a much brighter picture of the rural economy, admits that "until well past midcentury, agriculture in Buenos Aires remained almost as limited and rude" as during the colonial era.[27]

In spite of Bernadino Rivadavia's efforts to create a nation of sturdy yeomen on small farms during the 1820s, the agrarian dream never materialized on the Argentine plains. Although some ranchers grew wheat, many viewed farmers as unwanted competitors who pushed up land prices and threatened their monopoly on acquisition of the public domain. Tomás Anchorena, Rosas' cousin and alter ego, opposed renting land to foreigners who might farm it. Not until large landowners controlled the province's vast territory later in the century did terratenientes encourage farming. Rosas practiced arboriculture on a cautious, modest scale to supply the needs of his extensive ranching empire. Most of his estancias included orchards that produced fruit, nuts, and wood to construct corrals and buildings. His headquarters at Palermo drew admiring comments from visitors for its beautifully landscaped and wooded grounds. At "San Martín" Schöo planted orchards of nine thousand peach trees and seventeen hundred paraíso trees to complement existing groves. In mid-1847 he reported that most of the ranch's trees—orange, peach, olive, walnut, ombú, poplar, and Chinaberry—were growing well.[28]

Rosas, a cautious innovator, experimented carefully with new agricultural ideas. In 1836 he sent alfalfa seed to one of his managers to be planted along a riverbank. He instructed his manager to plant the seeds after a rain shower but strictly forbade plowing the earth. This taboo against plowing persisted among many ranchers until the twentieth century. Respectful of nature's precarious balance, appreciative of the great richness of the natural grasses, and fearful of erosion, Rosas hoped to reap the benefits of improved alfalfa pasturage without the risks and costs of plowing. He hoped that his "experiments" would yield the "great advantage" of fattening livestock with little investment in labor for farming. Rosas continued his agricultural experiments for several years but never agreed to slice open the pampean sod with a plow.[29]

Farmers during the Rosas era who sought to expand into ranching districts needed equal parts of patience and perseverance to survive. Juan Fugl, a Danish pioneer in Tandil, recalled many difficulties and disappointments in his autobiography, *Abriendo surcos*.[30] Natural disaster, such as severe drought in 1850, limited and distant porteño markets for wheat flour, and scavenging livestock plagued early efforts. Neighboring horses "loved wheat," and local officials, "no friends" of the farmer, refused to enforce ordinances against invading livestock. After Rosas' fall, the local justice acknowledged Fugl's right to control animals that entered his fields. Tandil gauchos, furious at being fined or having their livestock sold for eating a gringo's wheat, threatened Fugl. As a further complication, alcalde Ramón Zavala refused to enforce the justice's edicts against foraging animals. As farming became more common and important to the region, local officials began to uphold the rights of agriculturists.

To the north, in Azul, similar conflicts erupted between farmers and ranchers in 1855. Farmers on the *chacras*, or plots, near the city found support in an old unenforced Rivadavian decree of April 16, 1823, under which animals could not enter the exclusively agricultural zone extending one league (3.2 miles) in circumference around pampean towns. Stock owners whose animals violated the law could be fined 20 pesos per animal. Except for scattered pioneers such as Fugl and other immigrants, mid-century agriculture in the province was limited largely to partidos surrounding Buenos Aires and along the shores of the Río de la Plata. The agricultural zone near Buenos Aires produced a scant 9 percent more wheat than did the ranching zone near the frontier during the half-year period from late 1854 to early 1855. These figures hardly sustain Jonathan Brown's contention that agriculture was a vibrant part of the provincial economy during the first half of the nineteenth century, even taking into consideration the much larger geographical area of the ranching region. The ranching zone included 81 percent of provincial lands in 1838, less than 2 percent was devoted to agriculture. In 1854, ranch lands made up 78 percent of the provincial territory and agriculture about 6 percent—hardly a massive expansion of farming. In 1856 farming occupied 9 percent of provincial lands and ranching the remaining 91 percent.[31]

Although Argentine leaders gave lip service to the need for agriculture, none after Rivadavia championed the small farmer until Sarmiento took up the cause in the 1860s. Great admiration for the United States and a determination to civilize the "barbarian" plain motivated his agricultural colonization efforts, but the political and economic clout of the ranching elite stifled his vision of a Jacksonian prairie of family farms as it had Rivadavia's three decades earlier.[32]

In the latter half of the century, farming pockets gradually established themselves at scattered points across Buenos Aires province, and some wider support for agriculture emerged. On August 23, 1872, the editor of *La unión del sud* in Chascomús supported farming as a means of attracting immigrants to the underpopulated plains. Significantly, he emphasized the vast quantity of land available to *renters*, making no mention of purchasers. Except for limited subdivision in agricultural and mixed zones, latifundia remained. Subdivision of latifundia for sale as family farms appealed neither to terratenientes nor to their spokesmen.

At this time, several classes of pampean farmers developed who enjoyed only slightly more security and comfort than did native migrant ranch workers. James R. Scobie has documented the lives of pampean farmers during the late nineteenth century. A small minority of immigrants settled in officially or privately sponsored agricultural colonies. Called *colonos*, these men had some prospect of purchasing land and working toward a stable life, but most farmers labored as arrendatarios or *medianeros* (sharecroppers) who shifted from plot to plot, eking out a marginal existence in bountiful years and going into debt in others. Farmers enjoyed only meager amenities, yet their lives were better than those of seasonal farm workers. Some natives worked in the harvests, but *golondrinas*, or "swallows," who crossed the Atlantic from Italy and Spain each year, harvested most of the wheat, corn, and linseed crops.[33]

The precarious existence of one colony, at Baradero, illustrates the hardships and penury of establishing agriculture in the province. Guillermo Wilcken's report in 1873 on the condition of Argentine farming detailed the obstacles. Francisco Sola communicated to Felipe Senillosa in March 1872 that speculating interlopers were endangering the 150 colonist families at Baradero. The farmers, with ten and twelve year's residence on the land, lacked clear title and stood to lose the fruits of their decade-long struggle. They survived the threat to enjoy a bountiful harvest in 1876, but drought shriveled the corn harvest and prevented potato planting, bringing disaster the following year. By 1877 the colony had grown to 1,896 residents, mostly foreign-born. Swiss predominated, with 699 total, followed by 459 native Argentines, 352 Italians, 153 Basques, and 233 others. Italians and Spaniards comprised the majority of pampean farmers overall.[34]

Provincial authorities made only sporadic half-hearted efforts to promote farming. In only one instance did the provincial government actively sponsor an official colony. In November 1877 nine Russian-German Mennonite families settled with official aid on the still unsecured southern frontier in Olavarría. Within a few years the colony had grown to some 250 families totaling a thousand persons, as other nationalities joined the Mennonite founders. But this colony never grew or prospered as rapidly as did farming communities in neighboring Santa Fe province. In 1887 the provincial legislature enacted the only law to create official agricultural centers to attract immigrants. This last effort at official colonization quickly failed, and by the 1890s the notion was a dead cause. A lengthy polemic debating the reasons for failure persisted into the 1930s, but no further legislation to foster agriculture resulted.[35] The political power of the large landowners and their reluctance to alter traditional land tenure patterns, land usage, and social relations killed any possibility of large-scale farming in the province.

In contrast to the lackluster efforts of Buenos Aires province on behalf of agriculture, Santa Fe proved a spectacular success. Several factors converged to fuel the farming boom there and to retard its development in Buenos Aires. Livestock raising held a preferential position among landowners of both provinces, but the higher mean temperatures in Santa Fe made much of its land inappropriate for sheep raising. Estancieros in Buenos Aires province immersed themselves in the highly profitable merino wool cycle, whereas *santafecinos* had to seek other investment opportunities. Immigrant tenant farmers stood ready to occupy the fertile but under-utilized lands of the province. Higher labor demands for farming, compared with ranching, forced the provincial government to mount a heady immigration campaign. The landowner-controlled legislature decisively supported and promoted both immigration and agriculture. Colonies, spread out as they were along the frontier, also gave ranchers a buffer between their estancias and raiding Indians.[36] From the first colony established in 1856 at

Esperanza, farming spread quickly throughout Santa Fe province. By 1874 thirty colonies, populated by more than fifteen thousand persons, occupied nearly two hundred thousand hectares (494,200 acres). Not until the last decade of the century, when ranchers needed alfalfa for their purebred cattle, did export agriculture prosper in Buenos Aires province. Production of cereals for the porteño market occupied some farmers there, but agriculture remained the poor stepchild to ranching for most of the nineteenth century.[37]

Unlike Santa Fe, Buenos Aires province granted only meager support for agriculture. Tenant farmers, renting land on two- to five-year contracts, formed the great majority of farmers there. Contracts varied, some requiring an annual payment for rent and others stipulating sharecropping ratios of one-half, one-third, or one-quarter of the harvest (medianero, *terciero, cuartero*). In an early contract signed in 1847, Antonio and Pedro Bitancur rented farmlands in Quilmes from Tristán Baldez. The six-year contract specified equal sharing of harvest profits, making the renters medianeros. The agreement obligated Baldez to help keep cleared ditches that protected plant life for the first eight months and to provide a cart, plow, oxen, and vegetable and alfalfa seed for the first year's planting. The Bitancurs agreed to plant peach trees, to maintain the rented house in good repair, and to grow alfalfa.[38]

Tenancy, rather than ownership, persisted among farmers in Buenos Aires province throughout the century. According to a 1854 census, 57 percent of the nearly five thousand Argentine farmers in the province rented their holdings. About half of the 824 foreigners also rented. The massive wave of immigrants later in the century reversed the proportions of native and foreign farmers. The proportion of renters also rose as inflating land values pushed purchase prices beyond the reach of most. A typical tenancy cycle evolved to meet the needs of ranchers. During the first year a renter plowed the virgin plain and planted flax as a cash crop for the duration of the contract, except in the northern counties, where corn predominated. During the final year of tenancy, a farmer planted alfalfa on which the rancher grazed livestock after the renter had departed.[39]

Renters faced myriad problems. The short-term nature of contracts precluded building comfortable dwellings or making other improvements. Tenants lived in tiny, miserable, earthen hovels, planted no trees, built no fences, and added few amenities because they had to move to new lands every few years. In 1914 Herbert Gibson described the tenant's house as an "enlarged sardine can," with zinc roof, dirt floor, and mud walls. Contracts often obliged the sharecropper to bag and transport the landowner's share of the crop as well as his own, which increased his workload and expenses. Some owners required renters to buy and sell produce and supplies through them, thereby denying access to better prices on the open market. An exchange in 1915 between B. Edwards, manager of William Walker's estancia in Bolívar county, and a local merchant illuminates the farmer's plight. Edwards submitted a list of supplies to be filled by Sánchez Calac and Company in Daireaux and appended the following note: "You must take special care with the prices and remember that you are not dealing with a colonist." (Argentines generalized the term colono to include all farmers.) Edwards cautioned that he would not pay the exorbitant prices charged to agriculturists and threatened to take his considerable business to Buenos Aires if not satisfied.[40]

Godofredo Daireaux accurately summed up the landowners' attitude toward the farmer in 1908: The large rancher, he observed, "at heart cordially detests the settler, the husbandman, the people that come in swarms. He uses them for the time being because he cannot help himself, in order to fit his lands for carrying plenty of stock . . . As soon as possible, he sends them off to plough elsewhere, longing to realize his dream of seeing only on his land a maximum of cattle with a minimum of keepers." The estanciero's "deepest wish has ever been to reduce the staff to its simplest expression."[41] In short, ranchers used tenants only to avoid having to farm themselves.

However tenuous and primitive the life of the farmer, the migrant farm worker hired seasonally to sow and harvest crops lived an even more precarious existence. Farmers sometimes paid these workers in the tokens redeemable at the local pulpería, where inflated prices absorbed the bulk of the wage for bare necessities. In late 1891 farm workers at Olavarría complained of working 16-hour days for 1.5–2 pesos plus puchero and mate for breakfast and dinner.[42]

Seasonal wages varied with the supply of workers and the prices of agricultural goods. Daily harvest wages for farm workers ranged from 2.5 to 3 pesos between 1898 and 1904 and climbed to 4 pesos from 1905 to 1910. Monthly wages for sowing seed rose from 30 to 33 pesos between 1898 and 1904, then to 40 pesos from 1905 to 1910. Farmers felt squeezed between rising land rentals and what they considered to be high seasonal wages demanded by harvesting peons. High wages compared to those in Europe attracted masses of golondrinas, numbering perhaps more than two hundred thousand in 1908, but they returned to their native countries after the harvest. A scant 27 percent of the men who worked in agriculture enjoyed year-round employment in 1908. Like the migrant ranch worker, agricultural laborers faced long periods of unemployment, variable wages, and little prospect for long-term improvement in their economic condition.[43]

Farmers faced other problems in addition to wage and rental demands, including the continued presence of loose livestock that invaded, trampled, and devoured crops. In spite of a November 1870 law ordering ranchers to keep cattle enclosed and away from fields, fencing did not become common until more than a decade later. Luis Bousom, a French immigrant, complained to the Ayacucho municipal council in mid-1874 of the "great damage" that livestock caused to surrounding farmlands.[44] Immigrant farmers in Tandil faced similar difficulties. Following Fugl's lead, other Danes moved to the area, totaling about five hundred by 1885. The Scandinavians grew wheat and corn, built their own schools and church, and even provided night classes for men. Native Argentines admired their quiet industriousness but found them rather "cold and ceremonious." In 1885 Juan R. Petersen of the Danish community corralled horses owned by Juan Curuchet after the animals had trampled his crops. The Dane demanded 20 pesos per horse as indemnity, and Curuchet offered 10. In July 1893 Candido Zulillaga solicited permission from the Tandil municipal intendant, Juan Capdepont, to round up animals that had invaded his rented lands. The intendent granted him the required permit the same day it was requested. Two months later Luis Bilbao submitted a similar request, as conflict between ranchers and farmers continued.[45]

Opposition to farming remained strong among many of the ranching elite. Herbert Gibson, an influential rural expert and member of a prominent sheep-raising family, decried agriculture for destroying the pampa's rich, natural pastures—the same objection raised by Rosas when he attempted to sow alfalfa without plowing. Writing in the *Anales* of the Rural Society in 1890, Gibson warned that 1.2 million hectares (3 million acres) of cereal grains had already displaced four million sheep. The pampa had become "stained with colonies, agricultural centers, and stretches of public farmlands." Although he grudgingly acknowledged the need for farming, Gibson insisted that lands less suitable for livestock be utilized rather than the rich grasslands of the humid pampa. He believed, as did most large landowners, that livestock raising was and should remain the economic mainstay of the province. In his play of 1904, *La gringa*, Florencio Sánchez echoed Gibson's anti-farming sentiments and vividly portrayed the cultural conflict between gaucho and gringo in Santa Fe province: having lost his land to an Italian immigrant because of overdue loans, the gaucho Don Cantalicio laments: "And one day, a bit of land, the next day, another, has been seized by these foreigners to plow up. It's a shame, to break up fields where the grass grew like that."[46]

A Ch. Leonardi stressed the social benefits of agriculture in a rebuttal to Gibson's anti-farming essay. He attributed the "deplorable economic and social state of the majority of the rural population" to the lack of employment opportunities, which forced many of the rural poor to turn to crime to survive. Agriculture was needed to "uplift the character of our paisano, to give him work habits, to educate him." Agronomist Carlos D. Girola voiced support for farming on economic grounds. Because of great labor and transportation requirements, he argued that farming should receive preferential treatment over livestock production. Farmers needed access to fertile lands near rail lines, whereas ranchers could utilize outlying pasturelands. A few peons could herd livestock to market, but heavy, bulky farm produce required more workers and rail transport. Mindful of the dangers of a monocultural rural economy, Girola urged mixed livestock and agriculture as the most productive and secure means of developing the pampa.[47]

Catastrophic losses caused by natural disasters and economic reversals resulting from world market vagaries persuaded many ranchers to diversify into agriculture during the latter decades of the nineteenth century. *La prensa* of Belgrano urged estancieros to branch into nonlivestock activities. The paper noted that a sheep valued at 40 pesos in 1870 brought only 8 pesos in 1882, a fivefold drop in price. Furthermore, an estimated four million sheep perished in a hard freeze of May 1882, ruining many ranchers across the province. *La campaña* of Buenos Aires urged ranchers to improve pastures by placing land under cultivation by tenants. The paper cited Texas and Australia as examples of successful mixed rural economies. Many Argentine estancieros had come to understand and exploit the profitable symbiotic relationship between animal and crop production.[48]

The shifting attitude of terratenientes toward farming was also evidenced in publications by rural expert Miguel A. Lima. His 1876 guide to livestock raising, *El estanciero práctico* (The practical rancher), reflected the prevalent ambivalence toward fencing and farming. His second work, issued nine years latter, *El hacendado del porvenir* (The rancher of the future), stressed the centrality of agriculture to the rural economy. "The rancher," he wrote, "should be an agriculturist"; fencing, a topic of heated debate a decade earlier, was accepted on the modern ranch of the 1880s.[49] Few ranchers heeded Lima's advice literally and became farmers themselves, but most rented out lands to tenants.

Agriculture experienced unprecedented growth in the province around the turn of the century. In 1897, livestock accounted for nearly three-fourths of Argentina's total export earnings. Three years later agricultural earnings for the first time exceeded livestock export revenues by 50 to 46 percent. Farm products continued their dramatic rise through the next decade, at times accounting for as much as 61 percent of the nation's export income.[50]

The blossoming of agriculture little affected the overweening influence of terratenientes and did not alter the traditional pattern of land tenure. Figures for 1897 show renters farming three-fourths of the province's twelve thousand agricultural holdings, including 79 percent of all farmlands. Owners comprised only 28 percent of all farmers between 1906 and 1911, with renters 60 percent and sharecroppers 12 percent. By 1914 owners still accounted for only 31 percent of the province's nearly 48,000 farmers. Italians and Spaniards predominated, with Frenchmen a distant third. Fifty-five percent of all rental contracts ran for periods of less than three years. Thirty-eight percent of these short-term contracts included sharecropping provisions. Only 5 percent of all renters enjoyed contracts of more than five years' duration. Land rents ranged from 5 to 20 pesos per hectare (2.47 acres), varying with location, fertility, and demand.[51] Impermanency, uncertainty, marginal living: this was the lot of the tenant farmer and farm worker.

Despite his rosy evaluation of the provincial economy to mid-century, Jonathan Brown concurs with the constriction of opportunity for the gaucho and his way of life on the new pampa gringa of export capitalism: "Yet rising prices and wholesale speculation quickly put land out of reach of most rural residents. Wheat farming was accomplished on large ranches rather than exclusively on small farms.

The resulting incidence of tenant farming seems to have dampened opportunity in some parts of the pampa, and the arrival of foreign laborers marginalized many native-born workers in the countryside."[52] The elite leadership, culminating with the Generation of 'Eighty, led by Julio A. Roca, elected to supplant the native with the foreign—in culture, livestock, and people—on the new pampa of sheep, wire, and wheat.

10
Immigration
and
Xenophobia

Along with sheep ranching, fencing, and agriculture came the immigrant farmer, touching off the greatest social change on the pampa. Massive immigration, the social concomitant of rural economic diversification, wrought an abrupt and sweeping cultural and demographic transformation of rural society. Largely employed in farming, mechanical, and commercial pursuits shunned by natives, foreigners did not represent a direct economic threat to the gaucho. But they did herald and sometimes accompany changes that provoked negative and occasionally violent reactions among natives.

Migration, first from interior provinces and later from Europe, steadily increased the population of Buenos Aires province throughout the century. Argentine migrants, often ranch workers, altered pampean society little, but the millions of foreigners who fenced and farmed the pampa greatly changed rural life on the littoral. Despite the legal repression of the gaucho during the Rosas era, Buenos Aires province offered better economic opportunities than the even more repressive and economically stagnant interior. Progress on the littoral came at the expense of the interior, and peons migrated from the interior in search of employment. Internal migration swelled the provincial population in the countryside from 32,000 in 1797 to nearly double in 1822, to 81,000 in 1836, 184,000 in 1855, and 317,000 in 1869. A census of 1836 provides a portrait of ranching society during the Rosista dictatorship. Of 410 estancias in the partidos of Monte, San Antonio de Areco, Luján and Chascomús, 37 percent had fewer than 6 residents, 45 percent had 6–10, 12 percent had 11–15, and only 5 percent had 16 or more residents. Slave peons and servants worked on many ranches. In Monte there were 92 slaves laboring on 25 estancias, in Chascomús

202 on 63, and in San Antonio de Areco 76 on 15. Blacks constituted 13 percent of the total urban population of Monte, San Nicolás, and Luján and 8 percent of the rural total. Foreigners, still a rarity on the pampa, made up only 1 percent of the total population (107 of 10,605 persons) included in the census.[1]

A census of active (age fifteen to forty-nine) and inactive (age fifty and over) militiamen in Luján in 1851 adds further information about the male population at mid-century. Of 588 men enrolled for military service, ranchers (owners and renters) comprised 23 percent and ranch workers 56. Eighty-six percent of the estancieros and 73 percent of the workers were natives of the province. The remaining 27 percent of ranch laborers had migrated from interior provinces. Marriage patterns differed drastically for the two groups, with 78 percent of estancieros but only 17 percent of workers married.[2]

An 1854 census registered clearly the continuing native predominance in rural areas. Only 15,523 foreigners resided in the countryside, 11 percent of the total of nearly 140,000. Immigrants comprised only 7 percent of the province's 20,313 rural peons. On the other hand, 45 percent of the 1,464 provincial merchants were foreigners. Three-fourths of immigrants were men, with Spaniards predominating (26 percent), followed by English (19 percent), French (17 percent), and Italians (11 percent). Northern counties such as Exaltación de la Cruz showed the highest population densities (81.5 persons per square league, or 7.8 persons per square mile), followed by the central region, with 51.2 persons per square league (4.9 per square mile). The southern frontier, still plagued by Indian attacks, averaged only 21.5 persons per square league (2 per square mile).[3]

An 1862 census of Tandil's nearly 3,000 inhabitants showed the impact of a continuing current of internal migration from the interior to the littoral. Provincianos comprised 28 percent of the rural male population and 31 percent in the town of Tandil. Provincial women comprised 17 percent of the rural population and 26 percent of the urban. Livestock raising employed most people in the county, which remained 82 percent rural in 1862. Few foreigners braved the southern frontier, so Argentines comprised all but 6 percent of rural males and all but 1 percent of females in the countryside. Immigrants accounted for 23 percent of urban males, however, and Spaniards and French were the most numerous.[4]

The booming cattle industry of the littoral attracted peons from the early eighteenth century on. Workers mostly from Santiago del Estero

Table 6:
Internal Migration to
Buenos Aires Province, 1869–1914

Region	Percentage of Migrants		
	1869	**1895**	**1914**
Northwest	77	51	26
Pampa/littoral	9	23	53
Cuyo	9	14	10
Other	5	12	11
Total migrants counted in census	24,280	23,981	57,616

Source: Data from Zulma Recchini de Lattes and Alfredo E. Lattes, *Migraciones en la Argentina*, pp. 290–91, table A6.

Note: Northwest provinces include Santiago, Córdoba, and Tucumán; Pampa/littoral include Santa Fe, Entre Ríos, Corrientes, and La Pampa; Cuyo include Mendoza and San Luis.

rode southeast in search of employment. Of 24,280 internal migrants recorded in 1869 in Buenos Aires province, 77 percent came from the northwest provinces of Santiago del Estero, Córdoba, and Tucumán, and only 9 percent from the adjacent pampa. By 1895, the three provinces of the northwest contributed only 51 percent and the pampean provinces (Santa Fe, La Pampa, Entre Ríos, Corrientes) 23 percent. In 1914 only 26 percent of Buenos Aires province's 57,616 internal migrants came from the northwest; 53 percent came from pampean areas. The proportion from the western region of Cuyo remained roughly constant throughout the period. Table 6 summarizes internal migration patterns from 1869 to 1914. Internal migration indicates the bleak opportunities open to peons in the interior provinces.[5]

Migration from the interior paled in comparison with that from Europe during the last third of the century. A massive wave deposited 5.5 million Europeans in Argentina between 1857 and 1924. Foreigners, totaling about 15,500, accounted for only 11 percent of the population of Buenos Aires province in 1854. The proportion of foreigners rose steadily thereafter to 20 percent in 1869, 31 in 1895, and 34 in 1914. Few immigrants ventured beyond the humid pampa to the economically stagnant interior, preferring to remain in the port, in one of the pampean towns, or on a rented farm or ranch. Nearly one-third of all immigrants settled in the province and another three-tenths in the federal capital. The bulk of the newcomers were adult males, which sharply altered the sex ratio throughout the littoral. Italians, leading the invasion, ranged up to 71 percent of the total during the 1860s and did not fall below half until the twentieth century. Italy contributed nearly 51 percent of all immigrants from 1869 and 1895, compared with 20 percent from Spain. Between 1895 and 1914, however, Spaniards accounted for 41 percent and Italians 36 percent. By 1914 the once strongly native composition of the provincial population had been altered in all but the remotest counties. The rural population of 923,066 included nearly 120,000 Italians and 118,707 Spaniards (13 percent each); foreigners made up 30 percent of the total rural population and 39 percent of all rural males. Most of the immigrants flocked to the port or to another town. Natives, facing shrinking employment opportunities in livestock raising, also migrated to urban areas. The urban percentage of the provincial population rose from 28 in 1869 to 30 in 1881, 39 in 1895, and 55 in 1914. The pampa of cattle, gauchos, and estancias had become a plain of towns and immigrants. With World War I, the floodtide of immigrants was reduced to a trickle. The number of foreigners settling in the province fell from 46,000 in 1912 to 11,000 in 1914 and bottomed out at a scant 1,100 in 1918; but the cultural and demographic character of the pampa had been altered irrevocably.[6]

Most Argentine leaders favored immigration to populate their immense, labor-scarce nation. Rivadavia actively promoted immigration and agriculture during the 1820s. Juan Bautista Alberdi, spokesman for the anti-Rosas intellectuals called the Generation of 'Thirty-Seven, voiced attitudes common among the nation's liberal intellectuals. He considered Americans "nothing else than Europeans born in America" and urged the replacement of Indian elements by Anglo-Saxons and the transformation of the Indian through education into "an English laborer who works, consumes, and lives with dignity and comfort." He wrote, "The Indian has no place in our political and civil society." Alberdi, and later Sarmiento, recommended English classes at the university level. "How can one receive the example and civilizing action of the Anglo-Saxon race without understanding their language?" English, "the language of liberty, industry, and order" had become, in Alberdi's eyes, the lingua franca of the Argentine intelligensia.[7] Anglophilia and a concomitant disdain for native stock persisted among national and provincial leaders throughout the century.

Rosas' defeat of the pro-European unitarios forced a shift in official policies. Rosas did not inhibit spontaneous immigration, nor did he stimulate "artificial" immigration through special projects and incentives for foreigners. The fragile, frequently broken *pax Rosista* did not provide a propitious climate for attracting immigrants. Furthermore, laws of April 1829 and May 1831 subjected foreigners to service in the city militia and in the army.[8]

Rosas did promote selective immigration on a small scale by contracting young Spanish boys to work as peons on his estancias and in some government agencies. Teenagers and a few adult males worked at reduced wages under the guidance of Rosista foremen. Their wages rose gradually with experience and age, and they paid back their passage costs according to their own schedules. Once the passage had been repaid, the immigrants could and often did seek employment elsewhere. By 1849, ninety-five *gallegitos* (little Spaniards) worked at the general prison at Santos Lugares, nine with the police, thirteen at the port authority, six at the artillery park, and many others at various ranches. Managers at the estancias gave them mixed marks as workers. Ramírez at "Chacabuco" praised them in 1846 for their "great dexterity on horseback and intelligence for rural work." On the other hand, Schöo at "San Martín" found little to commend the youngsters. In a letter of July 25, 1844, he complained to Rosas of the "scant intelligence of my little Gallegos." At the end of the year he charged that the boys spurred and ran the horses unnecessarily and otherwise mistreated them. Schöo also found fault with the Spanish men who often broke tools and did not merit the wages they were paid. "I have never seen men as churlish as those" he grumbled in a letter of December 12, 1844, and suggested replacing them with boys who would work at reduced salaries. In 1846 and 1847 Schöo found it necessary to place several gallegitos in the stocks for thievery. Overall, he judged Spaniards to be far less desirable workers than other Europeans.[9]

Because of Rosas' policies and the instability of the nation, few foreigners chose to settle. MacCann remarked the dearth of immigrants in the countryside in the late 1840s. Having observed the gaucho's distaste for such foot work as cleaning and maintaining wells and ponds, he noted that "such work is therefore for the most part neglected, because there are not enough foreigners to do it." On the southern frontier in Tandil and Azul, Irish ditchdiggers commanded high wages because "few of their class come so far south, and the natives will never take a spade in their hands."[10]

Having overthrown Rosas, liberal Argentine leaders resurrected the Alberdian dictum "to govern is to populate" and incorporated immigration promotion into the national constitution of 1853, in which Alberdi's proposals to grant immigrants full citizens' rights and to encourage settlement from Europe (but not from neighboring Latin American nations) found realization. Porteño politicians viewed the immigrant as a means of countering deepseated federalist sentiment and caudillo power in the interior. Urban leaders hoped to build a new political constituency, as well as to gain much-needed manpower to speed the nation's economic growth.[11]

Immigration came to be viewed as a panacea for assuring and accelerating progress. Writing to Victorino Lastarría in early 1853, Sarmiento claimed that "we can in three years introduce 300,000 new settlers and drown in the waves of industry the creole rabble, inept, uncivil, and coarse, which stops our attempt to civilize the nation." *El nacional*, Sarmiento's newspaper, glowingly forecast that "immigration will bring everything—peace, abundance, civilization, the power of morality, order and liberty." Promoters like the Frenchman Augusto M. Brougnes extolled immigration's manifest blessings. According to his 1855 tract, landless, impoverished workers from Europe could find success and happiness in the Río de la Plata, with its healthful climate and abundant fertile land. The pampa's more than a million square miles held only twenty thousand farm families, leaving ample room for thousands more. Brougnes viewed immigration as the critical ingredient in a perfect blend of "industry plus land" that would hasten the advent of Argentina's golden age. Interest and optimism focused on the foreigner, but many boosters anticipated an additional benefit in that exposure to and commingling with Europeans would uplift and refine the creole masses culturally and racially. The *Revista del Plata* reported in 1861 that, "thanks to contact with [other] nationalities, the gaucho now does not wear the bota de potro, and like the foreigner, enjoys eating bread."[12] The dream of Alberdi and Sarmiento to destroy the caudillo-ridden, barbarian pampa and supplant it with a modern Europeanized civilization seemed a valid and attainable goal. Landowners envisioned yet another blessing from the foreign influx:

increased demand for their lands and hence rising land values. On May 12, 1872, *La voz del Saladillo* urged government promotion of immigration. Sparsely settled regions near the frontier, like Saladillo, could expand economically only with a growing population of immigrants.

But the more remote counties like Saladillo and the interior provinces gained few immigrants because of the preference for the agricultural and mixed areas near Buenos Aires. British sheep ranchers and shepherds settled in many of the northern counties within 150 kilometers (93 miles) of the capital. The Spanish writer Federico Rahola y Tremols sardonically characterized the English of Argentina as being like the English everywhere—"taking their bath, drinking their tea, downing their whiskey, reading *The Times*, feeling repugnance for the inferior races." But he conceded that they were the world's best animal breeders, a singular virtue on the pampa. In San Antonio de Areco, Irish predominated among foreign settlers until the late 1880s, when Italians outstripped them. In 1881 the British community comprised 36 percent of the county's foreign-born population and 9 percent of all residents. Neighboring Mercedes attracted Irish and Basque families. The Irish settled on small sheep ranches, which they usually rented. Michael and Edward Mulhall somewhat generously estimated the Irish population of the province in 1875 at thirty thousand, mostly in counties to the north and west of Buenos Aires. Scottish shepherds more frequently labored in counties south of the capital, such as San Vincente and Chascomús. One of the Scots, Robert Bruce, introduced milk pasteurizing equipment and first produced butter for sale commercially in Argentina.[13]

Other immigrant groups held a variety of jobs on the pampa. Italians and Spaniards often worked as pulperos, housekeepers, and hucksters, usually in urban areas, or as tenant farmers. Basques labored at diverse occupations ranging from innkeeper, artisan, and brickmason to shepherd and drover. The manager of William Walker's "25 de Mayo" estancia, J. B. MacDonald, wrote to his employer in 1900 praising his Basque employee José Ayastuy as "an excellent workman, strong and active, can do almost everything required about the place except horseback work, is a good cartman, ploughman, cut and stack alfalfa and general handyman."[14]

Immigrants and gauchos seldom competed directly for employment because the former did foot work and the latter mounted labor. Sheep ranching was one of the few areas of the rural economy in which gauchos and gringos competed. Both tended flocks and sheared the animals, but foreigners more often worked in counties near the port, whereas natives labored in regions to the south and west. To the gaucho, the horse represented an entire way of life. To the immigrant, it offered only another tool of work—and one inferior to the ox. The immigrant aspired to own land and reap its profits rather than to live an equestrian life. The division of labor by nationality appeared clearly in the 1895 census of a saladero in Azul. Seventeen Argentines monopolized the work of handling and killing cattle in the stockyard, chores akin to those on the traditional ranch. Thirty-six Italians and three Argentines worked in the grease-extracting and soap-making sections of the plant. Industrial and mechanical tasks generally fell to foreigners.[15]

Immigrants willingly accepted foot work scorned by gauchos like digging ditches, tending orchards, stretching fences, fashioning bricks, and sowing and harvesting crops. In a 1904 treatise, Godofredo Daireaux counseled ranchers to hire foreigners as foot peons whenever possible. Although they lacked equestrian skills, immigrants possessed expertise in carpentry, metal work, and other mechanical tasks vital to the modern estancia. The foreigner willingly accepted a sedentary life amid mechanical inventions, and he was thus better adapted than the creole to the twentieth-century pampa.[16]

Although the foreigner posed no direct economic threat to the native, he did personify the rapid, bewildering changes that altered forever the nature of pampean life. He dug ditches and erected fences that closed off free transit on the open range. He constructed and operated railroads that ended cattle and sheep drives to the porteño markets at Liniers and facilitated the spread of urban life and culture across the plains. The gringo ran his iron plow over the pampa, slicing away rich pasturelands and replanting cereals. He walked rather than rode horseback. The gaucho found ample reason to detest, disdain, and fear the gringo, and numerous incidents attest to this xenophobia.

Crossing the pampa in 1818, General William Miller sensed the native's contempt for the foreigner. "The gauchos regard with a sort of pitying disdain the timid or unskilled horseman." When Miller declined a proferred cigar, one gaucho remarked to another that the general "knows absolutely nothing; why, he cannot even smoke." Gerstaecker noted in 1849, as had many others, that the gaucho thoroughly detested foreigners. Although Rosas protected British interests in the province, he also suspected foreigners of pro-Unitarian sympathies and may have encouraged xenophobia in the countryside. His cousin, Tomás Anchorena, hated foreigners, whom he considered liberal, heretical thieves. An incident during Rosas' last month of rule, in January 1852, reflected the gaucho's scorn of the gringo. Seven men dressed in military uniforms robbed two foreigners, Pedro Oga and Fernando Nie, near San José de las Flores. The thieves, probably army deserters, took everything, leaving the two hapless immigrants stripped of both shirt and pants.[17] Although civilian clothing was doubtless useful to the thieves, the incident also indicates the ridicule and derision of the gaucho for the foreigner and his odd manners, speech, and actions.

A flare-up in Azul four years later revealed starkly the depth of native-foreign tensions. Colonel Silvio Olivieri, an Italian army officer, had organized a quasi-military agricultural colony named New Rome, which included both Italians and Argentines. In August 1856 Olivieri imprisoned sixteen creoles in a cave used as a jail at the colony. Following a month of fruitless negotiations and appeals, twenty other natives rebelled, killed the colonel, and released their imprisoned countrymen.[18]

The most horrifying and flagrant xenophobic assault on the pampa occurred on New Year's Day 1872 in Tandil. Although it was primarily a sheep- and cattle-raising area, Tandil had attracted immigrant wheat farmers numbering several hundred Danes, as well as Italians, Basques, and others. In early 1871, Geronimo G. de Solané, a curandero, arrived in the county. Solané (also called Tata Dios or Médico Dios), aged forty-five or fifty, set up a clinic and gained considerable fame and a popular following among the country people. He was an imposing figure, with a dark complexion, "penetrating gaze, thick, long white beard, well-kept, reaching nearly to the waist," and "long straight hair."[19] He possessed the "intelligence and penetrating liveliness of the sagacious gaucho."[20] The healer walked about majestically clad in an attractive, handwoven poncho of pampa cloth. Admirers and patients kissed his hand in reverence. The origins of Tata Dios remain a mystery. Some thought he was Bolivian, others Chilean, and one porteño newspaper identified him as a "secret agent of the Jesuits" sent to fight the spread of Masonry in Argentina. Solané was barely literate so left no personal documents indicating his history.[21]

Tata Dios practiced a skillful blend of miraculous cures, herbal remedies, and conventional Catholicism, preaching allegiance to Jesus

Christ and the popular Virgin of Luján. Many such practitioners traveled about the countryside effecting cures through a syncretic mixture of folk medicine, mysticism, and Catholicism. Solané, though perhaps more popular and successful than most curanderos, appeared to be nothing out of the ordinary to most Tandil residents.[22]

On New Year's Eve 1871, Jacinto Pérez, Solané's helper (called San Jacinto el Adivino), and Cruz Gutiérrez, second-in-command to Pérez, gathered together some forty or fifty gaucho adherents of Tata Dios. Pérez instructed the men to meet at the foot of *la piedra movediza*, a famous balancing rock in the granite hills above the town of Tandil. According to El Adivino, God would appear before the band to initiate the destruction by earthquake of the old society, giving rise to a new people. Antonio Ponce, an old shoemaker from Rauch, handed out red ribbons, symbols of the "cutthroats of the years 40 and 42 in Buenos Aires"—the violent Rosistas of the Mazorca, or Sociedad Popular Restauradora. The leaders also distributed arms and harangued the gauchos on the importance of their sacred mission: to kill foreigners and Masons.[23]

At dawn on New Year's Day 1872, the armed band invaded Independence Plaza in Tandil, shouting "Long live the republic! Long live religion! Death to gringos and Masons!" They freed the only prisoner in the city jail, an Indian named Nicolás Oliveira, who joined the group. Gathering more arms, they began a murderous rampage. Near the plaza they struck down their first victim, a forty-five-year-old Italian organ player who died of a fractured skull. Turning north, they fell upon a group of sleeping Basque carters at General Rodríguez Plaza in Arroyo Tandil and slit the throats of several. A Basque merchant met the same fate. The killers spared his Argentine wife but dispatched a young Italian peon. Several English settlers died at a store owned by a Mr. Thompson. The band slit the throats of the clerk and his wife, both in their mid-twenties. Another employee died of a knife wound in the chest and a bullet in the arm. Pressing northwest, the gaucho mob claimed additional victims at the pulpería: another Basque—the pulpero, Juan Chapar—his wife, two daughters aged four and five, and a five-month-old son all died with their throats slit. A sixteen-year-old employee, who appears to have been the only woman raped in the rampage, died in the same manner. Two others also died, a peon and the owner of a carting operation. The raiders destroyed the account books of the pulpería, filled with those mysterious little marks that held the gaucho in debt to the foreign merchant. A native, Honorio de la

Canal, rode up to the store during the attack. The killers spared his life when a black member of the band assured them that he was Argentine, not foreign.[24]

Leaving behind a path of carnage—17 dead, 14 with slit throats—the band turned toward the estancia of Ramón Santamarina, a wealthy Spanish Basque immigrant marked for death. Santamarina had arrived in Argentina at the age of sixteen and, through hard work as a carter and marriage into the land-rich Gómez family, had risen to status and wealth. To the hapless gaucho he probably epitomized the exploitative foreigner who profiteered from the labor of natives. Had he been present at the ranch he would have become the best-known victim of the tragedy. But the avengers, finding no one at the estancia, camped and rested.[25]

Tandil townspeople, awakening to the New Year, were stupified at the massacre. A thirty-man posse led by military commander José Ciriaco Gómez tracked the bloody trail of the gaucho band to the Santamarina ranch. On the morning of January 2 the posse engaged the band in battle, killed ten, and took eight prisoners. Most of the murderers escaped, but the posse killed the leader, Pérez, and captured his second-in-command, Cruz Gutiérrez, who, after trial, was executed by firing squad at the Tandil central plaza. Back in town, armed vigilantes patroled the streets as the stunned residents puzzled over the gauchos' motives and fearfully watched for further violence.[26]

Tata Dios remained at the ranch of Ramón Gómez, the site of his clinic and camp, during the massacre. Confronted by officials, he wept and disavowed any knowledge of or involvement in the grisly events. Solané refused further comment until an impartial justice of the peace had arrived from another county, before whom he agreed to testify. But he never had the opportunity: at midnight on the fifth of January, unknown assassins shot him to death through a small window in the jail cell. Whether he actually planned the massacre or whether his lieutenants acted without his knowledge remains unclear, though the latter seems more plausible, given the fact that he did not flee from the authorities. Equally mysterious is the identity of his murderers. Accomplices in the violent rampage may have shot the curandero to prevent him from testifying and implicating them, or the assassination may have been an act of vigilante justice. Fearing the influence of Tata Dios among powerful local officials, townspeople, probably foreigners, may have killed him to insure his punishment.[27]

Nearly all of the marauding band were unlettered provincianos.

Rural officials circulated descriptions of some of the escapees: Félix Juárez, black, bearded, age forty-five to fifty, from Tucumán; Mario Pérez, tall, swarthy, Indian features, age fifty, from Córdoba; José María Trejo, short and stout, Indian features, age forty, from Santiago del Estero; Geronimo Navarro, short, stout, flat-nosed, "smallpox eyes," from Buenos Aires province; and Leandro Quebedo, black, age thirty, from Buenos Aires province.[28]

A bizarre melange of xenophobia, religious zealotry, superstitious fanaticism, and greed motivated these humble gauchos to embark upon their mission as exterminating angels. Deeper structural causes, including latifundism and legal oppression of the gaucho, also played a role. An anonymous pamphlet published in 1871, entitled *Abusos y ruina de la campaña*, reflected the enmity toward foreigners and rural officials evident in the Tandil affair. The pamphleteer harshly criticized the many immigrants who sought an easy, prosperous life in Argentina without working. He castigated shiftless foreigners in Azul who assumed public office and thus gained fortunes at the expense of natives; Azul justice of the peace Galicia, for example, was said to have encouraged barter between immigrants and Indians while the latter stole from natives to gather trade goods.[29] Gauchos viewed their own social and economic difficulties through the same nativist lens as did the pamphleteer: gringos brought only trouble.

In an editorial published shortly after the massacre, *La nación* of Buenos Aires cited the "deplorable conditions" of the gaucho in the countryside as the central motivation for the crime. The government demanded six months of military service but held the gaucho for six years. The gaucho, having lost job, ranch, and family, reacted with violence and hatred against his oppressed social condition.[30] Martín Aguirre, an Uruguayan lawyer who defended the accused assassins in their February trial in Tandil, also blamed oppressive rural conditions for the gauchos' murderous behavior. He cited a lengthy litany of ills, including abuse by military commanders and rural justices, and lack of education, home, and access to honorable work; the gaucho was "disinherited by the nation," worse off than serfs of the Middle Ages. Aguirre divided rural society into two classes, the privileged landowners and the oppressed landless. He blamed the events at Tandil squarely on the government, whose policies condemned "an entire social class to perpetual indigence, to brutalization, to crime." Oppressed and uneducated, the rural proletariat offered "fertile ground" for the "perverse counsels" of the wily. "Simple, ignorant men," acting out of drunkenness and rage, easily fell prey to the fanaticism preached by Pérez. The Uruguayan's eloquent plea for reduced sentences fell upon deaf ears, but his defense poignantly evinced the social roots of the nativist reaction.[31]

Pérez had skillfully played upon many of the gaucho's fears, prejudices, and desires in his harangue on that fateful New Year's Eve. By offering salvation and a fortune in a new paradise, he appealed to both spiritual and material values. The naïve gauchos thought the destruction of foreigners would pave the way to a new era. No personal animosity existed between any of the victims and the assassins; the foreigners were killed simply because they were foreigners. The vicious extermination of the entire Chapar family at the pulpería most clearly manifests the gauchos' sentiments: the Basque pulpero represented the new pampa and the loss of a traditional, beloved way of life. The band destroyed the store's account books, wherein "little marks" inexorably strangled the gaucho's freedom and enslaved him economically. The attack upon the pulpería can be viewed as a literal attack on a new, capitalist pampa gringa of private property and of shrinking opportunity for the gaucho.[32]

Fugl, visiting in Denmark during the raid, carefully sifted through the complex events upon his return to Tandil. He detected evidence of more than a xenophobic rage by ignorant gauchos. According to him, justice Juan A. Figueroa hated foreigners because their agricultural life impinged upon the free movement of his herds. Fugl believed that Figueroa and military commander Gómez headed a conspiracy of landowners seeking to halt further encroachment by immigrant farmers. The conspiracy theory is tenuous at best, but it adds further weight to the intensity of creole nativism, not only among lowly gauchos, but also among the landed elite.[33]

The dreadful events of Tandil shook the province and the nation, and repercussions extended to Europe. Many feared uprisings elsewhere. Manuel R. Baudrix, a Tandil resident, wrote to a friend in Lobería on January 19, 1872, deploring the "fanaticism and ignorance that possessed those people" responsible for the massacre. He repeated a false rumor that more than twenty persons had met death near Las Calaveras with the "same cruelty and perverse intention" as the Tandil victims.[34] Fear and paranoia gripped the pampa. On January 13, Justice Pedro Roca of Chascomús reported "agents of Médico Dios" hiding in his county, and he instructed rural police to question anyone "unknown and suspicious" and to detain such persons unless identity could be ascertained.[35] Officials throughout the province arrested men with names or descriptions matching those of the escaped Tandil raiders. In January, police arrested Florentino Quevedo in Magdalena and another man with the same name in Junín but soon freed both. In April Patricio Maccrady arrested Marcelo Almirón in Chascomús on suspicion of being a Tandil fugitive, but he too was released.[36]

Curanderos met with strict scrutiny as officials moved to stifle other suspected conspiracies and the proliferation of fanatical cults. Police Commissioner Francisco Wright of Luján, for example, initiated a thorough investigation of Paulino Ajeda, a seventy-year-old healer residing in Giles. According to preliminary findings, Ajeda posed no threat. He had practiced in the area for three years, prescribing herbs and ministering to the people. Wright persisted with his investigation into the curandero's activities but found no evidence of wrongdoing.[37]

Representatives of the foreign community stood aghast at the "ruthless and wholesale massacre of foreigners" in Tandil. The *South American Journal and Brazil and River Plate Mail* of London called the episode as barbaric as the execution of Maximilian in Mexico in 1867. The paper pointed to inadequate rural communications as the major hindrance in bringing the escaped criminals to justice. British consul Frank Parish complained repeatedly about the government's lack of zeal in pursuing the murderers, who had slain British subjects among others. The atrocities dampened the enthusiasm of some Europeans to migrate to Argentina. Five years after the bloody events, "Justice" asked the editor of the Buenos Aires *Herald* why all ten men sentenced to death for the murders had not been executed. The *Herald* interpreted the government's actions as indicative of Argentine laxity in criminal punishment.[38]

The Tandil massacre stands at the extremity of Argentine rural nativism. Always disdainful of the gringo, the gaucho came to resent and fear him as a harbinger of doom for the traditional pampean way of life. Many passages in *Martín Fierro*, published the same year as the Tandil massacre, illustrate the gaucho's xenophobia. Hernández enunciated the unspoken protest of the inarticulate gaucho masses, whose actions took violent, not literary forms. In 1884, Francisco Fernández wrote a play entitled *Solané* that was based on the Tandil events. The work was seldom performed, but it faithfully captured the violent nativism of the gaucho attack. Sporadic if less spectacular incidents of native-foreign conflict ignited elsewhere on the pampa. In 1884 residents of the northern county of Lincoln (now Leandro Alem) fought with foreign railroad workers. Justice of the Peace Andrés Sein, fearing an attack upon the town by armed railroad construction workers, requested twenty extra provincial policemen to restore order. The British-owned and -constructed railways favored European over native workers.[39] Further, natives looked upon the rails spreading over the plains as threatening to the gaucho way of life.

The anarchist organ *El obrero* commented on native antipathy toward foreigners in 1892. Per capita meat consumption for Buenos Aires in 1891 stood at only 37 percent of the 1854 level and 28 percent of the 1822 figure. The "son of the country, the gaucho," blamed the gringo for his shrinking meat supply and vented his wrath upon the immigrant. According to this worker daily, the fault lay not with the foreigner but rather with the capitalist system that impoverished all laborers. Natives, however, could not overlook the coincidence between rising numbers of foreigners and falling meat supplies.[40] Economic anxieties, coupled with already inflamed cultural antipathies, increased native opposition to the foreigner.

Urban immigrants sensed the hostility of the native, but those on the pampa experienced it directly. At the Esperanza agricultural colony, the first established in Santa Fe province, the government stationed a picket of gaucho soldiers to defend against Indian raids. According to William Perkins, who inspected the colonies in the 1860s, colonists considered these "dregs of the *gaucho* population" to be "entirely useless, besides being prejudicial to the people by their horses damaging the crops." Perkins found the spectacle of "drunken gauchos" protecting sturdy Swiss and other European yeomen to be "supremely ridiculous." Colonists also came into conflict with native rural officials, especially the detested justice of the peace. Profound ethnic, religious, and economic divisions provoked numerous confrontations between farmers and government agents. Foreigners at Esperanza focused much of their political energies at the municipal level to establish local autonomy. Francisco Scardin, an Italo-Argentine doctor, listed the major enemies of the agriculturalist as "hurricanes, droughts, freezes, the justice of the peace."[41] Immigrants faced the hostility of the rural masses and the native landed elite, both fearful of the growing numbers, prosperity, and potential political power of the colonists.

Immigrant-native tensions burst out violently again in 1893. *La agricultura* decried the rural crime wave, especially the "innumerable cases" of robbery afflicting farmers in Santa Fe. According to this

journal, "the outlaw gaucho, who idles in the countryside," perpe-
trated most of the crimes. Colonists resorted to vigilante justice in one
case, lynching an infamous criminal, "the murderer Ferreira," without
concern for the requisites of law. Anti-gringo sentiment, high
throughout the period of massive immigration, reached fever pitch in
northern Buenos Aires and Santa Fe provinces during the agricultural
tenants' strike in September and October 1893. Native ranch workers
sacked farming communities and harassed and even killed a few
protesting farmers. The revolt provided an ideal context for xenophobic
rural ruffians to vent their rage against the immigrant farmer and his
infringement upon the open range.[42]

Florencio Sánchez, an Uruguayan expatriate who became one of
Argentina's most renowned playwrights, cast the native-foreign
conflict in bold relief in *La gringa*. Don Nicola, an Italian shopkeeper
and entrepreneur, views creoles as drunken, gambling wastrels with no
foresight or sense of progress. When a native named Prospero asks for
(and at the end of the play gains) the hand of his daughter Victoria in
marriage, Nicola retorts: "Marry, eh? Marry her inheritance! No! The
inheritance of the old gringo, to spend it in saloons and gamble at the
races. Lazy rascals! Get out! Learn to work first!" Don Cantalicio, an
old creole, hates the avaricious Nicola, who takes his land by
entrapping him with "little papers" for mortgages and loans. A native
peon voices similar disgust toward the Italian for making his daughters
work hard. "Pucha! Selfish gringos! Rotten with money and making
these poor little things work!" Another character, an Italian physician
named Dr. Buottini, callously proceeds with a card game after learning
that an injured man is a native, not an immigrant. The gaucho who
sought out the doctor bitterly complains, "It's certain that if the sick
man were Bertoni or some other rich gringo, he'd run down through the
cornfields!"[43]

Other works of Argentine literature also reflect anti-foreign
sentiments. Such works as *Juan Moreira*, a novel written in 1880 by
Eduardo Gutiérrez, portray foreigners in a negative light. Juan Antonio
Argerich provides another unflattering portrait in his 1884 novel
Inocentes o culpables: Novela naturalista. José María Miró, using the
pen name Julian Martel, vents anti-Semitic feelings in his 1891 novel
La bolsa; and *Quilito*, published the same year by Carlos María
Ocantos, is also anti-Semitic. Juan Alsina, the Argentine director of
immigration for some twenty years, criticized Jewish farmers who
settled in Entre Ríos for not assimilating into Argentine society. Like

most leaders, he feared the fragmenting social impact of separatist groups who would put their own interests before those of the nation. Alberto Gerchunoff, a Russian-born Jewish immigrant, refuted the charge of separatism in a 1910 work titled *Los gauchos judíos*. According to Gerchunoff, Jewish farmers, at least, maintained their religious values but adopted Argentine national values as well.[44]

Argentina's several million immigrants brought some desired benefits—much-needed manpower, increased land values, and cultural enrichment. But problems accompanied these blessings, and many of the intelligentsia came to reconsider the wisdom of vigorous immigration promotion. Sarmiento had early heralded the immigrant as a revitalizing and civilizing force to lift the nation out of the grasp of barbarian caudillos and ignorant rural masses. But in the last years of his life, his writings reveal a grave sense of disappointment with the fruits of massive immigration. Instead of myriad farms tilled by sturdy Anglo-Saxon yeomen, he saw throngs of Italians who represented no appreciable improvement over the backward native Spanish and mestizo population. A few months before his death in 1888, Sarmiento lamented that Argentina's most numerous European immigrants were also the "least cultured," the Italians. As a fervent supporter of education, he found the high rate of immigrant illiteracy, which he estimated at two-thirds, profoundly disturbing.[45]

"Minuit," writing in *La campaña* of Buenos Aires, had mixed feelings toward foreigners. Immigration brought needed laborers to the nation but also resulted in beggars and "turks" peddling junk on every street corner. Itinerant hucksters had invaded all parts of the capital. Reversing its earlier unequivocal support for immigration, *La campaña* issued a veiled call for restriction. Federico Tobal contrasted the foreigner unfavorably with an idealized image of the gaucho, who held "cultured customs and Christian habits" insofar as his primitive environment permitted. Lacking the gaucho's sound moral values, "pride and independence," the foreigner exuded avarice and materialism. Tobal preferred the gaucho's "romantic cult of honor and friendship, the dignity that ennobles," to the grasping habits of the gringo.[46] His viewpoint anticipated turn-of-the-century nationalists, who exalted the gaucho as the paragon of Argentine virtue and national identity.

Director of Immigration Juan A. Alsina pushed for a policy of selective immigration. In 1893 he complained about the "worthless" Brazilians, who aspired to a life of urban leisure and refused honest work. He saw them as adding nothing to the nation except an increase in mendicant ranks. Like all Argentine leaders, Alsina considered Europeans the only acceptable immigrants. A decade later, he further limited his definition of acceptable foreigners and proposed admitting only farmers with sufficient resources to purchase land. In this way he hoped to eliminate the "parasites" and "pseudo-merchants" that had troubled "Minuit" in 1884. He also modified the conventional wisdom that immigration was the key to national economic growth and social regeneration, terming it an "auxiliary factor" rather than the prime mover in national development. The immigration director wanted to attract enterprising farm families that would populate the countryside and spur agricultural growth but not compete with native workers.[47]

Argentine chief executives over the years modified official policy away from unconditional support for immigration. A content analysis of thirty-six presidential messages to the legislature from 1881 to 1916 reveals growing concern for the problem of assimilating the nation's millions of foreigners. Argentine presidents expressed increasing fear of immigrants as dangerous to the established social order and came to view restriction as partial remedy to the perplexing "social question" of urban worker unrest. But beyond the immediate political and economic difficulties engendered by foreign-born socialist and anarchist labor leaders, the nation's leaders feared the impact of newcomers and their alien ideas upon the native population.[48]

The cultural penetration of the immigrant masses troubled many Argentine intellectuals. Ernesto Quesada pointed up the corrupting influence of heavy Italian immigration upon the Spanish language. In rural areas a hybrid dialect called *cocoliche* fused strains of Italian, gauchesco and *lunfardo* (an urban lower-class argot). The dialect even gave rise to its own body of popular literature. Quesada expounded his misgivings in two books, *El problema del idioma nacional* (1900) and *El "criollismo" en la literatura argentina* (1902). In a 1911 novel entitled *El peligro*, Carlos María Ocantos expressed fears about fundamental linguistic and cultural changes being wrought by massive immigration and about the impact of all this upon Argentine national character. Miguel Cané expressed similar apprehensions tinged with a harsher xenophobia.[49]

By 1912 many observers agreed with Enrique de Cires that foreigners, far from being the hope of the future, instead brought increased crime, mendicancy, and social unrest. Cires charged that two-thirds of all criminals in Buenos Aires were foreigners, as were nearly all the beggars and anarchists. He harshly characterized the immigrant masses as "unserviceable . . . unpatriotic . . . people with no concept of work, vagrants, criminals." Cires held that vagrants and the unemployable immigrated in far greater numbers than the farmers the nation wanted and needed. His unfair, caustic appraisal represents the extremity of intellectual xenophobia, but the cultural nationalism touched off by Ricardo Rojas and furthered by Leopoldo Lugones and other writers clearly manifested the depth of national discontent with the fruits of immigration. The gaucho did not stand alone in his aversion to the gringo. In *Restauración nacionalista* (1909), Rojas called for a concerted national push in education to "Argentinize" the immigrant hordes. Dr. José María Ramos Mejía, nativist head of the National Council of Education, Carlos Octavio Bunge, and Enrique de Vedia also backed the drive to revitalize nationality through education. Ramos Mejía instituted a pledge of allegiance and other nationalistic reforms.[50]

By the time of the nation's centennial celebration in 1910, most of the intelligentsia understood that the dream of economic prosperity and social regeneration through immigration fostered by Alberdi, Sarmiento, Avellaneda, and others had not been realized. The gravity of the "social question," with its strikes, violence, and disruptions, forced many to reevaluate the relative merits of the foreigner and the native. The ruling elite, besieged and threatened by vociferous demands from immigrant workers, adeptly maneuvered to maintain power. The oligarchy resurrected the long-scorned gaucho and transformed him into a nostalgic, idealized, domesticated symbol of Argentine national virtue. Ironically, the gaucho, long despised by the elite, became its central ideological weapon in a battle against foreign-inspired demands for social justice and democracy.

11
Man to Myth:
Literary and
Symbolic Images

Gauchos disappeared as a recognizable social group in the last third of the nineteenth century, but literary and symbolic evocations persisted into the twentieth. Sarmiento had shaped the negative attitudes of many Argentines toward the gaucho with his compelling dichotomy of civilization versus barbarism. Hernández poetically and convincingly refuted Sarmiento's interpretation with *Martín Fierro*. The gaucho's disappearance, a necessity to Sarmiento and an avoidable tragedy to Hernández, set the stage for his mythical return in the works of twentieth-century nationalists and traditionalists. Seldom appreciated in life, the gaucho became the embodiment of Argentine character as the nation's thinkers and leaders reconstructed the past to suit twentieth-century political needs. Vanquished by the juggernaut of oppression and modernization, the gaucho persevered to gain a central place in Argentine thought and letters.

Journalist, educator, historian, political philosopher and practitioner, Sarmiento molded the thoughts and policies of the nation's Europeanizing elite. In *Facundo* he elaborated a racial and geographical interpretation of Argentine history and society that blamed the rise of the Rosista dictatorship and other ills on the inferiority of the mestizo population. The native's idleness and incapacity for hard work stemmed from the mixture of Spanish and inferior Indian blood. In letters to his friend Mary Mann, who translated *Facundo* into the English, Sarmiento decried the limitations imposed upon the nation by the "Indian and Spanish element." He complained of "our ignorant popular masses" and of "those ignorant masses, the poor whites," that retarded progress. His most extreme and revealing commentary on the gaucho came in instructions to General Mitre in 1861: "Do not try to save the blood of gauchos. It is a contribution that the country needs. Blood is the only thing they have in common with human beings."[1]

Sarmiento proposed four major policies to combat the barbarism of the countryside. First, like most Argentine leaders, he firmly believed in subjecting the rural population to strict control. The gambling and knife fighting that were common on the pampa called for strong countermeasures. In *Facundo* he suggested that "such customs need vigorous methods of repression, and to restrain hardened men, judges still more hardened are required."[2] Strong justices of the peace, alcaldes, and police zealously applied "vigorous methods of repression" throughout the countryside.

Through massive immigration from Europe, Sarmiento hoped to strengthen and purify the native race with an infusion of what he considered to be superior Anglo-Saxon blood. While natives secured the frontier and held back the Indian threat, industrious European settlers could cultivate the plains as they were doing in the United States. Sarmiento contrasted unfavorably the ramshackle huts and dirty children of creole holdings with the nicely painted and well-kept homes of immigrant settlers, epitomizing, respectively, backwardness and progress.[3]

Land reform and the promotion of agriculture formed another plank in this San Juan politician's program for national greatness. He recognized the links between Spanish-inspired latifundism and the social problems and civil unrest that plagued Argentina. As a tourist and diplomat, Sarmiento visited and greatly admired family farms in the United States, where he traveled in 1847 and again in the 1860s. A county fair, with its blend of solid agricultural and industrial progress, fascinated him. He desired to supplant great estates with family farms peopled by Anglo-Saxon immigrants. In 1868 he dedicated a new agricultural colony at Chivilcoy and declared it the basis of his entire program. Through farming he hoped to see "gauchos tranformed into peaceful residents" on a civilized pampa.[4] But as president he had no more success in eradicating latifundism than did other reformers. The terratenientes held fast.

Public education was the final element in Sarmiento's blueprint for civilization. In his speech at Chivilcoy in 1868 he pledged to "make one hundred Chivilcoys in the six years of my government and with land for each head of the family, with schools for your children." Landownership and education would uplift the gaucho and turn him from the plundering life of a montonero who followed some ruthless caudillo to a life of peace and productivity. He looked to American educator Horace Mann for inspiration in the philosophical and practical applications of public education.[5]

Given the profound and pervasive impact of Sarmiento's writings, especially his vision of pampean social dualism, the inception and execution of *Facundo* merit comment. He wrote his sweeping interpretation of pampean life and of his four gaucho archetypes (pathfinder, tracker, troubadour, and outlaw) without any firsthand knowledge of the great plain or its inhabitants. In a letter to Juan María Gutiérrez of May 1847, he confided: "You know that I have never crossed the pampa to Buenos Aires, having obtained a description of it from San Juan muleteers who cross it every year, from poets like Echeverría, and from the soldiers of the civil war." He also read travelers' journals and even cited Sir Walter Scott as an authority on the gaucho. When he first crossed the great plain, returning from exile with Urquiza's conquering forces in early 1852, Sarmiento felt overwhelmed by "the pampa, that I have described in *Facundo*, felt by intuition, but that I saw for the first time in my life!" In 1868 he repeated that his vision of the pampa had been intuitive: "I had described the pampa without having seen it."[6] Sarmiento's intuition led him to assess accurately some aspects of gaucho character, but his own political goals obstructed his vision on key points.

Facundo, more than a work of history or sociology as is often asserted, is a literary and polemical piece. The literary flavor derives from Sarmiento's admiration for North American and European literature, particularly the writings of James Fenimore Cooper. He modeled his baqueano on Cooper's Pathfinder and compared the outlaw gaucho with Cooper's Hawkeye or Trapper. In discussing the troubadour, he evoked images of the wandering minstrels of the Middle Ages.[7] Like most pro-European intellectuals in Argentina, Sarmiento sought to place his own work within a broader context of western letters—the benchmark of cultural worth.

But *Facundo*'s overriding purpose was political, not literary. The work is an imaginative, moving attack on the "barbarian" dictatorship of Rosas and on the forces that permitted his success. The gaucho of *Facundo* is not a historical figure, but rather a political metaphor for the rural masses that kept barbaric caudillos in power. Sarmiento preached the dogma that, to destroy the caudillo and civilize the pampa, the gaucho masses had to be eradicated. His political program, elaborated over several decades and effected in part during his presidency and after, sought that end. Subsequent presidents completed the destruction of the gaucho; but the anticipated regeneration and civilization did not follow.[8]

Other thinkers, including the romantic poet of the Generation of 'Thirty-Seven, Esteban Echeverría, shared Sarmiento's dualism. In *El dogma socialista*, published in 1837, Echeverría stated flatly that "Europe is the center of the civilization of the centuries and of humanitarian progress." Though he cautioned against blind cultural subjugation, he urged that Europeanized "social and civilized life" be spread throughout the nation from the cities to counter the influence of rural caudillos. Later intellectuals, including José Ingenieros, Adolfo Saldías, and Ernesto Quesada, promoted their own varieties of geographical determinism, each pitting a feudalistic, caudillo-ruled rural society against modern urban commercial and industrial centers. Ingenieros depicted the nation's history as a racial struggle between white "Euro-Argentines" who had won the country's independence and caudillos like Rosas and Facundo Quiroga, who were supported by the gaucho masses. In place of Sarmiento's urban civilization and rural barbarism, he posited white "Argentines" and mestizo gauchos.[9]

The urban fixation of the Spanish provided the structural basis for the dichotomous vision of Argentine life. The Spanish perpetuated the Roman practice of linking social status with municipal office-holding and urban life and had founded three hundred towns by 1600 in their American colonies. Urban outposts spearheaded their civilizing push by controlling and subjugating the hinterland—areas lacking in worth except insofar as they contributed to the city's well-being.[10]

Not everyone subscribed to the tidy rural-urban typology depicted by Sarmiento and others. Gerstaecker expressed the view at mid-century that "the worst people are said here, as in other countries, to be located in the capital itself." In 1886, Tobal painted an image of the gaucho as a noble savage maintaining his dignity and natural goodness in spite of the encroachments of the evil city. Walter Larden observed in 1911 that "in Argentina, it is not the gaucho class that is untrustworthy." Even Sarmiento recognized the oppression of the countryside by the city, admitting in *Facundo* that Buenos Aires sent "only chains, exterminating hordes, and petty subaltern tyrants" to the pampa rather than its civilizing "light, wealth, and prosperity."[11]

Sarmiento's dichotomy ignored the obvious and essential interrelations between city and country. In some ways civilization was the mother of barbarism because the extension of forts, settlements, and great estates displaced indigenous peoples and frontiersmen, provoking a violent reaction. Urban interests tried to impose their will upon the frontier with military force and to strip the uncivilized of their ability to resist. For example, Rosas and other leaders forbade the gaucho to carry his facón in towns. On the other hand, civilization could also be the child of barbarism. The colonial traffic in illegal hides, based on the labor of those classified as barbarian, built the economic power of the porteño elite. Thus civilization and barbarism coexisted, interacted, and merged in the Río de la Plata.[12]

Some intellectuals harshly criticized Sarmiento's vision of Argentine social reality. Juan Bautista Alberdi flatly asserted that the gaucho could only represent "barbarism in books that do not understand what civilization is." He aptly compared the gaucho with the English sailor and mechanic—"coarse, uncultured, rough"—but central to the nation's economic vitality. Manuel Gálvez, a twentieth-century nationalist and admirer of Rosas, dismissed all of *Facundo* except the introduction as a "truculent and vulgar pamphlet, written by an improvising journalist."[13]

The strongest reaction to Sarmiento came from José Hernández. Even as Sarmiento had created his fanciful polemic in reaction to the cruel oppression of Rosas, Hernández reacted to the administration of Sarmiento and the porteño elite by showing that urban "civilization" also manifested corruption, repression, and viciousness. By standing *Facundo* on its head and presenting the city as the source of national social ills and political despotism, Hernández successfully challenged Sarmiento's simplistic dualism and illuminated the greater complexity of Argentine social reality.

In the vigorous, vibrant stanzas of *Martín Fierro*, Hernández drew upon a venerable, lively national literary heritage. Although elite cultural tastes aped movements and dictates from Europe, several strains of autochthonous literature developed during the nineteenth century. Native writers pursued various paths in emphasizing Argentina's New World experience and traditions. "Indianists" focused on indigenous cultural antecedents, whereas "Americanists" sought out broader roots common to the Americas. *Gauchismo*, creolism, and nationalism were the three sometimes overlapping strains that played off New World images and types (sometimes nativistically) against foreign influences. Hernández marked the zenith of gaucho-inspired poetry; his liveliness of verse and clarity of vision were never equaled.[14]

Gauchesco poetry utilized the rustic dialect of the pampa, which provoked scorn and derision from cosmopolitan critics and linguistic purists. The poems invariably presented an epic narrative with a gaucho protagonist and employed both particular and transcendental themes. Though they drew inspiration from folklore, from the products of illiterate, anonymous authors, gauchesco poets were cultured, lettered men who maintained a proximity to and veracity in describing rural life. Bartolomé Hidalgo, the father of gauchesco poetry, moved the genre from the realm of oral anonymous verse to written culture with his *Diálogos patrióticos*, published in 1820. Following Hidalgo's inspiration, Juan Gualberto Godoy and Hilario Ascasubi wrote numerous poems, many heavily political and polemical. Estanislao del Campo added his superbly satirical *Fausto* in 1870, and the Uruguayan master Antonio D. Lussich published *Los tres gauchos orientales* early in 1872. Lussich dedicated his work to his friend Hernández, who drew inspiration from it for the first part of *Martín Fierro*, published later in 1872. Because they employed grammatically correct Castillian rather than dialect, the writings of Juan María Gutiérrez, Bartolomé Mitre, and Rafael Obligado comprise a parallel group of modified gauchesco poetry. Although sometimes classified with gauchesco works, *La cautiva* by Echeverría utilizes Castilian, not dialect, is romanticized and not realistic, and fails to treat the gaucho.[15]

The powerbrokers of Argentine culture never accepted gauchesco poetry as legitimate because of its humble dialect and political content. Entertaining, quaint, picturesque, fit for popular consumption, the poems did not gain elite acceptance in their own time. The porteño cultural elite turned a deaf ear to gauchesco poets as literary figures but acknowledged the truthfulness of the social and political commentary in some of their writing.[16] From its inception, gauchesco poetry resonated with political opinion and polemic. Bartolomé Hidalgo, writing in the blush of independence nationalism, glorified the gaucho as the paragon of patriotism, valor, and religion. Through his delightful character Paulino Lucero, Hilario Ascasubi attacked Rosas, *"El ilustro conculador de las leyes"* (illustrious infringer of the laws). Estanislao del Campo's *Gobierno gaucho* (1870) decried such rural social ills as conscription, passports, latifundia, abusive officials, and mercenary merchants—problems pilloried by Hernández two years later.[17]

Hernández was a political activist as well as a poet. Fighting beside the federalist caudillos of Entre Ríos—Justo José de Urquiza and Ricardo López Jordan—against Mitre and Sarmiento, speaking out in the provincial legislature, writing prose and poetic attacks, he put his political beliefs into intense, often violent action. In reaction to Sarmiento, Hernández posited Buenos Aires as the locus of the nation's political ills, and through Fierro he voiced his political commentary:

> there's some dirty linen here to be washed
> and I won't give up till it's done . . .
> I sing giving opinions
> and that's my kind of song.[18]

An intense federalism, grounded in a consistent set of classical nineteenth-century liberal beliefs, characterized this poet's political philosophy. In the pages of his journal, *El Río de la Plata*, he lashed out against the unitarios and their centralizing policies. Reacting to Sarmiento's hostile depiction of Angel Vicente Peñalosa (El Chacho), he published a more sympathetic sketch of the La Rioja caudillo in 1863. Of El Chacho's death, he wrote that "the savage unitarios are celebrating . . . the unitario party has another crime to write on the page of its horrible offenses."[19] But Hernández insisted upon a legitimate federalism as epitomized by Urquiza or López Jordan rather than the porteño pseudo-federalism of Rosas. In *El Río de la Plata* of October 3, 1869, he attacked the "dictatorship of Rosas . . . a tyranny of twenty years." And in *Martín Fierro* he compared the mistreatment of frontier troops with that accorded at Rosas' headquarters: "it was just like Palermo— / they'd give you such a time in the stocks / that it would leave you sick."[20] Speaking to the Chamber of Deputies on November 19, 1880, he criticized Rosas for denying the nation a constitution and added that "for twenty years he tyrannized, despotized, and bloodied the country."[21]

Hernández strenuously demanded policies that would end the city's oppression of the countryside and uplift the gaucho to his rightful position as a citizen with full rights in the republic. Contrary to Sarmiento, who called for more "vigorous methods of repression," Hernández urged that the rural population be freed from oppression. In

El Río de la Plata of August 19, 1869, he focused upon the hated frontier service as the most visible and onerous evidence of the city's exploitation of the countryside. "What more monstrous contradiction than that which converts the citizen of the countryside into the guardian of the interests of the capital more than his own . . . ? Frontier service seems to have been conceived as a terrible punishment for the son of the countryside." In the issue for September 26, 1869, he called for an end to the draft lottery as the "only means of giving security and quietude to the countryside."

Unlike Sarmiento and the ruling elite, Hernández did not view massive immigration as a panacea for national progress. Reacting to a pro-immigration article in Sarmiento's *El nacional*, the poet expressed disenchantment with the fruits of the foreign influx. He charged that immigration had filled the cities with an "army of bootblacks, of lottery numbers sellers," rather than populating the desert. "Immigration, without capital and without jobs, is an element of turmoil, disorder, and backwardness." Always concerned for the welfare of the native, Hernández feared that masses of foreigners would drive working-class wages even lower. Foreigners appear in *Martín Fierro* only in caricature as Hernández gave vent to the native's disdain for the gringo, worthless in an equestrian frontier society.[22]

On the issues of land reform and education, however, Hernández concurred with Sarmiento. The poet charged that latifundism left rich lands lying in "sterility and abandon . . . There are no poorer or more backward countries than those where property is divided among a few privileged classes." Whereas Sarmiento concerned himself with attracting foreign farmers, Hernández wished to see latifundia subdivided among native workers. In his *Instrucción del estanciero* (Instruction to the rancher), published in 1881, he reiterated the need to establish a system of colonies for rural native workers. He understood and accepted the passing of a strictly pastoral society and its herdsmen as an inevitable part of the nation's agricultural and industrial progress but demanded government aid to the gaucho in making the transition— aid that the liberal elite never provided.[23]

Hernández urged public education as well as agricultural and livestock vocational training for the rural population. In a letter to the editors of the eighth edition of *Martín Fierro* in 1874, he expressed the hope that his work would awaken in the gaucho a desire to read. Fierro lamented his lack of education in the second half of the poem:

> The only schooling I ever had,
> Was a life of suffering;
> Don't be surprised if at the game,
> I've made mistakes;—that's not my shame—
> It's mighty little a man can know,
> If he's never learnt anything.[24]

During the decade in which he published his epic, Hernández abandoned his violent rebelliousness and militancy in favor of institutional reform through the political system. His alteration in tactics is clearly evinced by changes from the first to the second part of the poem, which was published seven years later. He joined the ranks of other reformers called the Generation of 'Seventy—Leandro Alem, Manuel Zuitana, Bernardo Solveyra, Aristobulo del Valle, Rufino Varela—to attempt to alter the shape of provincial politics, supporting the federalization of Buenos Aires and backing Roca's "peace and administration" politics of accommodation. In 1882 he expressed the need for "peace, liberty, and roads," and he came to accept Sarmiento's premise that Argentina required institutional reform and technological advancement in order to prosper.[25] The outlaw of the first part of *Martín Fierro* became a hard-working, practical paisano seeking stability and social acceptance in the second part. Recognizing the inadequacy of old gaucho ways in modernizing society, Fierro counseled adaptation and compromise, not rebellion. Urging the paisano to value friendship, respect others, work hard, solve problems nonviolently, and avoid drink, Fierro set new priorities: "The gaucho should have house, school, church and rights." Whereas the old gaucho domador was praised in part one, Fierro expressed admiration for a gentler manner of taming in part two. Viejo Vizcacha represents the shiftless, laughable, worldly-wise creole who had lived beyond his time. As Fierro's son recalled of him, "My guardian was one of the old sort / and there aren't many of them left now." Hernández accurately captured the transition taking place from the gaucho of the pampa criolla to the domesticated peon of the pampa gringa.[26]

The disappearance of the gaucho and his transformation into a dependent peon attracted other commentary. Some observers contended that the gaucho had actually disappeared early in the nineteenth century, during the independence wars. Others linked his demise to the shrinking number of wild cattle at mid-century. Still others asserted that he had never disappeared at all, but rather lived on albeit in altered form. Adolfo Bioy Casares, a writer and collaborator of Jorge Luis Borges, wryly noted that several generations of witnesses had asserted that the gaucho "only existed in the past, preferably seventy years before each of these affirmations." Nostalgia frequently prompted observers to date the decline of the gaucho to the previous generation; indeed, "it is true that his deplorable extinction occasionally appears to us as the most enduring characteristic of the gaucho."[27]

The difficulty in dating the gaucho's demise stems from the conundrum of defining who and what he was. Depending upon the scope and nature of the definition, a social group meeting the criteria could be found to vanish at almost any point during the Argentine past. Enrique de Gandia, defining the gaucho as a colonial cattle thief and vagrant, saw him being transformed early in the nineteenth century into a soldier for independence or a montonero for a provincial caudillo. Rosas supposedly delivered the coup de grâce by shutting up these free-roving horsemen into military barracks. Others saw the gaucho losing his livelihood and traditional way of life when the enormous herds of wild cattle gave way to domesticated animals tended by salaried workers. According to Gibson, the early nineteenth century witnessed "the nomad *gaucho* of the colonial period converted into the loyal *gaucho* of the *estancia*."[28]

At the opposite extreme from those who see the gaucho vanishing early in the century stand such writers as Manuel Gálvez, Ricardo Güiraldes, and José Agustín de Basualdo, who assert that he did not disappear at all. Focusing upon the character and values of the gaucho, they find that essential traits and traditions have been perpetuated by a reduced group into the present century. As Güiraldes noted in 1926, "the gaucho has neither died nor has he authorized us to dispose of his life with such impertinence." In 1868 Wilfred Latham perceptively traced the social processes that gradually altered the gaucho. Farming and sheep ranching displaced him from the traditional cattle herding role, and incompetent, dishonest officials and onerous military duty denied him security and an incentive to work. Recognizing the tremendous loss and waste in the gaucho's extinction, Latham asked, "Why should so much excellent material be cast adrift on the plains, homeless and hunted?" He accurately identified the same conditions criticized by Hernández, which brought the gaucho as a social group to an end during the last third of the century.[29]

As the historical gaucho receded from the pampa, new, conflicting images appeared. Some commentators shed no tears over the gaucho's demise and welcomed his successor—the quiet, obedient, industrious paisano. Others, less impressed with the domesticated creole worker and the strident, demanding immigrant, generated a wistful, nostalgic vision of the old gaucho and his virtues. *La vanguardia* uncharacteristically lauded the gaucho on November 10, 1894, the birthday of José Hernández, who had died eight years earlier. Quoting thoughts by Antonio Piñero from *La agricultura*, this socialist organ presented an idyllic portrait of the old gaucho—proud, virile, well-dressed, honorable, free to roam and work as he chose. His successors, the unlettered "rural proletariat," represented a "miserably dressed . . . degenerate racial type" vastly inferior to the gaucho of old. The government had contributed to the process of degeneration because each administration would "decrease the number of schools but increase the police." Juan José de Lezica in 1901 recalled the independence, pride, loyalty, hospitality, bravery, and strength of the gaucho. He unfavorably contrasted the humble, servile paisano of the modern estancia with the magnificent centaur of yesteryear. The modern creole stood as but a "shadow" of the gaucho, "pale, weak, prematurely old." The gaucho had been "savage, strong, and master of the desert," but the paisano labored as "a slave," bullied by gringo foremen and weakened by alcohol. Even police officials became wistful about the old gaucho—a sentiment never voiced while he yet roamed the plains and escaped their clutches. In a 1902 editorial on "Rustling," *Revista de policía* lamented the passing of the old "philanthropic gaucho" who had bravely and willingly died for his country. In his place arose the "rascal, egoistic, trouble-making gaucho" who completely lacked noble impulses.[30]

Ernesto Quesada also deplored the passing of the "true gaucho"— noble, loyal, free, taciturn, proud, and contemplative—whom fencing, farming, and immigrants had pushed from the plains and forced to flee to the interior. In a pseudo-psychological interpretation of Argentine character published in 1904, Emilio Zuccarini contrasted the gaucho with his successor of the late 1880s and early 1890s, the *atorrante* (vagrant, loafer). The atorrante neither worked nor asked alms, but rather subsisted as a lost, wandering soul overrun and debased by civilization. The old gaucho, the epitome of individualism, rebelled against all forms of authority and sought out the quietude and tranquillity of the remote, solitary pampa.[31]

As the nation approached its centennial celebration of the first shots of independence in 1810, several nationalistic writers elevated the gaucho to the position of paragon of argentinidad. Ricardo Rojas, Leopoldo Lugones, and Manuel Gálvez forged a new image of the gaucho by resurrecting him from his historically despised position and exalting him as the quintessence of national virtue. These three nationalists, born in the interior provinces, viewed the interior rather than the immigrant-saturated littoral as the legitimate repository of Argentina's cultural heritage. Lugones published *Guerra gaucha* in 1905 and *Odas seculares* in 1910, but his interpretive lectures on *Martín Fierro*, delivered before an audience of the cultural elite at the Odeón Theater during May 1913 brought to completion the apotheosis of the gaucho. To Lugones, the wars of independence had initiated the "calamities of the gaucho," which persisted until his disappearance later in the century. He censured the nation's oligarchic leadership for facilitating the "extinction of the gaucho, an essential element of nationality." His lectures, published under the title *El payador* in 1916, mark the beginning of elite acceptance of the rehabilitated gaucho, and of Hernández' poetry as culturally significant. Rojas wrote *El país de la selva* in 1907 and *Blason de plata* in 1910, but his major contribution to cultural nationalism came in *La restauración nacionalista* (1909). The recommendations to reform the nation's educational policies rang with strident nationalism and called for rejection of the Europeanizing cosmopolitanism that dictated porteño cultural tastes.[32]

Lezica, Quesada, Zuccarini, and other writers contrasted the peon of the modern ranch unfavorably with the old gaucho. Some twentieth-century novelists extended the rehabilitation even further, imbuing the modern paisano with romanticized virtues of the gaucho. Benito Lynch and Ricardo Güiraldes presented paisanos as retaining the wily sense of humor and the sound traditional values of the gaucho but shedding his anti-social qualities. Lynch, who frequently set his characters in the humid pampa near Dolores, depicted the domesticated peon in *Los caranchos de la Florida* (1917), *Raquela* (1918), and *El romance de un gaucho* (1930). *Don Segundo Sombra*, based on the life and character of an old paisano whom Güiraldes knew in San Antonio de Areco, also reflected a positive image of the tamed gaucho of the modern plain. Don Segundo—strong, capable, loyal, honest—passes on his wisdom to a young boy whom he tutors for many years. As the lad reaches manhood, Sombra commends him: "You've become a man—better than a man, a gaucho. The one who knows the world's evils because he has lived through them is tempered to overcome them."[33]

The landed elite found final victory in the characters depicted by

Lynch and Güiraldes—tractable, forbearing, obedient peons of the new ranching industry. The twentieth-century paisano met the real and idealized expectations of the elite that had strived throughout the century to convert the gaucho into a dependent peon. As historical figures, both the gaucho and his modern-day incarnation, the paisano, gave way to mythical images consonant with the viewpoint and needs of the province's landed oligarchy. The metamorphosis was complete: as the peon replaced the gaucho, so idealized images replaced them both in the nation's literature and thought.

In 1918, Charles Darbyshire recorded a terse but apt epitaph for the domesticated peon of the pampa gringa: "The gaucho, as a rule, cannot read or write. When he dies—after possibly thirty or more years' service—he leaves no effects, no savings bank account; the owner of the estancia puts together a rude coffin and a bullock-cart takes the corpse to the nearest cemetery."[34]

"Gaucho"—only the name remained, but the mundane reality recorded by Darbyshire accurately bespoke the unhappy life and death of the gaucho during the nineteenth century. Vanquished in reality, the gaucho still rides a romanticized frontier pampa as an idealized myth and political symbol. His qualities, real and imagined, represent an essential ingredient in the continuous quest by Argentines to define the essence of their national character. Oppressed and downtrodden in life, the gaucho has achieved immortality in the nation's literary and ideological formation—a partial counterpoint to the sad realities of his persecuted existence in the nineteenth century.

Appendixes

Appendix A:
Population Growth,
Buenos Aires Province, 1778–1914

	City	Countryside	Total	Gauchos
1778	24,205	12,905	37,110	3,226
1797	40,000	32,168	72,168	8,042
1822	55,416	63,230	118,646	15,808
1836	62,228	80,729	142,957	20,182
1854/55	90,076	183,861	273,937	45,965
1864	140,000	254,832	394,832	63,708
1869	177,787	317,320	495,107	79,330
1881	351,298	526,581	877,879	—
1890	519,865	764,166	1,284,031	—
1895	663,854	921,168	1,585,022	—
1904	950,891	1,463,535	2,414,426	—
1914	1,575,814	2,066,165	3,641,979	—

Sources: Argentine Republic, *Tercer censo nacional . . . 1914*, 4: 501; Benito Díaz, *Rosas, Buenos Aires y la organización nacional*, pp. 154, 264; John Lynch, *Argentine Dictator*, p. 93; Jonathan C. Brown, *A Socioeconomic History of Argentina, 1776–1860*, p. 163; see n. 2 of Introduction on estimate of gaucho population.

Appendix B:
Livestock and Wheat Production,
Buenos Aires Province and Argentina, 1866–1914

Number of Livestock (in millions)

	Sheep		Cattle		Horses	
	Province	*Nation*	*Province*	*Nation*	*Province*	*Nation*
1866	60	—	6	—	1.8	—
1875	45.5	57.5	5.1	13.3	1.5	3.9
1881	57.8	67.4	4.8	11.9	2.4	4.1
1888	51.6	66.7	8.7	22.0	1.7	4.3
1895	52.4	74.4	7.7	21.7	1.7	4.4
1908	34.6	67.2	10.4	29.1	2.5	7.5
1914	18.8	43.2	9.1	25.9	2.8	8.3

Area Sown in Wheat (in thousands of acres)

	Province	*Nation*
1866	—	—
1875	—	—
1881	220	—
1888	610	2,014
1895	907	5,066
1908	4,811	11,994
1914	5,691	16,311

Source: Data from Roberto Cortés Conde, *El progreso argentino, 1880–1914*, pp. 277–78.

Appendix C:
Changing Composition
of Argentine Exports, 1822–1919

	Hides	Salted Meat	Wool	Wheat	All Livestock	All Agriculture
	Percentage of Total Exports by Product				*All Livestock*	*All Agriculture*
1822	65	10	1	—	—	—
1825	55	9	—	—	—	—
1836	68	10	8	1	—	—
1850	65	8	11	—	—	—
1859	32	14	34	—	—	—
1875–79	38	8	53	0.3	—	—
1880–84	32	5	58	1.7	89	7
1885–89	—	—	—	—	81	17
1890–94	26	2	38	20	66	29
1895–99	—	—	—	—	64	31
1900–04	14	1	26	22	49	47
1905–09	—	—	—	—	39	58
1910–14	12	0.3	14	21	45	51
1915–19	—	—	—	—	55	39

Sources: John Lynch, *Argentine Dictator*, p. 83; Jonathan C. Brown, *A Socioeconomic History of Argentina, 1776–1860*; p. 81; Carlos F. Díaz Alejandro, *Essays on the Economic History of the Argentine Republic* (New Haven: Yale University Press, 1970), p. 5; Felipe Arana, *Historia económica y social argentina* (Buenos Aires: El Coloquio, 1969), pp. 216, 219–20.

Notes

Abbreviations

AGN	Archivo General de la Nación (Buenos Aires)
AHMT	Archivo Histórico Municipal de Tandil (Tandil)
AHPBA	Archivo Histórico de la Provincia de Buenos Aires "Ricardo Levene" (La Plata)
ASRA	*Anales de la Sociedad Rural Argentina* (Buenos Aires)
HAHR	*Hispanic American Historical Review*
Walker, ITDT	Instituto Torcuato Di Tella (Buenos Aires)

Introduction

1. Roberto Cortés Conde, *El progreso argentino, 1880–1914*, pp. 277–78; Buenos Aires Province, *Censo general de la provincia de Buenos Aires . . . 1881*, p. 491.

2. Ricardo Rodríguez Molas, "El gaucho y la modernización," *Polémica* 22 (Oct. 1970): 45; Benito Díaz, *Rosas, Buenos Aires y la organización nacional*, pp. 154, 264; Jonathan C. Brown, *A Socioeconomic History of Argentina, 1776–1860*, p. 163. This estimate of the gaucho population is based on an 1854 provincial census, which classified 40 percent of rural males as peons and 22 percent as "other." I classify the peons as gauchos and about half of the "others" as gauchos so that, with the number of men and women about equal, 25 percent of the total population of the countryside would be gauchos. Given the greater proportion of men in frontier regions and the undernumeration of migrants, this yields a conservative estimate of the gaucho population. See Appendix A for provincial population growth from 1778 to 1914.

3. E. Bradford Burns, *The Poverty of Progress*, pp. 22–23, 60–62, 94, 123, 146–47; Domingo Faustino Sarmiento, *Facundo*, translated as *Life in the Argentine Republic in the Days of the Tyrants*, pp. 1–72. On Argentine historiography, see Jorge A. Bossio, *Argentina: La historiografía en crisis*; Horacio Juan Cuccorese, *Historia crítica de la historiografía socioeconómica argentina del siglo XX*; Miguel Angel Scenna, *Los que escribieron nuestra historia*; and Héctor José Tanzi, *Historiografía argentina contemporánea*.

4. Compare my interpretation with Brown, *Socioeconomic History*, pp. 146–200. See my review of Brown in *The Times of the Americas*, Apr. 15, 1981, p. 11; see also reviews by Roger M. Haigh, *HAHR* 60 (Aug. 1980): 477–78, Vera Blinn Reber, *American Historical Review* 85 (Apr. 1980): 488–89, and Carl E. Solberg, *Agricultural History* 54 (Apr. 1980): 373–74.

5. My findings are consonant with those of Ricardo Rodríguez Molas, *Historia social del gaucho*; Miguel Angel Cárcano, *Evolución histórica del régimen de la tierra pública, 1810–1916*; Andrés M. Carretero, *Los Anchorena* and *La propiedad de la tierra en la época de Rosas*; Jacinto Oddone, *La burguesía terrateniente argentina*; James R. Scobie, *Revolution on the Pampas*; Carl E. Solberg, "Farm Workers and the Myth of Export-Led Development in Argentina," *The Americas* 31 (Oct. 1974): 121–38; Solberg, "Rural Unrest and Agrarian Policy in Argentina, 1912–1930," *Journal of Inter-American Studies and World Affairs* 13 (Jan. 1971): 18–52; John Lynch, *Argentine Dictator*, pp. 101–16; George Reid Andrews, *The Afro-Argentines of Buenos Aires, 1800–1900*; José P. Barrán and Benjamín Nahum, *Historia rural del Uruguay moderno*.

6. On Rosista or revisionist historiography, see Roberto Etchepareborda, *Rosas: Controvertida historiografía*; Tulio Halperín Donghi, *El revisionismo histórico argentino*; Clifton B. Kroeber, *Rosas y la revisión de la historia argentina*, trans. J. L. Muñoz Azpiri (Buenos Aires: Fondo Editor Argentino, 1964); Arturo Jauretche, *Política nacional y revisionismo histórico* (Buenos Aires: Peña and Lillo, 1974); José María Rosa, *Historia del revisionismo y otros ensayos* (Buenos Aires: Merlin, 1968).

Chapter 1

1. Federico Tobal, "Los libros populares de Eduardo Gutiérrez," 5 pts., *La nación*, Mar. 4, 1886; Ernesto Quesada, "El criollismo en la literatura argentina," *Estudios* 1:3 (1902): 258–59, 265; Emilio A. Criado, *El "Martín Fierro"*, pp. 14–15.

2. Vicente Rossi, *El gaucho*, pp. 20–21, 24–30; Pablo Blanco Acevedo, "El gaucho," *Revista del Instituto Histórico y Geográfico del Uruguay* 5 (Aug. 1927): 441–44; Aníbal Cardoso, "Los atribútos del gaucho colonial," *Boletín de la Junta de Historia y Numismática Americana* 5 (1928): 79–87.

3. Emilio Angel Coni, *El gaucho*, pp. 15, 56–57, 79; Martiniano Leguizamón, "La cuna del gaucho," *Boletín de la Junta de Historia y Numismática Americana* 7 (1930): 165; Arturo Costa Alvarez, *El castellano en la Argentina*, pp. 308–9; Manuel Gálvez, *La Argentina en nuestros libros*, pp. 37–38; see also Charles G. Lobb, "The Historical Geography of the Cattle Regions along Brazil's Southern Frontier," pp. 11–14.

4. Jorge Juan y Santacilia and Antonio de Ulloa, *Noticias secretas de América, siglo XVIII*, 2:247. Luis C. Pinto first pointed out this early use of the term in *Entre gauchos y gaúchos*, p. 156. Ricardo Rodríguez Molas, "Antigüedad y significado histórico de la palabra 'gaucho,' 1774–1805," *Boletín del Instituto de Historia Argentina "Dr. Emilio Ravignani"* 1 (Apr. 1956): 145.

5. Emeric Essex Vidal, *Picturesque Illustrations of Buenos Ayres and Montevideo*, p. 89.

6. Antonio Jorge Pérez Amuchástegui, *Mentadidades argentinas*, p. 221; Martiniano Leguizamón, *Recuerdos de la tierra*, p. 202.

7. Rodríguez Molas, "Antigüedad y significado," p. 145; Rómulo Muñiz, *El gaucho*, pp. 129–34; Madaline Wallis Nichols, *The Gaucho*, pp. 7–10.

8. Alonso Carrío de la Vandera [pseud. Concolorcorvo], *El lazarillo*, pp. 54–55, 142, 150, 154; Félix de Azara, *Descripción de los cuadrupedos de Paraguay*, 2 vols. (Madrid, 1802), 2:208; Azara, *Descripción e historia del Paraguay y del Río de la Plata*, 2:202; Nichols, *The Gaucho*, pp. 8–9.

9. Sergio Villalobos R., *Comercio y contrabando en el Río de la Plata y Chile, 1700–1811*; Nichols, *The Gaucho*, pp. 29–35; Jonathan C. Brown, *A Socioeconomic History of Argentina, 1776–1860*, pp. 9–10, 23–26, 31–32.

10. Cited in Tom B. Jones, *South America Rediscovered*, p. 78.

11. Pérez Amuchástegui, *Mentadidades*, pp. 221–26; Nichols, *The Gaucho*, pp. 54–57; Ricardo Rodríguez Molas, *Historia social del gaucho*, pp. 186–92, 196–201; George Reid Andrews, *The Afro-Argentines of Buenos Aires, 1800–1900*, pp. 124–25; Carlos Mario Storni, "Las disposiciones de los códigos rurales en materia laboral y sus raíces históricas," *Revista de historia del derecho* 7 (1973): 188.

12. Henry Marie Brackenridge, *Voyage to South America*, 1:304; Alexander Caldcleugh, *Travels in South America*, 1:144; J. A. B. Beaumont, *Travels in Buenos Ayres*, p. 60; S. Samuel Trifilo, "The Gaucho: Some Impressions by Early Nineteenth-Century English Travelers," *Mid-America* 40 (July 1958): 175; Luis. C. Pinto, *El gaucho y sus detractores*, pp. 125, 198–203.

13. Robert Proctor, *Narrative of a Journey Across the Cordillera of the Andes*, pp. 14–16; Edmond Temple, *Travels in Various Parts of Peru*, 1:60.

14. Report by Francis Baylies, July 24, 1832, doc. 70 in William R. Manning, ed., *Diplomatic Correspondence of the United States*, 1:130.

15. Charles Darwin, *Journal and Remarks, 1832–1836*, pp. 147, 197–98.

16. Newspaper found in Tribunales Comercio, Letter L, 1860–1868, legajo 171, Archivo General de la Nación (Buenos Aires, hereafter AGN).

17. James Peden to Secretary of State William L. Marcy, Nov. 23, 1855, in Manning, *Diplomatic Correspondence*, 1:581; Domingo F. Sarmiento, *Facundo*, translated as *Life in the Argentine Republic in the Days of the Tyrants*, pp. 1–72, 113–33; Lucas Ayarragaray, *La anarquía argentina y el caudillismo*, pp. 254–56.

18. Thomas Joseph Hutchinson, *Buenos Ayres and Argentine Gleanings*, p. 283 and *The Parana*, pp. 87–93.

19. Paul Groussac, *Popular Customs and Beliefs of the Argentine Provinces* (Chicago: Donohue, Henneberry, 1893), pp. 9–10; see also Nichols, *The Gaucho*, pp. 60–63; Fernando O. Assunção, *El gaucho*, pp. 365–66.

20. Frederick Mann Page, "Remarks on the Gaucho and His Dialect," *Modern Language Notes* 8 (Jan. 1893): 19, 21.

21. Leopoldo Lugones, *El payador*, pp. 52–56, 69, 71, 156; Juan José de Lezica, "Lo que dice un gaucho viejo," *Revista nacional* 31 (Mar. 1901): 293, 298; Groussac, *Popular Customs*, pp. 10–11; Criado, *El "Martín Fierro,"* pp. 14–17.

22. Francis Bond Head, *Rough Notes*, pp. 44–45; Adolfo Bioy Casares,

Memoria sobre la pampa y los gauchos, pp. 44–46; Nichols, *The Gaucho*, p. 17.

23. G. A. Cohen, *Karl Marx's Theory of History: A Defense* (Princeton: Princeton University Press, 1978), pp. 65, 68, 76.

24. Martínez Estrada, *Muerte*, 1:251; Walter Larden, *Estancia Life*, pp. 310–312; Nichols, *The Gaucho*, p. 17.

Chapter 2

1. Robert Bontine Cunninghame Graham, *Rodeo*, p. 65.

2. Thomas A. Turner, *Argentina and the Argentines: Notes and Impressions of a Five Years' Sojourn in the Argentine Republic, 1885–1890* (London: Swan Sonnenschein, 1892), p. 223.

3. Alonsio Carrío de la Vandera [Concolorcorvo], *El lazarillo*, p. 70; Anthony Zachariah Helms, *Travels from Buenos Ayres*, p. 10.

4. Robert Proctor, *Narrative of a Journey across the Cordillera of the Andes*, pp. 6, 7, 13; Rodríguez quoted in Antonio G. del Valle, *Recordando el pasado*, 1:39–40.

5. Francis Bond Head, *Rough Notes*, pp. 2–4; John Anthony King, *Twenty-four Years in the Argentine Republic*, pp. 433–434; Edmond Temple, *Travels in Various Parts of Peru*, 1:68.

6. William Henry Hudson, *Far Away and Long Ago*, p. 5; Jonathan C. Brown, *A Socioeconomic History of Argentina, 1776–1860*, p. 124.

7. On Luro, see Carlos Antonio Moncaut, *Pampas y estancias*, p. 83. Robert Elwes, *A Sketcher's Tour round the World*, pp. 111, 124–25.

8. George Catlin, *Last Rambles amongst the Indians of the Rocky Mountains and the Andes*, p. 263.

9. Elwes, *Sketcher's Tour*, p. 119; George Augustus Peabody, *South American Journals, 1858–1859*, p. 121.

10. William MacCann, *Two Thousand Miles' Ride through the Argentine Provinces*, 1:140; Carlos Walker Martínez, *Páginas de un viaje al través de la América del sur* (Santiago, Chile: Independiente, 1876), p. 114; Cunninghame Graham, *Rodeo*, pp. 70, 72.

11. Frederick Jackson Turner, "The Significance of the Frontier in American History," in *The Frontier in American History*, pp. 24, 30, 35, 37.

12. Emilio Daireaux, *Vida y costumbres en La Plata*, 2:197–202; Domingo F. Sarmiento, *Facundo*, translated as *Life in the Argentine Republic in the Days of the Tyrants*, pp. 1–37.

13. David M. Potter, *People of Plenty*, pp. 124, 155–65; Walter Prescott Webb, *The Great Frontier*, pp. 8–28.

14. Ezequiel Martínez Estrada, *X-Ray of the Pampa*, p. 68; Roberto Cortés

Conde, "The Different Role of the Frontier in Argentine History," pp. 5–11.

15. Both quoted in Potter, *People of Plenty*, pp. 79, 92.

16. Michael G. Mulhall and Edward T. Mulhall, *Handbook of the River Plate Republics*, pp. 104–5; Cunninghame Graham, *Rodeo*, pp. 65–66; quotation from Thomas Falkner, *A Description of Patagonia and the Adjoining Parts of South America*, p. 39.

17. Juan Agustín García, *La ciudad indiana*, pp. 67, 89–90; Alfredo J. Montoya, *Historia de los saladeros argentinos*, pp. 12–13, 37–38; Carrío de la Vandera, *El lazarillo*, pp. 55, 63–64; quotation from Helms, *Travels*, p. 9.

18. Félix de Azara, *Memoria sobre el estado rural del Río de la Plata y otros informes*, p. 5; Brackenridge, *Voyage*, 1:222, 286; Temple, *Travels*, 1:60–61.

19. Charles Darwin, *Journal and Remarks, 1832–1836*, p. 198; MacCann, *Two Thousand Miles' Ride*, 1:138–39; see also Richard Arthur Seymour, *Pioneering in the Pampas*, p. 26; Catlin, *Last Rambles*, pp. 256–57.

20. MacCann, *Two Thousand Miles' Ride*, 1:64; poem in Alvaro Yunque, "Estudio Preliminar," in Alvaro Barros, *Fronteras y territorios federales de las pampas del sur*, p. 12.

21. Alexander Caldcleugh, *Travels in South America*, 1:171–72.

22. Emeric Essex Vidal, *Picturesque Illustrations of Buenos Ayres and Montevideo*, p. 24; Joseph Andrews, *Journey from Buenos Ayres through the Provinces of Córdova, Tucumán and Salta, to Potosí*, 1:28.

23. William Henry Hudson, *The Naturalist in La Plata*, pp. 350–51; Ricardo Güiraldes, *Don Segundo Sombra*, p. 173.

24. Horacio Jorge Becco, ed., *Antología de la poesia gauchesca*, pp. 1657–58; Domingo F. Sarmiento, *El Chacho*, p. 71.

25. Elwes, *Sketcher's Tour*, p. 120.

26. Nathaniel Holmes Bishop, *The Pampas and the Andes*, pp. 79–80.

27. Thomas Woodbine Hinchliff, *South American Sketches*, p. 392.

28. Alfredo Ebelot, *Frontera sur*, pp. 138–39.

29. Wilfred Latham, *The States of the River Plate*, pp. 13, 14.

30. Quotation from Proctor, *Narrative*, p. 15; Ruben Franklin Mayer, *El país que se busca a si mismo*, pp. 169–71.

31. Robert M. Denhardt, *The Horse of the Americas*, pp. 251–62.

32. José Ortega y Gassett, "Intimidades," in *Obras completas*, 2:639.

Chapter 3

1. Azara and Lastarria cited in Juan Alvarez, *Las guerras civiles argentinas*, pp. 67–68; Emilio Daireaux, *Vida y costumbres en La Plata*, 2:213, 231.

2. John Lynch, *Argentine Dictator*, p. 253; Roberto Cortés Conde, *El progreso argentino, 1880–1914*, pp. 277–78. See Appendix B on the number of livestock in the province.

3. José María Jurado, "La estancia en Buenos Aires," *ASRA* 9:7 (1875): 220–21.

4. Godofredo Daireaux, *La cría del ganado en la estancia moderna*, pp. 387–88; Adrián Patroni, *Los trabajadores en la Argentina*, p. 138.

5. Florentino Ameghino, *Las secas y las inundaciones en la provincia de Buenos Aires*, 2d ed. (Buenos Aires: Lajouane, 1886), p. 98.

6. Argentine Republic, *Censo agropecuario nacional: la ganadería y la agricultura en 1908*, 1:376–77.

7. Reports by María Herrera de Peredo to Juan Manuel de Rosas, 1842–44, AGN X 26 4 2.

8. Damián Lan and Pedro Cruz Mendoza, "Apreciación del costo de la producción de carne," *Boletín del Ministerio de Agricultura* 15 (Jan. 1913): 131; "Diario," June 1900–, pp. 130–472, uncatalogued, records of the William Walker estancias, Instituto Torcuato Di Tella (Buenos Aires), hereafter Walker, ITDT.

9. Carlos Mario Storni, "Las disposiciones de los códigos rurales en materia laboral y sus raíces históricos," *Revista de historia del derecho* 7 (1973): 177–81; Alejandro Magariños Cervantes, *Estudios históricos, políticos y sociales sobre el Río de la Plata*, 1:300.

10. George Reid Andrews, *The Afro-Argentines of Buenos Aires, 1800–1900*, pp. 38, 48–49, 56–57, 62.

11. Jonathan C. Brown, "A Nineteenth-Century Cattle Empire," *Agricultural History* 52 (Jan. 1978): 168; Manuscript census summary, 1836, AGN X 25 2 5; Andrews, *Afro-Argentines*, pp. 56–57, 98. Arnold Strickon has asserted that slaves were not used as ranch workers; see Strickon, "The Euro-American Ranching Complex," in Anthony Leeds and Andrew P. Vayda, eds., *Man, Culture and Animals*, pp. 242–43.

12. Recopilación de leyes, justice of the peace of Lobos, Feb. 9, 1846, AGN X 17 7 4; Andrews, *Afro-Argentines*, p. 57.

13. John Lynch, *Argentine Dictator*, p. 150; Páez to Rosas, Dec. 17, 1842, and Schöo to Rosas, Dec. 15, 1842, AGN X 26 3 2.

14. Páez to Rosas, Jan. 2, 1843, and Apr. 13, 1843, AGN X 26 3 2.

15. Ramírez to Rosas, May 26, 1847, AGN X 26 5 4; Brown, "Nineteenth-Century Cattle Empire," p. 168; Schöo to Rosas, June 30, 1849, AGN X 26 8 3.

16. Walker, ITDT; Juan Bialet Masse, *El estado de las clases obreras*

argentinas a comienzos del siglo, pp. 119–23; Ricardo Rodríguez Molas, "El gaucho y la modernización," *Polémica* 22 (Oct. 1970): 45.

17. Emeric Essex Vidal, *Picturesque Illustrations of Buenos Ayres and Montevideo*, pp. 71–72; Wilfred Latham, *The States of the River Plate*, pp. 44–45; quotations from William Henry Hudson, *Far Away and Long Ago*, pp. 40–41. See Appendix C on changing livestock production.

18. Rosas to Ramírez, Mar. 18, July 21, 1846, AGN X 26 5 5; see Juan Manuel de Rosas, *Instrucciones a los mayordomos de estancias*.

19. Martiniano Leguizamón, *Recuerdos de la tierra*, p. 195; Vidal, *Picturesque Illustrations*, pp. 71–72; William MacCann, *Two Thousand Miles' Ride through the Argentine Provinces*, 1:24.

20. Hudson, *Far Away*, p. 10; see also Benjamín Vicuña MacKenna, *Páginas de mi diario durante tres años de viaje, 1853–1854–1855*, pp. 428–29; Noél H. Sbarra, *Historia del alambrado en la Argentina*, pp. 68–69; Octavio P. Alais, *Libro criollo*, pp. 83–85; José Hernández, *Instrucción del estanciero*, pp. 178–79.

21. Reports by Schöo, Mar.–Sept. 1846, AGN X 26 6 3; Apr.–June 1846, AGN X 26 8 3; see also Hernández, *Instrucción*, pp. 185–86; Alais, *Libro criollo*, pp. 30–33.

22. Report by Schöo, July 8, 1847, AGN X 26 6 3; Michael G. Mulhall and Edward T. Mulhall, *Handbook of the River Plate Republics*, pp. 108–9; Alais, *Libro criollo*, pp. 8–14; Carlos Antonio Moncaut, *Pampas y estancias*, pp. 53–56.

23. Francis Bond Head, *Rough Notes*, pp. 48, 53, 81–82; Charles Darwin, *Journal and Remarks, 1832–1836*, p. 111.

24. Schöo to Rosas, Oct. 15, 1842, AGN X 26 1 5; Ramírez to Rosas, July 18, 1846, AGN X 26 5 5.

25. MacDonald to Walker, Apr. 29, 1900, "25 de Mayo, Craig" records, Walker, ITDT; MacKitchie to Walker, Nov. 12, 1912, "500" records, p. 402, Walker, ITDT.

26. Diógenes Muñiz, Luis Ricardo Fors, and Agustín B. Gambier, eds., *La policía de la provincia de Buenos Aires*, p. 442.

27. Pedro Calderón to Rosas, May 1, July 16, 1849, AGN X 26 8 4; quotation from MacCann, *Two Thousand Miles' Ride*, 1:216.

28. José María Jurado, "La estancia en Buenos Aires," *ASRA* 9:7 (1875): 218; Ricardo Güiraldes, *Don Segundo Sombra*, pp. 43–66; Alais, *Libro criollo*, pp. 22–26; E. Daireaux, *Vida*, 2:231.

29. José Agustín de Basualdo, *El gaucho argentino*, pp. 125–27; Schöo to Rosas, Aug. 31, 1843, and report for June–Aug. 1843, AGN X 26 3 2.

30. Platon Alexandrovich Chikhachev, *A Trip across the Pampas of Buenos Aires, 1836–1837*, pp. 54–55; Schöo to Rosas, Dec. 1, 1843, AGN X 26 6 3; Alcides d' Orbigny, *Viaje a la América meridional realizado de 1826 a 1833*, 2:502–9.

31. Head, *Rough Notes*, p. 47; Nathaniel Holmes Bishop, *The Pampas and the Andes*, p. 92.

32. *La tribuna*, Apr. 19, 1855.

33. Richard Arthur Seymour, *Pioneering in the Pampas*, pp. 100–102; *Livestock Journal*, Dec. 28, 1878, repr. in *El Plata industrial y agrícola* 2 (Mar. 10, 1879): 49.

34. Carlos Lemée, *El domador*, pp. 9–31, 229–56; see also Alais, *Libro criollo*, pp. 34–38.

35. Carlos Lemée, *El estanciero*, pp. 272–309; Walter Larden, *Estancia Life*, pp. 81–82.

36. Sansón Carrasco, "Una hierra," *ASRA* 30 (Mar. 31, 1895): 71–72.

37. Hernández, *Instrucción*, pp. 366–74; E. Daireaux, *Vida*, 2:231–32.

38. Hernández, *Instrucción*, p. 359.

39. Godofredo Daireaux, *La cría del ganado en la estancia moderna*, pp. 90–91.

40. Schöo to Rosas, June 30, 1849, AGN X 26 8 4; "Cuentas corrientes," vol. 2, pp. 29–30, 33, Walker, ITDT.

41. A. R. Fernández, *Prontuario informativo de la provincia de Buenos Aires*, vol. 2 (Buenos Aires: Campañía Sud-Americana de Billetes de Banco, 1903), pp. 37–38.

42. Patroni, *Los trabajadores*, pp. 138–40; Juan M. Pisano, "El proletariado rural," p. 190. See also Juan Bialet Masse, *Informe sobre el estado de las clases obreras en el interior de la República*, vol. 1.

43. Pedro Bergés, "Industria lechera—la mano de obra del ordeñe, modo de abaratarla y formularla," *ASRA* 46 (Mar. 1912): 136–37; Benito Lynch, *El estanciero* (Buenos Aires: Rosso, 1933), p. 16; Luis C. Pinto, *El gaucho y sus detractores*, p. 24; David E. López, "Cowboy Strikes and Unions," *Labor History* 18 (Summer 1977): 328–29.

44. Ricardo Rodríguez Molas, *Historia social del gaucho*, pp. 490–91; José V. Liceaga, *Las carnes en la economia argentina*, p. 26 gives meat prices; wages are in Roberto Cortés Conde, "Tendencias en la evolución de los salarios reales en Argentina, 1880–1910: Resultados preliminares," working paper 74, Centro de Investigaciones Económicas, Instituto Torcuato Di Tella (Buenos Aires, 1975), p. 20.

45. Carmen Llorens de Azar and Elena Kachanovsky, "Precios unitarios de

artículos de consumo y servicios, capital federal y provincias, 1901–1963," pt. 1; working paper 12, Centro de Investigaciones Económicas, Instituto Torcuato Di Tella (Buenos Aires, 1965), pp. 66–92.

46. Gordon Ross, *Argentina and Uruguay* (London: Methuen, 1917), pp. 14–15; Muñiz et al., *La policía*, pp. 307, 320, 324.

47. Hobart A. Spalding, Jr., comp., *La clase trabajadora argentina*, p. 19.

48. Sebastián Marotta, *El movimiento sindical argentino*, 1:282; *La vanguardia*, Dec. 19, 1906.

49. López, "Cowboy Strikes," pp. 330–336; Dardo Cuneo, "Las dos corrientes del movimiento obrero en el 90," *Revista de historia* 7:1 (1957): 72; Jorge N. Solomonoff, *Ideologías del movimiento obrero y conflicto social*, pp. 170–71; Jorge Abelardo Ramos, *Revolución y contrarevolución en la Argentina: del patriciado a la oligarquía, 1862–1904*, 5th rev. ed. (Buenos Aires: Plus Ultra, 1973), pp. 280–86.

50. *El obrero*, Feb. 7, 1894, p. 4. For a sympathetic overview of FORA, see Diego Abad de Santillán, *La FORA*, pp. 41–240; *La vanguardia*, Aug. 3, 1895, p. 3, and Nov. 11, 1906, p. 1. See reprints from *La agricultura* on the plight of native workers in the interior provinces in *La vanguardia*, Feb. 1, Feb. 8, Aug. 1, 1896; Feb. 17, May 26, Dec. 1, 1900; Jan. 15, May 1, May 12, July 11, July 12, Sept. 14, Sept. 21, Dec. 19, 1906. See Richard J. Walter, "The Socialist Press in Turn-of-the-Century Argentina," *The Americas* 37 (July 1980): 8–19, 23–24, for a commentary on labor newspapers.

51. James R. Scobie, *Revolution on the Pampas*, pp. 61–67.

52. *La vanguardia*, Dec. 23, 1906, p. 1; Rodolfo Puiggrós, *El Yrigoyenismo* (Buenos Aires: Jorge Alvarez, 1965), pp. 124–25, 128–29.

53. *La vanguardia*, Feb. 21, 1910, p. 2.

54. Richard J. Walter, *The Socialist Party of Argentina, 1890–1930*, p. 230; *La vanguardia*, Sept. 8, 1910, p. 1; quotations from *La vanguardia*, Oct. 8, 1910, p. 1.

55. Nicolás Repetto, *Mí paso por la política*, 1:41; Walter, *Socialist Party*, pp. 53, 55, 70, 132; Carl E. Solberg, *Immigration and Nationalism*, p. 156; Lauzet quoted in Marotta, *El movimiento*, 2:43.

56. Argentine Republic, *Tercer censo nacional . . . de 1914*, 4:215–16; *La organización*, Oct. 22, 1902. For a slightly different version of the congress, see Marotta, *El movimiento*, 1:139–40. On the sheep shearers' strike in Patagonia, see Osvaldo Bayer, *La Patagonia rebelde* (Mexico City: Nueva Imagen, 1980).

57. *ASRA* 39 (Feb. 20, 1904): 34–35; *La agricultura* 12 (Dec. 29, 1904): 549, and 12 (Mar. 3, 1904): 27.

58. *La agricultura* 13 (Feb. 23, 1905): 127, and 13 (Apr. 13, 1905): 205; *El eco de Tandil*, Oct. 12, Nov. 9, 1905. *La semana rural* treats the question of labor unrest frequently from 1905 to 1907.

59. *La vanguardia*, July 17, 31, 1912; Plácido Grela, *El grito de Alcorta*, p. 343; Walter, *Socialist Party*, pp. 127–28; Juan B. Justo, "La cuestión agraria," in *Discursos y escritos políticos*, pp. 140, 155.

60. *Giornale La vanguardia*, quoted in July 31, Oct. 24, 1912; see also Walter, *Socialist Party*, p. 129.

61. Sociedad Rural Argentina, *Tiempos de epopeya, 1866–1966*, p. 96.

Chapter 4

1. Félix de Azara, *Descripción e historia del Paraguay y del Río de la Plata*, 2:200; Francis Bond Head, *Rough Notes*, p. 24; Samuel Greene Arnold, *Viaje por América del sur, 1847–1848*, p. 203.

2. Alexander Caldcleugh, *Travels in South America*, 1:251; Robert Proctor, *Narrative of a Journey across the Cordillera of the Andes*, pp. 16–17; see also Frederick Gerstaecker, *Narrative of a Journey round the World*, pp. 56–57; Arnold, *Viaje*, p. 200. Madaline Wallis Nichols accepts the negative impressions of pampean women as accurate; see *The Gaucho*, p. 13.

3. Pellegrini quoted in *Revista del Plata* 2 (Sept. 1854): 218; Miguel A. Lima, *El hacendado del porvenir*, p. 163; Julio Mafud, *Psicología de la viveza criolla*, pp. 46–47.

4. Sosa testimony in Buenos Aires Province, *Antecedentes y fundamentos del proyecto de código rural*, pp. 28–29, 191; Ramírez to Rosas, Nov. 8, 1844, AGN X 43 2 8; Ramírez to Rosas, May 6, 1846; Rosas to Ramírez, July 21, 1846, AGN X 26 5 5.

5. Xavier Marmier, *Buenos Aires y Montevideo en 1850*, p. 75; *La Patria* (Olavarría), Apr. 11, 1897, p. 1; Daniel Granada, *Reseña histórico-descriptiva de antiguas y modernas supersticiones del Río de la Plata*, p. 80.

6. Emilio Daireaux, *Vida y costumbres en La Plata*, 2:233; Nicanor Magnanini, *El gaucho "surero" de la provincia de Buenos Aires*, pp. 139–40, 166, 169–71.

7. John Mawe, *Travels in the Interior of Brazil*, p. 47. The nature of land tenure on the pampa is discussed in Chapter 6.

8. Census (*padrón*), Tandil, 1862, Archivo Histórico Municipal de Tandil (hereafter AHMT); John Lynch, *Argentine Dictator* (p. 103), quotes Charles Mansfield that, in Corrientes province, "about one woman in fifty of the poor is married."

9. Caldcleugh, *Travels*, 1:251; Hugo Miatello, *El hogar agrícola*, p. 27;

Benoit Ferry and Susheela Singh, "Breast-Feeding: A Vital Factor in Birth Intervals," *People* (International Planned Parenthood Federation) 7:4 (1980): 19–20. Data based on A. K. Jain and J. Bongaarts, "Socio-biological Factors in Exposure to Child-Bearing: Breast-Feeding and Its Fertility Effects," paper presented to the World Fertility Survey Conference, London, July 1980.

10. Argentine Republic, *Tercer censo . . . de 1914*, 4:77, 81; O. Andrew Collver, *Birth Rates in Latin America: New Estimates of Historical Trends and Fluctuations* (Berkeley: International Population and Urban Research Center, 1965), pp. 26–27; Carlos P. Salas, *Elementos para un estudio de la demografía de la provincia de Buenos Aires*, p. 8; George Reid Andrews, *The Afro-Argentines of Buenos Aires, 1800–1900*, p. 72.

11. Buenos Aires Province, *Anuario estadístico, 1896*, pt. 1, pp. 67, 75, 83; Carlos P. Salas, *Elementos para un estudio de la demografía de la provincia de Buenos Aires*, pp. 47–49; Argentine Republic, *La población y el movimiento demográfico de la República Argentina en el período 1910–1925*, p. 76.

12. Bird to Walker, Sept. 10, 1896, copiador de cartas, no. 1, 1896–1898, Walker, ITDT; Salas, *Elementos*, pp. 47–48.

13. Head, *Rough Notes*, pp. 19–21; Martiniano Leguizamón, *Recuerdos de la tierra*, pp. 91–98; William Henry Hudson, *Far Away and Long Ago*, pp. 5–9, 45–63, 77; see also Robert Elwes, *A Sketcher's Tour round the World*, p. 130; Benjamín Vicuña MacKenna, *Páginas de mi diario durante tres años de viaje, 1853–1854–1855*, p. 469.

14. Lina Beck-Bernard, *Cinco años en la Confederación Argentina, 1857–1862*, pp. 172–73, 262–66; Martiniano Leguizamón, "Nueva noticia del gaucho," *Boletín de la Junta de Historia y Numismática Americana* 9 (1936): 165.

15. Accounts by Juan José Becán, Dec. 1838, AGN X 25 6 6, and Jan. 1840, AGN X 25 8 3; Reports by Dionisio Schöo, Dec. 5, 1845, AGN X 26 5 5, and July 8, 1847, AGN X 26 6 3.

16. Carlos Antonio Moncaut, *Pampas y estancias*, pp. 181–82.

17. Richard Arthur Seymour, *Pioneering in the Pampas*, p. 145.

18. Accounts for Rosas' estancias, AGN X 43 2 8, and AGN X 26 6 3; Office of Labor circular, 1872, AHMT.

19. Argentine Republic, second national census, 1895, MS returns, bk. 841, AGN; quotation in *La vanguardia*, Oct. 1, 1898, p. 1.

20. Henri Armaignac, *Viajes por las pampas argentinas*, p. 155; Herrera de Pinedo-Rosas correspondence, 1841–1842, AGN X 26 1 5; Argentine Republic, second national census, 1895, MS returns, bk. 842, no. 1152, and bk. 843, no. 1165, AGN.

21. Ezequiel Martínez Estrada, *X-Ray of the Pampa*, p. 29; Leopoldo Lugones, *El payador*, p. 57.

22. E. F. Sánchez Zinny, *Integración del folklore argentino*, p. 103.

23. Domingo F. Sarmiento, *Obras de D. F. Sarmiento*, vol. 38: *Conflictos y armonias de las razas en América*, p. 168; William MacCann, *Two Thousand Miles' Ride through the Argentine Provinces*, 2:20; Ann M. Pescatello, *Power and Pawn*, p. 163.

24. Alfredo Ebelot, *Frontera sur*, pp. 157–60; see also Manuel Prado, *La guerra al malón*, p. 60; Argentine Republic, first national census, 1869, MS returns, bk. 73, AGN.

25. Letter of Oct. 24, 1862, to justice of the peace of Tandil, 1862, AHMT; Pescatello, *Power and Pawn*, p. 164.

26. Edward Larocque Tinker, *The Horsemen of the Americas and the Literature They Inspired*, pp. 27–28; report by Francis Baylies in William R. Manning, ed., *Diplomatic Correspondence of the United States*, 1:133; MacCann, *Two Thousand Miles' Ride*, 1:86.

27. Municipality of Tandil, *Memoria . . . de 1875 y 1876*, p. ix; *Memoria . . . de 1886*, p. 11; Argentine Republic, second national census, 1895, MS returns, bk. 841, AGN.

28. Police reports, 1900, AHMT; quotation in *El eco de Tandil*, Mar. 19, 1905.

29. Angel Héctor Azeves, *Ayacucho*, pp. 199, 212–15; Oscar Ricardo Melli, *Historia de Carmen de Areco, 1771–1970* (La Plata: Archivo Histórico de la Provincia de Buenos Aires "Ricardo Levene," 1974), pp. 278, 280, 287; Pescatello, *Power and Pawn*, p. 165; Beck-Bernard, *Cinco años*, pp. 136–37; Pedro Inchauspe, *Reivindicación del gaucho*, p. 174; Argentine Republic, first national census, 1869, MS returns, bks. 49, 113, 123, AGN.

30. Justice of the peace of San Andrés de Giles, 1877, 56 3 1, Archivo Histórico de la Provincia de Buenos Aires "Ricardo Levene" (La Plata), hereafter AHPBA; *El oeste*, cited in Melli, *Historia*, p. 282; *La patria* (Olavarría), Feb. 9, 16, 1899.

31. Buenos Aires Province, *Anuario estadístico, 1896*, pt. 2, p. 66; *El orden* (Mercedes), Jan. 29, Mar. 10, Apr. 17, 25, 30, Sept. 14, 16, 17, 1909; *La patria* (Olavarría), Feb. 26, 27, 1909.

Chapter 5

1. Emeric Essex Vidal, *Picturesque Illustrations of Buenos Aires and Montevideo*, p. 71; Carlos Antonio Moncaut, *Estancias bonaerenses*, pp. 41–52; Yuyú Guzmán, *Estancias de Azul*, "Loma Pampa" sect., unpag.

2. Mario A. López Osornio, *Viviendas en la pampa*, pp. 33–35, 41, 49–66, 79; quotations from John Miers, *Travels in Chile and La Plata*, 1:14–15.

3. Robert Proctor, *Narrative of a Journey across the Cordillera of the Andes*, p. 24; William Henry Hudson, *Far Away and Long Ago*, pp. 22–23; see also Samuel Haigh, *Bosquejos de Buenos Aires, Chile y Perú*, pp. 46, 53.

4. Charles Darwin, *Journal and Remarks, 1832–1836*, p. 149; William Hadfield, *Brazil, the River Plate, and the Falkland Islands*, p. 321; Virginia Carreño, *Estancias y estancieros*, pp. 113–14, 117; Hudson, *Far Away*, p. 288; Schöo to Rosas, Aug. 31, Oct. 15, 1842, AGN X 26 1 5.

5. Hudson, *Far Away*, p. 110; see also Inventory, AGN X 27 1 5.

6. William MacCann, *Two Thousand Miles' Ride through the Argentine Provinces*, 1:30–32, 43–45, 78; George A. Peabody, *South American Journals, 1858–1859*, p. 122.

7. Guzmán, *Estancias*, "Santa Catalina" sect., unpag.

8. Michael G. Mulhall and Edward T. Mulhall, *Handbook of the River Plate Republics*, p. 109; J. V. Lastarria, "La Pampa: Fragmentos," *ASRA* 3 (Mar. 31, 1868): 79; Argentine Republic, *Primer censo de la República Argentina, 1869*, p. 89; Buenos Aires Province, *Censo agrícolo-pecuario de la provincia . . . de 1888*, pp. 243, 297; Argentine Republic, *Segundo censo de la República Argentina, mayo de 1895*, 3:27.

9. Carlos Lemée, *El paisano*, p. 97; Juan B. Justo, *El programa socialista del campo*, pp. 8–9.

10. Juan A. Alsina, *El obrero en la República Argentina*, p. 222; Buenos Aires Province, *Diario de Sesiones, 1914*, p. 466; Hugo Miatello, *El hogar agrícola*, pp. 5, 8–11, 27.

11. Frederick Gerstaecker, *Gerstaecker's Travels*, p. 35; Woodbine Parish, *Buenos Ayres, and the Provinces of Rio de la Plata*, p. 338; see also Ricardo Rodríguez Molas, *Historia social del gaucho*, pp. 150–52, 156.

12. Xavier Marmier, *Buenos Aires y Montevideo en 1850*, pp. 25–26; Charles B. Mansfield, *Paraguay, Brazil, and the Plate*, p. 128.

13. Peabody, *South American Journals*, p. 125; Godofredo Daireaux, *Costumbres criollos*, pp. 146–50.

14. Ezequiel Martínez Estrada, *X-Ray of the Pampa*, pp. 52–53, Domingo F. Sarmiento, *Facundo*, translated as *Life in the Argentine Republic in the Days of the Tyrants*, pp. 49–50.

15. MacCann, *Two Thousand Miles' Ride*, 1:47; on the autochthonous origin of the boot, see Luis C. Pinto, "La bota de potro: Un auténtico calzado rioplatense," *Boletín del Instituto Bonaerense de Numismática y Antigüedades*

9 (1961): 19; Gutiérrez, Fernández Blanco, and Gainza cited in Buenos Aires Province, *Antecedentes y fundamentos del proyecto de código rural*, pp. 31, 176, 202.

16. Frederick Gerstaecker, *Narrative of a Journey round the World*, pp. 54–55; Henri Armaignac, *Viajes por las pampas argentinas*, pp. 57, 59–60.

17. Francisco Bauzá, *Estudios literarios* (Montevideo: Librería Nacional, 1885), pp. 249–50; Sarmiento quoted in John Lynch, *Argentine Dictator*, p. 322; Octavio P. Alais, *Libro criollo*, pp. 86–88; Federico Rahola y Tremols, *Sangre nueva: Impresiones de un viaje a la América del sud* (Buenos Aires: Institución Cultural Española, 1943), p. 67; Daniel Granada, *Reseña histórico-descriptiva de antiguas y modernas supersticiones del Río de la Plata*, p. 79; Rodríguez Molas, *Historia social*, pp. 478–80.

18. Rodríguez Molas, *Historia social*, pp. 142–45.

19. Félix Coluccio, *Diccionario folklórico argentino*, 1:64, 275; 2:306–7.

20. Vidal, *Picturesque Illustrations*, pp. 68–69; Alexander Caldcleugh, *Travels in South America during the Years 1819–20–21*, 1:152; MacCann, *Two Thousand Miles' Ride*, 1:24; Juan Fugl, *Abriendo surcos*, pp. 47–48.

21. Jean León Pallière, *Diario de viaje por la América del sud*, p. 105; Gerstaecker, *Travels*, p. 69; Burmeister, *Viaje*, 1:125–26. Samuel Greene Arnold, *Viaje por América del sur, 1847–1848*, pp. 173–75.

22. Edwin Clark, *A Visit to South America* (London: Dean and Son, 1878), p. 153; Lemée, *El paisano*, pp. 42–43; Godofredo Daireaux, *La cría del ganado en la estancia moderna*, p. 96.

23. MacCann, *Two Thousand Miles' Ride*, 1:24; Haigh, *Bosquejos*, p. 41; see also Granada, *Reseña*, pp. 219–34; Amaro Villanueva, *El mate*, pp. 31–34.

24. Poem quoted in Eduardo Jorge Bosco, *El gaucho a través de los testimonios extranjeros, 1773–1870*, p. 74.

25. Carlos Pellegrini, "Mate," *Revista del Plata* 1 (Dec. 1853): 54–55; Armaignac, *Viajes*, pp. 41–42.

26. *ASRA* (1879): 148; Julio Lesage, "Efectos fisiológicos del mate," *ASRA* 41:11–12 (1908): 96–99.

27. G. Daireaux, *La cría*, pp. 95–96; Coni quoted in Luis C. Pinto, *El gaucho y sus detractores*, p. 27; Julio Díaz Usandivaras, *"La nacionalidad y el mate,"* *Nativa* 2 (May 31, 1925), n.p.

28. Martiniano Leguizamón, *Recuerdos de la tierra*, pp. 41–48; Coluccio, *Diccionario*, 1:151–52; 2:312–13, 499–501; Félix Coluccio, *Fiestas y costumbres de América* (Buenos Aires: Poseidón, 1954), pp. 61–73.

29. J. A. B. Beaumont, *Travels in Buenos Ayres*, pp. 202–3; see also Coluccio, *Fiestas*, pp. 111–12.

30. Alfredo Ebelot, *La pampa*, pp. 13–16; Armaignac, *Viajes*, p. 141; Coluccio, *Fiestas*, p. 112; Augusto Raúl Cortazar, *Folklore argentino*, pp. 199–238; Pedro N. Sarciat, *El pago de Chapaleofú hasta la fundación del pueblo de Rauch por Don Francisco M. Letamendi* (Buenos Aires: Julio Suárez, 1945), p. 209.

31. Robert B. Cunninghame Graham, *The Ipané*, p. 42; Rodríguez Molas, *Historia social*, p. 477.

32. Alonso Carrío de la Vandera [Concolorcorvo], *El lazarillo*, pp. 55, 69, 142; Proctor, *Narrative*, p. 11.

33. José Hernández, *La vuelta de Martín Fierro* (Buenos Aires, 1879), pt. 7; Rafael Obligado, *Santos Vega*, in Horacio J. Becco, ed., *Antología de la poesia gauchesca*, pp. 1661–74; Coluccio, *Diccionario*, 2:356–61; Sarmiento, *Facundo*, translated as *Life in the Argentine Republic*, pp. 41–45.

34. J. A. Hammerton, *The Argentine through English Eyes and a Summer in Uruguay* (London: Hodder and Stoughton, n.d.), p. 250.

35. José María Salaverría, *Vida de Martín Fierro*, pp. 178–79; Stephen Paullada, *Rawhide and Song*, pp. 164–68; quotation from Sarmiento, *Facundo*, translated as *Life in the Argentine Republic*, p. 44; see also Marcelino M. Román, *Itinerario del payador* (Buenos Aires: Lautaro, 1957), pp. 121, 143–48, 160–61.

36. Coluccio, *Diccionario*, 1:182; 2:367, 502; Alais, *Libro criollo*, pp. 123–24; song verses from Paullada, *Rawhide and Song*, pp. 55–56, 154–61.

37. Frederick Mann Page, "Remarks on the Gaucho and His Dialect," *Modern Language Notes* 8 (Jan. 1893): 21–22; MacCann, *Two Thousand Miles' Ride*, 1:47; see also Eduardo Acevedo, "El sentimiento de lo cómico en el carácter argentino," *Revista de filosofía* 1 (Nov. 1915): 452; Elbio Bernárdez Jacques, *Muestrario gaucho* (Buenos Aires: Ciordia y Rodríguez, 1953), p. 10.

38. *El hurón*, Apr. 21, 1867, p. 3; Jorge Páez, *Del truquiflor a la rayuela*, pp. 42–46.

39. Azara cited in Granada, *Reseña*, p. 272; Juldain cited in Nueva Era, *Bodas de oro, 1919–1969* (Tandil: Nueva Era, 1969), unpag.; see also Walter Larden, *Estancia Life*, p. 91; Alais, *Libro criollo*, pp. 102–3; Páez, *Del truquiflor*, pp. 40–42.

40. MacCann, *Two Thousand Miles' Ride*, 1:47; Coluccio, *Diccionario*, 2:472–73; Páez, *Del truquiflor*, pp. 35–40.

41. Eduardo Augusto Hopkins, *Memoria acompañando un proyecto de ley*, p. 109; Oliver Aquíleo González, "El juego y sus modalidades," *Revista de policía* 1 (Aug. 1900): 49–52; anonymous, "Leyes contra el cuatrerismo," *Revista de policía* 2 (May 1900): 375–76.

42. Alais, *Libro criollo*, pp. 98–101; Correspondence, 1900, AHMT;

Osvaldo L. Fontana, "La primera aldea," in *Tandil en la historia*, unpag.

43. Wilfred Latham, *The States of the River Plate*, pp. 56–59; Thomas Joseph Hutchinson, *The Paraná*, pp. 97–100; Robert Elwes, *A Sketcher's Tour round the World*, p. 109; Thomas Joseph Hutchinson, *Buenos Ayres and Argentine Gleanings*, pp. 51–52.

44. Peabody, *South American Journals, 1858–1859*, p. 128; Thomas A. Turner, *Argentina and the Argentines: Notes and Impressions of a Five Years' Sojourn in the Argentine Republic, 1885–1890* (London: Swan Sonnenschein, 1892), pp. 201–2.

45. William Henry Hudson, *Tales of the Pampa*, pp. 245–53; poem from Becco, *Antología*, p. 1652; Páez, *Del truquiflor*, pp. 26–27.

46. Darwin, *Journal*, p. 51; George Catlin, *Last Rambles amongst the Indians of the Rocky Mountains and the Andes*, p. 265; MacCann, *Two Thousand Miles' Ride*, 1:164.

47. Rosas to Ramírez, Sept. 20, 1844, AGN X 43 2 8; Alfredo J. Montoya, *Historia de los saladeros argentinos*, pp. 45–46; Lynch, *Argentine Dictator*, pp. 25, 43, 45, 125, 154.

48. Policía 1852, AHMT; Buenos Aires Province, *Registro oficial*, 1853, pp. 70–71; *La tribuna*, Aug. 19, 20, 1853; articles 259–65 of the provincial rural code in Aurelio Prado y Rojas, comp., *Leyes y decretos promulgados en la provincia de Buenos Aires desde 1810 a 1876*, 6:538–39.

49. Buenos Aires Province, *Memoria*, 1871–1872, pp. 703–4; Emilio Daireaux, *Vida y costumbres en La Plata*, 2:230–31.

50. *ASRA* 16 (July 1882): 133–34; Ernesto Raúl Hernández, *Recopilación de leyes agrarias vinculadas a la ganadería*, pp. 65–66.

51. *El orden*, Jan. 6, 1909; *El municipio* (Buenos Aires), Sept. 8, 19, 1909.

52. *La patria* (Olavarría), June 29, 1899, and Feb. 15, July 2, 1900; *La patria* (Dolores), Feb. 16, 1900, p. 2.

Chapter 6

1. Alfredo J. Montoya, *La ganadería y la industria de salazón de carnes en el período 1810–1862*, pp. 31–32.

2. Juan Agustín García, *La ciudad indiana*, pp. 20, 23, 48; Sagastí quoted in Montoya, *La ganadería*, pp. 49–50.

3. Montoya, *La ganadería*, pp. 49–50; Rómulo Muñiz, *El gaucho*, pp. 73–81.

4. Emilio A. Coni, *La verdad sobre la enfiteusis de Rivadavia*, pp. 6–7, 67–69; Gallardo quoted in Montoya, *La ganadería*, pp. 25–26, 34–35; John Lynch, *Argentine Dictator*, pp. 21, 56.

5. Samuel Schneider, *Proyección histórico del gaucho*, pp. 31, 95–96;

Luis C. Despontín, *El derecho de trabajo*, p. 356; Ricardo Rodríguez Molas, *Historia social del gaucho*, p. 315; Andrés M. Carretero, *La propiedad de la tierra en la época de Rosas*, pp. 45–47.

6. Milciades Peña, *El paraíso terrateniente: Federales y unitarios forjan la civilización de cuero*, 3d. ed. (Buenos Aires: Fichas, 1975), p. 59; Juan José Sebreli, *Apogeo y ocaso de los Anchorena*, pp. 190, 194; Rodolfo Puiggrós, *El Yrigoyenismo* (Buenos Aires: Jorge Alvarez, 1965), pp. 89–90; José P. Barrán and Benjamín Nahum, *Historia rural de Uruguay moderno*, 3:197.

7. Agüero quoted in Montoya, *La ganadería*, pp. 9–10; Sebreli, *Apogeo*, p. 200; Diana Hernando, "Casa y familia," pp. 21–22; Susan Migden Socolow, *The Merchants of Buenos Aires, 1778–1810*, p. 177; Lynch, *Argentine Dictator*, pp. 43–45.

8. Horacio Juan Cuccorese, "Historia sobre los orígenes de la Sociedad Rural Argentina," *Humanidades* 35 (1960): 23, 29–32; Alfredo Estévez, "La contribución directa, 1821–1852," *Revista de ciencias económicas* 48 (Apr. 1960): 182–83; Montoya, *La ganadería*, pp. 11–12; Lynch, *Argentine Dictator*, p. 56.

9. Tulio Halperín Donghi, "La expansión ganadera en la campaña de Buenos Aires, 1810–1852," *Desarrollo económico* 3 (Apr. 1963): 69, 71, 75, 91; Coni, *La verdad*, pp. 67–69; Carretero, *La Propiedad*, pp. 13–14; Miron Burgin, *The Economic Aspects of Argentine Federalism, 1820–1852*, pp. 249, 255; quotation from Domingo F. Sarmiento, *Inmigración y colonización*, vol. 23 of *Obras*, p. 292; Lynch, *Argentine Dictator*, p. 74.

10. Quotation from Lynch, *Argentine Dictator*, p. 98; Emilio Delpech, *Una vida en la gran Argentina*, pp. 154–58; Andrés M. Carretero, *Los Anchorena*, pp. 167–68, 187–88; Jonathan C. Brown, "A Nineteenth–Century Cattle Empire," *Agricultural History* 52 (Jan. 1978): 164 (Rosas data compiled by Eduardo Sagier), and *A Socioeconomic History of Argentina, 1776–1860*, pp. 149–50, 153, 179, 200; Vela data in Contribución directa, 1843, cuarteles 5, 6, AHMT (document erroneously filed in legajo for 1893).

11. Quotation from Enrique M. Barba, "Rosas y Buenos Aires," *Todo es historia* 10 (Mar. 1977): 9; see also Carretero, *Los Anchorena*, p. 11; Sebreli, *Apogeo*, p. 205; Juan Carlos Vedoya, "Tierras sin dueños," *Todo es historia* 8 (Dec. 1974): 82–83, 88–89.

12. Lynch, *Argentine Dictator*, pp. 68–69; Contribución directa, 1846, AGN X 26 5 4; Estévez, "La contribución directa," pp. 123–234; Carretero, *La propiedad*, p. 14.

13. Buenos Aires Province, *Registro estadístico*, 1854, pt. 2, table 10; Brown, *Socioeconomic History*, p. 152.

14. Alfredo Ebelot, *Frontera sur*, p. 163; Miguel Angel Cárcano, *Evolución histórico del régimen de la tierra pública, 1810–1916*, pp. 111–34, 147–63, 181–83, 247–64; Fernando E. Barba, *Los autonomistas del 70*, pp. 35–51; Manuel Bejarano, "Inmigración y estructuras tradicionales en Buenos Aires, 1854–1930," in Torcuato S. Di Tella and Tulio Halperín Donghi, comps., *Los fragmentos del poder*, pp. 84–86.

15. *Revista del Plata* 2 (1854): 313; Machado quoted in María Ines Cárdenas de Monner Sans, *Martín Fierro y la conciencia nacional*, pp. 87–88.

16. Nicolás Avellaneda, *Estudio sobre las leyes de tierras públicas*, pp. 146–47; Cárcano, *Evolución*, p. 163; Sarmiento letter, May 20, 1866, *Cartas de Sarmiento a la Señora María Mann*, p. 145.

17. *ASRA* 1 (Sept. 1866): 8.

18. Henri Armaignac, *Viajes por las pampas argentinas*, p. 78; Oscar Ricardo Melli, *Guardia Nacional: Orígenes del partido y ciudad de Chacabuco, 1865–1890* (La Plata: Archivo Histórico de la Provincia de Buenos Aires "Ricardo Levene," 1967), p. 191; Buenos Aires Province, *Contribución directa . . . de 1863*, pp. 128–29; Contribución directa, no. 39, 1872, pink file, AHMT; Hernando, "Casa y familia," p. 43.

19. *La tribuna*, Aug. 11, 16, 17, 1854, (all) p. 2; Cuccorese, "Historia sobre," pp. 36–40.

20. Cuccorese, "Historia sobre," pp. 42–47.

21. *ASRA* 9 (Sept. 30, 1875): 338–39; Barrán and Nahum, *Historia rural*, 3:192, 199.

22. Horacio Juan Cuccorese, "La conservación de carnes en la Argentina," *Trabajos y comunicaciones* 14 (1965): 84, 87, 93–95. For a general history of the Rural Society, see *ASRA* 75 (July 1941): 531–90.

23. Walter Larden, *Estancia Life*, pp. 42–43.

24. *La aspiración*, Aug. 12, 13, 1876; Carlos D'Amico, *Siete años en el gobierno de la provincia de Buenos Aires*, pp. 83–85.

25. *ASRA* 16 (May 1882): 94; Ezequiel Gallo and Roberto Cortés Conde, *Argentina*, pp. 55–56, 101–3.

26. *Revista de ganadería* 4 (June 8, 1882): 716; *El eco de Tandil*, Dec. 31, 1882.

27. Godofredo Huss, "Breve reseña de la legislación agraria argentina," report to Minister of Agriculture Victorino de la Plaza, n. d., Archivo Victorino de la Plaza, bk. 1, p. 5, AGN VII 4 6 1; Cárcano, *Evolución*, p. 181; quotations from Federico Tobal, "Los libros populares de Eduardo Gutiérrez," *La nación*, Feb. 16, Mar. 2, 1886.

28. Bejarano, "Inmigración," pp. 106–11; Carlos D. Girola, *Investiga-*

ción agrícola en la República Argentina, p. 258; *La agricultura* 3 (Sept. 12, 1895): 704–6, and 3 (Oct. 24, 1895): 820.

29. *La patria* (Dolores), Mar. 29, 1900, p. 2; *La agricultura* 11 (Apr. 11, 1903): 272, and 11 (Sept. 3, 1903): 623.

30. *La agricultura* 12 (Apr. 28, 1904): 173.

31. Ibid., Aug. 26, 1904: 478–79; Girola, *Investigación*, p. 264.

32. Martínez cited in *La unión* (Lomas de Zamora), Oct. 27, 1905, p. 1; Walker letter of Nov. 12, 1904, Copiador, letters of 1904–1905, p. 156, Walker, ITDT.

33. *La prensa* (Buenos Aires), May 25, 1910, p. 30; Argentine Republic, *Tercer censo nacional . . . de 1914*, 5:751, and 6:577, 679.

34. Cárcano, *Evolución*, pp. 385, 388–89; Oscar E. Cornblit, Ezequiel Gallo, and Alfredo A. O'Connell, "La generación del ochenta y su proyecto: Antecedentes y consequencias," in Torcuato S. Di Tella, Gino Germani, and Jorge Graciarena, eds., *Argentina: Sociedad de masas* (Buenos Aires: EUDEBA, 1965), p. 20.

35. Poem from José Hernández, *The Gaucho Martín Fierro*, trans. Ward, p. 163, lines 2113–18; see also Cárcano, *Evolución*, p. 516; Carl E. Solberg, "Farm Workers and the Myth of Export-Led Development in Argentina," *The Americas* 31 (Oct. 1974): 121–23, 136.

Chapter 7

1. Austin T. Turk, *Criminality and Legal Order*, pp. 25, 31–32; William J. Chambliss, "Functional and Conflict Theories of Crime," in Chambliss and Milton Mankoff, eds., *Whose Law? What Order? A Conflict Approach to Criminality*, pp. 4, 7–9.

2. Turk, *Criminality*, pp. xii–xiii, 9–10; Johan Thorsten Sellin, *Culture Conflict and Crime: A Report to the Subcommittee on Delinquency of the Committee on Personality and Culture* (New York: Social Science Research Council, 1938), p. 66; Rolf Dahrendorf, "Out of Utopia: Toward a Reconstruction of Sociological Analysis," *American Journal of Sociology* 64 (Sept. 1958): 115–27; Richard Quinney, "Crime Control in Capitalist Society," in Ian P. Taylor, Paul Walton, and Jock Young, eds., *Critical Criminology*, p. 192; Richard Quinney, *The Social Reality of Crime*, pp. 15–16, 21.

3. Douglas Hay, "Property, Authority and the Criminal Law," in Hay et al., *Albion's Fatal Tree*, p. 19; Edward P. Thompson, *Whigs and Hunters*, pp. 197, 262; Sellin, *Culture Conflict*, p. 22.

4. E. Bradford Burns, *The Poverty of Progress*, pp. 5–17, 60–62; Stanley

Diamond, "The Rule of Law versus the Order of Custom," *Social Research* 38 (Spring 1971): 47–48; Madaline Wallis Nichols, *The Gaucho*, pp. 8–10, 22–35; Ricardo Rodríguez Molas, *Historia social del gaucho*, pp. 60–69.

5. On rural labor conditions and debt peonage elsewhere, see the dialogue between Arnold J. Bauer, "Rural Workers in Spanish America," *HAHR* 59 (Feb. 1979): 34–78, also Brian Loveman, "Critique of Arnold J. Bauer's 'Rural Workers in Spanish America,' " and Bauer's "Reply," *HAHR* 59 (Aug. 1979): 478–85, 486–89; William Chambliss, "A Sociological Analysis of the Law of Vagrancy," *Social Problems* 12 (Summer 1964): 67–77.

6. Ricardo Rodríguez Molas, "Realidad social del gaucho rioplatense, 1653–1852," *Universidad* 55 (Jan. 1963): 105–6; Gastón Gori, *Vagos y mal entretenidos*, pp. 10–12; I. A. A. Thompson, "A Map of Crime in Sixteenth-Century Spain," *Economic History Review* 21 (Aug. 1968): 249; Norman F. Martin, *Los vagabundos en la Nueva España, siglo XVI* (Mexico City: Jus, 1957), pp. xiii–xxi, 167.

7. Jonathan C. Brown, *A Socioeconomic History of Argentina, 1776–1860*, p. 161; Rodríguez Molas, "Realidad social," pp. 117–18, and *Historia social*, pp. 114–16, 171; Carlos M. Storni, "Acerca de la 'papeleta' y los juzgados de paz de la campaña bonaerense," *Revista del Instituto de Historia del Derecho "Ricardo Levene"* 20 (1969): 153; Juan Agustín García, *La ciudad indiana*, pp. 182–83.

8. Storni, "Acerca de la 'papeleta,' " pp. 154–55; Rodríguez Molas, "Realidad social," p. 129. "Papeleta" usually referred to a military enrollment form (army or, more commonly, national guard), but it also meant working paper in some archival documents.

9. Benito Díaz, *Juzgados de paz de la campaña de la provincia de Buenos Aires, 1821–1854*, pp. 104–5, 202–3; Buenos Aires Province, *Registro oficial*, 1822, pp. 69, 170, 277; *Registro oficial*, 1823, pp. 63, 77; *Registro oficial*, 1824, p. 81.

10. Díaz, *Juzgados de paz*, p. 24; Gori, *Vagos*, pp. 25, 37; José León Pagano, *Criminalidad argentina*, pp. 119–24; John Lynch, *Argentine Dictator*, pp. 25, 125, 154; see the passport issued to Ramón Leat, Oct. 20, 1849, Policía 1849, AGN X 26 8 3; report by justice of the peace of Las Flores, Dec. 31, 1851, AGN X 21 2 4. Rosas' decree of Oct. 6, 1831, required both a passport and an enrollment form. See also Alfredo J. Montoya, *Historia de los saladeros argentinos*, pp. 45–46, 57, 60; Rodríguez Molas, *Historia social*, pp. 229–34.

11. Clasificaciones 1851, AGN X 43 2 7. This legajo holds numerous cases of sentences adjusted to age; see also Lynch, *Argentine Dictator*, pp. 169–71, 211–13, 298–99.

12. Solano Rocha case in letter from Díaz to Rosas, July 28, 1839, AGN X 25 6 6; Clasificación de Bartolo Díaz, Apr. 1, 1846, AGN X 21 1 1.

13. Buenos Aires Province, *Registro oficial,* 1852, pp. 10–11, 181–82; *Registro oficial,* 1853, pp. 73–74. On Urquiza's economic interests as rancher and saladerista, see Saladero, "Once de setiembre," 1859–1860, sección mercantil, vols. 360–68, AGN VII; and Manuel Macchi, *Urquiza: El saladerista* (Buenos Aires, 1971).

14. Ruíz to Minister of War Yreneo Portela, Nov. 12, 1853, AGN X 18 9 1; Gainza cited in Buenos Aires Province, *Antecedentes y fundamentos del proyecto de código rural,* p. 201.

15. Letters from justice of the peace of Matanza, July 9, 1855, Oct. 18, 1855, AGN X 19 3 6; Buenos Aires Province, *Antecedentes,* p. 189; law quoted from Buenos Aires Province, *Diario de sesiones,* 1858, "Proyectos," pp. 22–23.

16. Marcos Estrada, "Antecedentes para la historia del desarrollo agrícola y ganadero argentino," *ASRA* 98 (Sept. 1964): 52; Carlos M. Storni, "Las disposiciones de los códigos rurales en materia laboral y sus raíces históricas," *Revista de historia del derecho* 7 (1973): 193–95; María Teresa Villafañe Casal, "Antecedentes del código rural de la provincia de Buenos Aires," *Comunicaciones: Serie campaña Bonaerense,* 1:6.

17. Donna J. Guy, "The Rural Working Class in Nineteenth-Century Argentina," *Latin American Research Review* 13:1 (1978): 138–39; rural code reprinted in Ernesto Raúl Hernández, *Recopilación de leyes agrarias vinculadas a la ganadería,* pp. 8–45.

18. Storni, "Acerca de la 'papeleta,' " pp. 158–59; Luis A. Despontín, *El derecho de trabajo,* p. 356; legal brief, July 31, 1869, doc. 118, bk. 423, AGN X 34 8 3.

19. *La voz de Saladillo,* Jan. 26, 1873, p. 1, and Feb. 23, 1873, p. 1; see also Mar. 9, Mar. 16, 1873; *El centinela del norte,* Mar. 19, 1873, pp. 2–3; *ASRA* 13 (June 1879): 210–11; José María Jurado, "La estancia en Buenos Aires," *ASRA* 9:2 (1875): 37; legal briefs, 1880, AHMT. See Lynch, *Argentine Dictator,* p. 32, on rural-urban elite cooperation.

20. Storni, "Acerca de la 'papeleta,' " p. 161.

21. Alberto A. Durañona, *Indice general de leyes, decretos y resoluciones desde el año 1810 a 1920,* 1:211; Francis Bond Head, *Rough Notes,* p. 300; Alcides d'Orbigny, *Viaje a la América meridional realizado de 1826 a 1833,* 2:520–21.

22. Gómez and Pereyra cases in legal briefs, AGN X 21 2 4, and X 21 1 1; Policía 1851, AHMT; Osvaldo L. Fontana, "La primera aldea," in *Tandil en la*

historia, unpag.; quotation from John Anthony King, *Twenty-four Years in the Argentine Republic*, p. 325.

23. John S. Pendleton to Daniel Webster, Sept. 23, 1852, in William R. Manning, ed., *Diplomatic Correspondence of the United States*, 1:534; Thomas Woodbine Hinchliff, *South American Sketches*, pp. 89, 195.

24. Quotations from Robert Crawford, *Across the Pampas and the Andes*, pp. 115–16; Carlos D'Amico, *Siete años en el gobierno de la provincia de Buenos Aires*, p. 99; *El eco de Tandil*, July 23, 1886.

25. Borges to Gainza, Junín, Nov. 3, 1872, doc. 6340, legajo 43, Documentos del Museo Histórico Nacional, AGN; Richard Arthur Seymour, *Pioneering in the Pampas*, pp. 52–53, 74–75, 150.

26. Alexander Caldcleugh, *Travels in South America during the Years 1819–20–21*, 1:179–180; Ezequiel Martínez Estrada, *X-Ray of the Pampa*, pp. 52–53; d'Orbigny, *Viaje*, 2:497–98; Robert Proctor, *Narrative of a Journey across the Cordillera of the Andes*, p. 16.

27. Domingo F. Sarmiento, *Facundo*, translated as *Life in the Argentine Republic during the Days of the Tyrants*, pp. 39–41, 49–50; Eric J. Hobsbawm, *Bandits*, p. 17. For folkloric sources of social banditry on the pampa, see José Hernández, *Martín Fierro* (Buenos Aires, 1872) and *La vuelta de Martín Fierro* (Buenos Aires, 1979), and Eduardo Gutiérrez, *Juan Moreira* (Buenos Aires, 1880).

28. Arthur E. Shaw, *Forty Years in the Argentine Republic*, p. 225; Policía 1852, and Policía 1862, AHMT: Juez de Crímen 1872, 38 4 313, AHPBA; Diógenes Muñiz, Luis Ricardo For, and Agustín B. Gambier, eds., *La policía de la provincia de Buenos Aires*, p. 421.

29. Silvio R. Duncan Baretta and John Markoff, "Civilization and Barbarism," *Comparative Studies in Society and History* 20 (Oct. 1978): 606; Federico Oberti, "La propiedad privada y el gaucho," *Historia* 3 (Apr. 1958): 140; see also Pagano, *Criminalidad argentina*, pp. 15–28, 81–87; Rodríguez Molas, *Historia social*, pp. 48–52, 487–504; Horacio C. E. Giberti, *Historia económica de la ganadería argentina*, pp. 172–90; Burns, *The Poverty of Progress*, pp. 60–62, 147.

30. García to O'Gorman, July 18, 1871, bk. 475, AGN X 34 11 5; *ASRA* 7 (Sept. 30, 1873): 289–90, 307–13, also 257–59, 335–43, 353–62.

31. Justice of the peace of Ensenada, 1875, 9 4 19, 684, AHPBA; *Revista de ganadería* 2 (May 5, 1880): 275, also 2 (Oct. 28, 1880): 382; Fernando O. Assunção, *El gaucho*, p. 182; Rodríguez Molas, *Historia social*, pp. 465–67.

32. Marion M. Mulhall, *Between the Amazon and the Andes*, pp. 26–27.

33. *ASRA* 7 (Sept. 30, 1873): 307–13, and 16 (Aug. 1882): 182; *La patria*

(Dolores), Mar. 1, 1900, p. 2; Mar. 18, 1900, p. 2; Apr. 14, 1909, p. 1; Chambliss, "Functional and Conflict Theories," p. 7. On the fencing of illicit goods, see Richard W. Slatta, "Pulperías and Contraband Capitalism in Nineteenth-Century Buenos Aires Province," *The Americas* 38 (Jan. 1982): 347–62.

34. Muñiz, *La policía de la provincia,* following p. 98.

35. *Boletín de la Liga Agraria de la Provincia de Buenos Aires* 2:15 (1898): 323–25, and 3:12 (1899): 375–76.

36. *Revista de policía* 2 (Dec. 1901): 183–89; Pagano, *Criminalidad argentina,* pp. 257–72.

37. Buenos Aires Province, *Registro oficial,* 1854, pp. 107–11; *Registro oficial,* 1857, pp. 71–72; *Registro oficial,* 1884, p. 874; Díaz, *Juzgados de paz,* pp. 23, 95, 146; Carlos Tejedor, *Manual de jueces de paz en las demandas civiles y asuntos administrativos.*

38. Baylies in Manning, *Diplomatic Correspondence,* 1:135; Charles Darwin, *Journal and Remarks, 1832–1836,* pp. 198–99; Xavier Marmier, *Buenos Aires y Montevideo en 1850,* p. 61; Lynch, *Argentine Dictator,* pp. 116–17.

39. Ortubia quoted in Juez de Crímen 1872, 38 4 314, AHPBA; Gori, *Vagos,* pp. 62–63.

40. Fernando E. Barba, *Los autonomistas del 70,* pp. 15–16, 60–61; Ataúlfo Pérez Aznar, "La política traditional y la Argentina moderna," *Revista de la universidad* 20–21 (Jan. 1966–July 1967): 213–14.

41. Machado quotation from *El eco de Tandil,* June 16, 1886, p. 1 (emphasis added); Sarmiento quoted in María Ines Cárdenas de Monner Sans, *Martín Fierro y la conciencia nacional,* p. 13; see also Díaz, *Juzgados de paz,* pp. 163–78.

42. Hobsbawm, *Bandits,* pp. 33, 35–36.

43. Marcos A. Herrera, "Martín Fierro y la ley penal," *Universidad* 86 (Jan. 1977): 97–98; Hay, "Property, Authority," pp. 13–14.

Chapter 8

1. José Hernández, *The Gaucho Martín Fierro: Adapted from the Spanish,* p. 72.

2. Ricardo Levene, *A History of Argentina,* p. 393; Hernández, *The Gaucho Martín Fierro: Adapted from the Spanish,* p. 87; see also Ataúlfo Pérez Aznar, "La política traditional y la Argentina moderna," *Revista de la universidad* 20–21 (Jan. 1966–July 1967): 207–8, and Fernando O. Assunção, *El gaucho,* p. 183.

3. Esteban Echeverría, *Dogma socialista y otras páginas políticas*, p. 53; William Henry Hudson, *Tales of the Pampa*, p. 247; Walter Larden, *Estancia Life*, p. 302; see also José Luis Romero, *A History of Argentine Political Thought*, pp. 67, 101.

4. Ricardo Rodríguez Molas, *Historia social del gaucho*, pp. 186–88; Alcides d'Orbigny, *Viaje a la América meridional realizado de 1826 a 1833*, 2: 496, 520–21; quotation from Benito Díaz, *Juzgados de paz de la campaña de la provincia de Buenos Aires, 1821–1854*, pp. 120–23.

5. John Lynch, *Argentine Dictator*, pp. 194–95; Pedro Inchauspe, *Reivindicación del gaucho*, p. 27; Peter Campbell Scarlett, *South America and the Pacific*, 1:272; Páez to Rosas, July 8, 1839, AGN X 25 6 6; Páez to Rosas, Dec. 18, 1839, Feb. 6, 1840, AGN X 25 7 1; Paéz quotation from Páez to Rosas, Sept. 8, 1841, AGN X 26 2 4; Haedo quoted in Alfredo J. Montoya, *La ganadería y la industria de salazón de carnes en el periódo 1810–1862*, p. 45.

6. Morton cited in Carlos Antonio Moncaut, *Pampas y estancias*, pp. 199–200; William MacCann, *Two Thousand Miles' Ride through the Argentine Provinces*, 1:144–45; Rosas quoted in Osvaldo L. Fontana, "La primera aldea," in *Tandil en la historia*, unpag.; Augusto G. Rodríguez, *Reseña histórica del Ejército Argentino, 1862–1930*, p. 38; Alberto A. Durañona, ed., *Indice general de leyes, decretos y resoluciones desde el año 1810 a 1920*, 1:375–77.

7. *La tribuna*, Oct. 1, 1853, p. 1; Fontana, "La primera aldea," unpag.; justice of the peace 1852, AHMT: María Ines Cárdenas de Monner Sans, *Martín Fierro y la conciencia nacional*, p. 67.

8. Document 997, AGN X 19 3 6; *La tribuna*, July 27, 1854, p. 3; May 16, 1854, p. 4; May 21, 1854, p. 4.

9. *El industrial*, Jan. 23, 1856; *La tribuna*, Aug. 24, 1854, p. 2; military rosters, Sept. 2, 1855, Fuerte Argentina, AGN X 19 3 3.

10. Military census, Mar. 4, 1855; report by Minister of War Manuel de Escalada, AGN X 19 3 6; Peden to Secretary of State William L. Marcy, Mar. 26, 1856, doc. 276 in William R. Manning, ed., *Diplomatic Correspondence of the United States*, 1:586; William Hadfield, *Brazil, the River Plate, and the Falkland Islands*, p. 324.

11. Alfred J. Tapson, "Indian Warfare on the Pampas during the Colonial Period," *HAHR* 42 (Feb. 1962): 5–7, 12–13. On changing frontier lines, see maps in Martín Suárez, *Atlas histórico militar argentino* (Buenos Aires: Círculo Militar, 1974), p. 322; and Jonathan C. Brown, *A Socioeconomic History of Argentina, 1776–1860*, p. 126.

12. MacCann, *Two Thousand Miles' Ride*, 1:165; Juan Fugl, *Abriendo*

surcos, pp. 75–77; population figures from Daniel E. Pérez, *Los italianos en Tandil: Centenario de la Sociedad Italiana de Socorros Mutuos* (Tandil: Sociedad Italiana de Socorros Mutuos, 1977), pp. 37–39. Raids described in *La reforma pacífica,* Apr. 13–14, 1857, pp. 2–3, and Apr. 15, 25, 1857.

13. Viera petition of Mar. 17, 1852, AGN X 27 1 5; Del Campillo to Urquiza, Dec. 30, 1855, cited in James R. Scobie, *La lucha por la consolidación de la nacionalidad argentina, 1852–1862,* p. 155.

14. Quotations from Pendleton to Webster, Sept. 23, 1852, doc. 246, in Manning, *Diplomatic Correspondence,* 1:534; Mitre to Obligado, June 2, 1855, cited in José Arena, Julio H. Cortés, and Alberto Valverde, *Ensayo histórico del partido de Olavarría,* pp. 251, 256, 259.

15. *La tribuna,* Apr. 18, 1855, pp. 1–2.

16. Cárdenas de Monner Sans, *Martín Fierro,* p. 69.

17. Viliarino and Dillon cited in Buenos Aires Province, *Antecedentes y fundamentos del proyecto de código rural,* pp. 144–45, 247; *La reforma pacífica,* Dec. 8, 1857, p. 1; Alsina to Mitre, Sept. 24, 1859, quoted in Cárdenas de Monner Sans, *Martín Fierro,* p. 40.

18. Angel Héctor Azeves, *Ayacucho,* p. 19; Enrique Bourges, Pablo Constantini, and Fernando Suárez, ''Polémica pública sobre la guerra del Paraguay,'' *Documentos de Polémica* 22 (Feb. 1973): 167–69, 181; Henri Armaignac, *Viajes por las pampas argentinas,* pp. 194–95.

19. María Teresa Villafañe Casal, ''La guerra del Paraguay,'' *Comunicaciones: Serie campaña bonaerense,* 2:5; Buenos Aires Province, *Memoria,* 1867, 2:156.

20. Avellaneda quoted in Buenos Aires Province, *Memoria,* 1867, pp. lxxxvi, 34–35; Olivera quoted in Emilio Frers, *Cuestiones agrarias y económicas,* 2:22–23; Molina quoted in Sociedad Rural Argentina, *Tiempos de epopeya, 1866–1966,* pp. 62–63; *ASRA* 1 (Jan. 31, 1867): 139.

21. Barros to Gainza, Feb. 23, 1869, Documentos del Museo Histórico Nacional, doc. 4085, leg. 34, AGN; Campos to Victoria, May 27, 1879, AGN X 43 6 10; Argentine Republic, first national census, 1869, MS returns, bk. 73, AGN.

22. Rivas quoted in Cárdenas de Monner Sans, *Martín Fierro,* pp. 89–90; Alvaro Barros, *Fronteras y territorios de las pampas del sur,* p. 107; poem from Hernández, *The Gaucho Martín Fierro: Adapted from the Spanish,* p. 40.

23. Gainza letter quoted in *ASRA* 4 (Feb. 28, 1870): 37–38; Barros, *Fronteras,* pp. 104, 107, 115–19, 121.

24. *El Río de la Plata,* Aug. 19, 22, 1869, repr. in Antonio Páges Larraya, *Prosas de Martín Fierro,* pp. 197–200, 206–8; Rómulo Muñiz, *El gaucho,* p. 97.

25. Jurado speech in Buenos Aires Province, *Diario de sesiones,* 1872, p. 420; Rural Society to Emilio Castro, Oct. 14, 1871, quoted in Estanislao S. Zeballos, *La conquista de quince mil leguas,* pp. 281–86.

26. *La redención,* May 4, 1873, pp. 27–29; *El progreso de Flores,* June 15, 29, 1873; *El progreso de Quilmes,* July 6, 20, Aug. 10, 31, 1873.

27. Manuel Prado, *La guerra al malón,* pp. 45–46, 54, 79–81; Robert Crawford, *Across the Pampas and the Andes,* pp. 120–21.

28. Alfredo Ebelot, *Frontera sur,* pp. 102–4, 133–37.

29. Juan Carlos Walther, La conquista del desierto, pp. 384, 415; Estanislao S. Zeballos, *Callvucurá y la dinastía de los piedra,* pp. 166–67; Antonio G. del Valle, *Recordando el pasado,* 1:303; quotation from *El fraile,* Oct. 5, 1876.

30. Sociedad Rural Argentina, *Tiempos,* pp. 44–45; Alfred Hasbrouck, "The Conquest of the Desert," *HAHR,* 15 (May 1935): 225–26; Zeballos, *La conquista,* pp. 279–80; see also Richard Owen Perry, "The Argentine Frontier."

31. *La campaña,* Apr. 25, 29, 1883.

32. Oscar Ricardo Melli, *Guardia nacional: Orígenes del partido y ciudad de Chacabuco, 1865–1890* (La Plata: Archivo Histórico de la Provincia de Buenos Aires "Ricardo Levene," 1967), p. 223; Carlos D'Amico, *Siete años en el gobierno de la provincia de Buenos Aires,* p. 91; quotation from telegram, García to Gainza, June 13, 1880, Documentos del Museo Histórico Nacional, doc. 9257, leg. 55, AGN; see also doc. 9229.

33. Rodríguez, *Reseña histórica,* pp. 31, 72, 75, 94.

34. *La opinión pública,* Feb. 11, 1888; Rodríguez Molas, *Historia social,* pp. 468–69.

35. *La vanguardia,* July 9, 1898; *La patria,* Sept. 17, 1899; *La palabra libre,* Dec. 9, 1900.

36. Carl E. Solberg, *Immigration and Nationalism,* p. 144; *La vanguardia,* Jan. 17–18, 1910.

37. Juan Zorilla de San Martín, "A trabajar en paz," in *Conferencias y discursos* (Montevideo: Ministerio de Instrucción Pública y Previsión Social, 1965), 2:19.

Chapter 9

1. *ASRA* "Numero especial en español" (1910): 163.

2. *ASRA* 9:6 (1875): 185; Gordon Ross, *Argentina and Uruguay* (London: Methuen, 1917), pp. 266–67, 270; Jonathan C. Brown, *A Socioeconomic History of Argentina, 1776–1860,* p. 79.

3. Carlos Lemée, *La agricultura y la ganadería en la República Argentina*, p. 342.

4. John Lynch, *Argentine Dictator*, pp. 25, 74–75; Juan José Becán to Rosas, Jan. 5, 1839, AGN X 25 6 6; Schöo to Rosas, Jan. 19, 1849, AGN X 26 8 3.

5. Alfredo J. Montoya, *La ganadería y la industria de salazón de carnes en el período 1810–1862*, pp. 110–17, 125; Ricardo M. Ortíz, *Historia económica de la Argentina*, p. 94.

6. Lemée, *La agricultura*, p. 347; Justo Maeso quoted in Montoya, *La ganadería*, pp. 14–15; Brown, *Socioeconomic History*, pp. 138–40; Registro de marcas, no. 15, 1852, Ganado 1852, AHMT.

7. Emilio Delpech, *Una vida en la gran Argentina*, pp. 82–84; see also José Pedro Barrán, *Historia uruguaya*, 4:110–11; José Panettieri, *La crisis ganadera*.

8. Montoya, *La ganadería*, p. 125; Ortíz, *Historia*, p. 94; Estanislao S. Zeballos, *Descripcioñ amena de la República Argentina*, 3:323–29; Raymond H. Pulley, "The Railroad and Argentine National Development, 1852–1914," *The Americas* 23 (July 1966): 69.

9. Argentine Republic, *Segundo censo de la República Argentina, mayo de 1895*, 3:215; on sheep breeds, see Herbert Gibson, "Nuestras razas ovinas," *Revista de ganadería, veterinaria y agricultura* 5 (Mar. 1907): 129–50; and John Hannah, *Sheep-Husbandry in Buenos Ayres*.

10. Carlos Antonio Moncaut, *Pampas y estancias*, pp. 175–82; Octavio P. Alais, *Libro criollo*, pp. 15–21, 125–26.

11. Accounts kept by Juan José Becán, Dec. 1838, AGN X 25 6 6; May 1840, AGN X 25 8 3; Dionisio Schöo, Dec. 5, 1845, AGN X 26 5 5; July 8, 1847, AGN X 26 6 3; Wilfred Latham, *The States of the River Plate*, p. 32; Miguel A. Lima, *El estanciero práctico*, p. 128.

12. José P. Barrán and Benjamín Nahum, *Historia rural del Uruguay moderno*, 3:220–22; Ricardo Rodríguez Molas, "El gaucho y la modernización," *Polémica* 22 (Oct. 1970): 50; Bird to Walker, Nov. 12, 1904, Copiador de cartas, 1904–1905, p. 156, Walker, ITDT.

13. Barrán, *Historia uruguaya*, 4:75; Barrán and Nahum, *Historia rural*, 3:192, 199.

14. Thomas Joseph Hutchinson, *The Paraná*, p. 121; Rodríguez Molas, "El gaucho," p. 50; Argentine Republic, first national census, 1869, MS returns, bks. 48–49, AGN; Latham, *States of the River Plate*, p. 27; Zeballos, *Descripción*, 3:309.

15. *La prensa* (Buenos Aires), Jan. 16, 1891, p. 4; *La patria*, Apr. 11, 1897, p. 1.

16. *La agricultura* 1 (Mar. 9, 1893): 96; 1 (June 1, 1893): 269; 1 (Sept. 28, 1893): 518–20; Pedro A..Vinent, "Las máquinas de esquilar," *ASRA* 29 (Nov. 1894): 260–63; see also *ASRA* 29 (Oct. 1894): 233–39.

17. Barrán and Nahum, *Historia rural,* 3:220–22.

18. MacKitchie to Walker, Oct. 20, 1912, Estancia "500," pp. 387–88, Walker, ITDT.

19. Brown, *Socioeconomic History,* pp. 133, 135.

20. Horacio C. E. Giberti, *Historia económica de la ganadería argentina,* pp. 116, 154; Sarmiento quoted in Sociedad Rural Argentina, *Tiempos de epopeya, 1866–1966,* p. 34; see also Prudencio de la Cruz Mendoza, *Historia de la ganadería argentina,* pp. 162–68. Brown incorrectly gives 1864 as the date of first fencing, *Socioeconomic History,* p. 135.

21. Noél H. Sbarra, "Historia de un pionero," *Boletín de la Academia Nacional de Historia* 35 (1964): 362, 369; Giberti, *Historia económica,* p. 154.

22. Thomas Woodbine Hinchliff, *South American Sketches,* p. 103; Buenos Aires Province, *Diario de sesiones,* 1872, pp. 357–58; Raúl Jacob, *Consequencias sociales de alambramiento, 1872–1880,* p. 43.

23. Jacob, *Consequencias,* p. 47; Noél H. Sbarra, *Historia del alambrado en la Argentina,* pp. 114, 117; *Revista de ganadería Huss y Cía.,* 2 (May 25, 1880): 284–85; *ASRA* 11 (Mar. 1881): 61; quotation from Lemée, *La agricultura,* p. 351.

24. *La prensa* (Buenos Aires), Jan. 1, 1894; see also E. Bradford Burns, *The Poverty of Progress,* pp. 8–12.

25. *La vanguardia,* May 5, 1894; Edmundo Wernicke, *Memorias de un portón de estancia y otros relatos camperos: Amena historia de la vida rural argentina en el siglo XIX* (Buenos Aires: Kraft, 1946), pp. 52–53, 115, 182.

26. Sbarra, *Historia del alambrado,* pp. 111–15, and *Historia de las aguadas y el molino,* pp. 36–41, 45–46, 157–68.

27. Juan Agustín García, *La ciudad indiana,* pp. 17, 50, 61; Ricardo Rodríguez Molas, *Historia social del gaucho,* p. 169; James R. Scobie, *Revolution on the Pampas,* pp. 9–13, 115; José Luis Romero, *A History of Argentine Political Thought,* pp. 26, 43–44; quotation from Brown, *Socioeconomic History,* p. 141.

28. Schöo to Rosas, Sept. 1, 1845, AGN X 43 2 8, and June 7, 1847, AGN X 26 6 3. Also Miron Burgin, *The Economic Aspects of Argentine Federalism, 1820–1852,* p. 24.

29. Rosas to Peredo, July 14, 1836, AGN X 25 2 5; Apr. 30, 1838, AGN X 25 5 4.

30. Juan Fugl, *Abriendo surcos,* pp. 48–51, 57, 59–60.

31. Justice of the peace of Azul, Dec. 5, 1855, 9 4 7, AHPBA; Brown,

Socioeconomic History, pp. 130, 132, 236; Buenos Aires Province, *Registro estadístico*, 1856, pt. 2, table following p. 72.

32. Lemée, *La agricultura*, p. 109; Domingo F. Sarmiento, *Discursos populares*, vol. 21 of *Obras de D. F. Sarmiento*, p. 246.

33. Scobie, *Revolution*, pp. 53–54, 58–61.

34. Guillermo Wilcken, *Las colonias: Informe sobre el estado actual de las colonias agrícolas de la república presentado a la Comisión Central de Inmigración* (Buenos Aires: Tipos á Vapor de la Sociedad Anónima, 1873), pp. 253–54; *El economista* 1 (May 1, 1877): 194.

35. Argentine Republic, *Memoria*, 1879, pp. xxxiv–xxxv; Alexis Peyret, *Une visite aux colonies de la République argentine*, pp. 323–27; Manuel Bejarano, "Inmigración y estructuras tradicionales en Buenos Aires, 1854–1930," in Torcuato S. Di Tella and Tulio Halperín Donghi, comps., *Los fragmentos del poder*, pp. 106–7, 111.

36. Ezequiel Gallo, "Ocupación de tierras y colonización agrícola en Santa Fe, 1870–1895," working paper 64, Centro de Estudios Sociales, Instituto Torcuato Di Tella, pp. 12–14; Rolf Sternberg, "Farms and Farmers in an Estanciero World, 1856–1914," p. 366.

37. Ricardo Napp, et al., *La République argentine*, pp. 440, 487–95; Sternberg, "Farms and Farmers," p. 368; Peyret, *Une visite*, pp. 317–36; see also William Perkins, *The Colonies of Santa Fe;* Roberto Schopflocher, *Historia de la colonización agrícola en Argentina*, pp. 32–79.

38. Contract, doc. 2809, Documentos del Museo Histórico Nacional, leg. 24, AGN.

39. Buenos Aires Province, *Registro estadístico*, 1854, pt. 2, table 10; Horacio C. E. Giberti, *El desarrollo agrario argentino*, p. 21; Scobie, *Revolution*, pp. 58–60.

40. Gibson quoted in Carl E. Solberg, "Rural Unrest and Agrarian Policy in Argentina, 1912–1930," *Journal of Inter-American Studies and World Affairs* 13 (Jan. 1971): 20–22; Pablo Guglieri, *Las memorias de un hombre de campo*, pp. 60–61; Edwards to Sánchez Calc, June 17, 1915, maroon folder, Walker, ITDT.

41. Godofredo Daireaux, "Estancias in Argentina," in *Censo agropecuario nacional . . . 1908*, 3:15.

42. *El obrero*, Dec. 5, 1891, p. 3.

43. ASRA "Numero especial en español" (1910): 132–33; Argentine Republic, *Censo agropecuario nacional . . . 1908*, 2:385.

44. Angel Héctor Azeves, *Ayacucho*, pp. 230–31.

45. *La reforma* (Mercedes), Oct. 20, 1876; *El eco de Tandil*, Dec. 16, 1884; Curuchet to justice of the peace of Tandil, green banded leg. 1885,

AHMT; request by Zulillaga, July 4, 1893, also Bilbao, Sept. 9, 1893, AHMT.

46. Herbert Gibson, "La agricultura en la provincia de Buenos Aires," *ASRA* 24 (Dec. 31, 1890): 795–97; Florencio Sánchez, *La gringa*, act II.

47. Ch. Leonardi, "La agricultura en la provincia de Buenos Aires (contestación al Señor Gibson)," *ASRA* 25 (Jan. 31, 1891): 26–27; Carlos D. Girola, *Investigación agrícola en la República Argentina*, pp. 263, 278–79.

48. *La prensa*, June 18, 1882; *La campaña*, Jan. 28, 31, 1883.

49. Miguel Lima, *El hacendado del porvenir*, pp. 20, 32.

50. Juan Alvarez, *Temas de historia económica argentina*, p. 198; *ASRA* "Numero especial en español" (1910): 163.

51. Buenos Aires Province, *Anuario estadístico*, 1897, pt. 3, p. 439; Barba, "El desarrollo," p. 8; Argentine Republic, *Tercer censo nacional . . . de 1914*, 5:741, 837.

52. Brown, *Socioeconomic History*, p. 228.

Chapter 10

1. John Lynch, *Argentine Dictator*, p. 93; MS census summary, 1836, AGN X 25 2 4; Donna J. Guy, "The Rural Working Class in Nineteenth-Century Argentina," *Latin American Research Review* 13:1 (1978): 135, 138–39, 143. See Appendix A for population growth, 1778–1914.

2. List by Justice of the Peace Roque Duro, Sept. 24, 1851, AGN X 43 2 5.

3. Buenos Aires Province, *Registro estadístico*, 1854, pt. 2, p. 39, tables 9 and 10; Argentine Republic, *Primer censo de la República Argentina, 1869*, pp. 17–18.

4. Census *(padrón)*, 1862, Tandil, AHMT.

5. Ricardo Rodríguez Molas, "Algunos aspectos de la economia rural bonaerense en los siglos XVII y XVIII," *Revista de la Universidad* 8 (May 1959): 148; Zulma Recchini de Lattes and Alfredo E. Lattes, *Migraciones en la Argentina*, pp. 290–91, table A6; Guy, "Rural Working Class," pp. 135, 138–39, 143.

6. Argentine Republic, *Segundo censo de la República Argentina, mayo de 1895*, 2:53, 56, 62; Argentine Republic, *Tercer censo nacional . . . 1914*, 2:219–20; Buenos Aires Province, *Registro estadístico*, 1854, pt. 2, p. 39; Vicente Vásquez-Presedo, *El caso argentino*, p. 26; see also Julio Mafud, *Psicología de la viveza criolla*, pp. 54–56; Argentine Republic, *Résumen estadístico del movimiento migratorio de la República Argentina, años 1857–1924*, pp. 4–5, 34–35; José P. Podestá, *La pequeña propiedad rural en la República Argentina*, p. 17; Alfredo E. Lattes, *La migración como factor de cambio de la población en la Argentina*, p. 40.

7. Quotations from Juan Bautista Alberdi, *Bases y puntos de partida,* pp. 77–78; see also 82–83, 90.

8. Buenos Aires Province, *Registro oficial,* 1829, p. 26; 1831, p. 78.

9. Rosas to Schöo, June 3, 1843, AGN X 26 3 2; report of June 30, 1849, AGN X 26 8 4; Ramírez quotation in Ramírez to Rosas, July 18, 1846, AGN X 26 5 5; Schöo quotations in Schöo to Rosas, July 25, 1844, AGN X 26 4 1 and Dec. 12, 1844, AGN X 43 2 8; see also May 31, 1846, AGN X 26 5 4; Mar. 2, 1847, AGN X 26 6 3.

10. William MacCann, *Two Thousand Miles' Ride through the Argentine Provinces,* 1:56–57, 99.

11. Donald S. Castro, "The Development of Argentine Immigration Policy, 1852–1914," pp. 17–18; Benito Díaz, *Juzgados de paz de la campaña de la provincia de Buenos Aires, 1821–1854,* pp. 191–92.

12. Sarmiento to Lastarría, quoted in Castro, "Development," p. 14; *El nacional,* Jan. 25, 1854; Augusto M. Brougnes, *Extinción del pauperismo agrícola,* pp. 4–5; *Revista del plata* 2 (Mar. 1861): 100.

13. Federico Rahola y Tremols, *Sangre nueva: Impresiones de un viaje a la América del sud* (Buenos Aires: Institución Cultural Española, 1943), p. 72; Oscar Ricardo Melli, *Historia de Carmen de Areco, 1771–1970* (La Plata: Archivo Histórico de la Provincia de Buenos Aires "Ricardo Levene," 1974), pp. 222–29; Michael G. Mulhall and Edward T. Mulhall, *Handbook of the River Plate Republics,* 102–3; Virginia Carreño, *Estancias y estancieros,* pp. 30–31.

14. MacDonald to Walker, Mar. 5, 1900, Copiador no. 5, Walker, ITDT: Mulhall and Mulhall, *Handbook,* pp. 102–3.

15. Gastón Gori, *Ha pasado la nostalgia,* pp. 145–50, and *La pampa sin gaucho;* Argentine Republic, second national census, 1895, MS returns, bk. 666, nos. 249–50, AGN.

16. Godofredo Daireaux, *La cría del ganado en la estancia moderna,* p. 91.

17. Quotation from William Miller, *Memoirs of General Miller,* 1:161–62; Lynch, *Argentine Dictator,* pp. 260–63; Frederick Gerstaecker, *Narrative of a Journey round the World,* p. 33; Vicente Letamendi of Pilá to Felipe Vela of Tandil, Jan. 30, 1852, AHMT.

18. María Ines Cárdenas de Monner Sans, *Martín Fierro y la conciencia nacional,* pp. 83–84.

19. Osvaldo L. Fontana, "Tata Dios," in *Tandil en la historia,* unpag.

20. Antonio G. del Valle, *Recordando el pasado,* 2:515, 549.

21. Hugo Nario, *Tata Dios,* pp. 67–69.

22. Daniel Granada, *Reseña histórico-descriptiva de antiguas y modernas supersticiones del Río de la Plata,* pp. 369, 371.

23. Doc. 21, book 506, AGN X 35 2 3; Del Valle, *Recordando,* 2:518–19.

24. Del Valle, *Recordando,* 2:520; Nario, *Tata Dios,* pp. 102, 107; see also accounts in *La prensa* (Buenos Aires), Jan. 10, 12, 13, 16, 19, 20, 1872.

25. Del Valle, *Recordando,* 2:521–22; Nario, *Tata Dios,* pp. 108–9, 119–20, 130–32; Emilio Delpech, *Una vida en la gran Argentina,* pp. 25–27, 141–42; Ramón Gorraiz Beloqui, *Tandil a través de un siglo,* p. 102.

26. Del Valle, *Recordando,* 2:523, 541; Nario, *Tata Dios,* p. 124.

27. Del Valle, *Recordando,* 2:524–30; Nario, *Tata Dios,* pp. 116–17; José María Suárez García and Juan Manuel Ortíz, *Historia de la parroquia de Tandil hasta 1896* (Tandil: Minerva, 1954), p. 29.

28. Police circulars, doc. 6, bk. 506, AGN X 35 2 3.

29. Anonymous, *Abusos y ruina de la campaña: Apuntes de en viajero argentino* (Buenos Aires: Imprenta y Litografía á Vapor de la Sociedad Anónima, 1871), pp. 7–10.

30. *La nación,* Jan. 16, 1872.

31. Del Valle, *Recordando,* 2: 576–81, 585.

32. Gorraiz Beloqui, *Tandil,* pp. 99–102, 108; Juan Carlos Torre, "Los crímenes de Tata Dios, el mesías gaucho," *Todo es historia* 1 (Aug. 1967): 44–45.

33. Juan Fugl, *Abriendo surcos,* pp. 126, 143; Torre, "Los crímenes," pp. 42–43; see also Roberto Etchepareborda, "La estructura socio-política argentina y la generación del ochenta," *Latin American Research Review* 13:1 (1978): 128–29.

34. Baudrix letter on display, Museo Fuerte Independencia, Tandil.

35. Roca to Enrique O'Gorman, Jan. 13, 1872, doc. 9, bk. 506, AGN X 35 2 3.

36. Police reports, Jan. 11, Jan. 17, Apr. 17, Apr. 25, 1872, docs. 13, 15, 17, 64, bk. 506, ACN X 35 2 3.

37. Wright to O'Gorman, Jan. 14, 1872, doc. 12, bk. 506, AGN X 35 2 3.

38. *South American Journal and Brazil and River Plate Mail,* Feb. 22, 1872, p. 8; and May 7, 1872, p. 7; *Herald,* Mar. 1, 1877.

39. José Hernández, *The Gaucho Martín Fierro: Adapted from the Spanish,* pp. 16, 38–41; Andrés R. Allende, *Historia del pueblo y del partido de Lincoln en el siglo XIX,* pp. 208–9.

40. El Obrero, June 18, 1892.

41. William Perkins, *The Colonies of Santa Fe,* p. 35; Ezequiel Gallo, "Conflictos socio-políticos en las colonias agrícolas de Santa Fe, 1870–1880," working paper 87, Centro de Estudios Sociales, Instituto Torcuato Di Tella, p. 30; Francisco Scardín, *La Argentina y el trabajo,* pp. 208–9.

42. *La agricultura* 1 (Apr. 27, 1893): 187; Ezequiel Gallo, *Farmers in Revolt*, pp. 64–65.

43. Florencio Sánchez, *La gringa*, end act I, act II; Antonio Jorge Pérez Amuchástegui, *Mentalidades argentinas*, pp. 438–39.

44. Solberg, *Immigration and Nationalism*, pp. 135–36, 143, 148–49.

45. Domingo F. Sarmiento, *Condición del extranjero en América*, pp. 456–57, 533; Nilda Díaz, "Sarmiento y el tema de la inmigración," *Boletín de literatura argentina* 1 (Aug. 1966): 88–89; Solberg, *Immigration and Nationalism*, pp. 132–33.

46. *La campaña*, Feb. 17, 1884; Federico Tobal, "Los libros populares de Eduardo Gutiérrez," *La nación*, Mar. 2, 1886, p. 4.

47. Argentine Republic, *Memoria*, 1893, pp. 39–40; *ASRA* 38 (Apr. 30, 1903): 793–95.

48. Jorge N. Solomonoff, *Ideologías del movimiento obrero y conflicto social*, p. 219.

49. Solberg, *Immigration and Nationalism*, pp. 139–40; Ernesto Quesada, "El criollismo en la literatura argentina," *Estudios* 1:3 (1902): 301–2, 306.

50. Enrique de Cires, "La inmigración en Buenos Aires," *Revista argentina de ciencias políticas* 2 (Sept. 1912): 737, 741; Solberg, *Immigration and Nationalism*, pp. 144–46; Hobart A. Spalding, Jr., "Education in Argentina, 1890–1914: The Limits of Oligarchical Reform," *Journal of Interdisciplinary History* 3 (Summer 1972): 43.

Chapter 11

1. Quoted in Leroy R. Shelton, "The Gaucho in the Works of Sarmiento," p. 47; Domingo F. Sarmiento, *Facundo*, translated as *Life in the Argentine Republic in the Days of the Tyrants*, pp. 10–11; letters of Mar. 6, 1865, Jan. 15, Feb. 25, 1867, in Sarmiento, *Cartas de Sarmiento a la Señora María Mann*, pp. 7, 24, 29.

2. Sarmiento, *Facundo*, translated as *Life in the Argentine Republic*, pp. 48–52.

3. Ibid., p. 11; Sarmiento, *Argirópolis: Capital de los estados confederados*, vol. 13 of *Obras de D. F. Sarmiento*, pp. 89, 94, 97–99.

4. Sarmiento, *Discursos populares*, vol. 21 of *Obras de D. F. Sarmiento*, pp. 260–67; Shelton, "The Gaucho," p. 44; Miguel Angel Cárcano, *Evolución histórica del régimen de la tierra pública, 1810–1916*, pp. 142–43; Elda Clayton Patton, *Sarmiento in the United States* (Evansville, Ind.: Univ. of Evansville Press, 1976), pp. 68–69, 127, 140.

5. Quotation from Sarmiento, *Discursos*, p. 266; Sarmiento, *Informes sobre educación*, vol. 44 of *Obras de D. F. Sarmiento*, pp. 313–14, 319.

6. Quotation from Sarmiento, *Campaña en el Ejército Grande*, vol. 14 of *Obras de D. F. Sarmiento*, p. 159; also *Facundo*, translated as *Life in the Argentine Republic*, p. 12; and *Discursos*, p. 258; Enrique Williams Alzaga, *La pampa en la novela argentina*, p. 97.

7. Sarmiento, *Facundo*, translated as *Life in the Argentine Republic*, pp. 25–26, 35–39, 41.

8. Luis C. Pinto, *El gaucho y sus detractores*, pp. 99, 112.

9. Esteban Echeverría, *Dogma socialista y otras páginas políticas*, pp. 21, 116; José Ingenieros, "La formación de una raza argentina," *Revista de filosofía* 1 (Nov. 1915): 473, 475–77; see also Wilbert E. Moore, "Rural-Urban Conflict in Argentine Sociological Theories," *Rural Sociology* 6 (June 1941): 138–41.

10. Alistair Hennessey, *The Frontier in Latin American History*, p. 47.

11. Frederick Gerstaecker, *Gerstaecker's Travels*, p. 50; Tobal in *La nación*, Mar. 2, 1886; Walter Larden, *Estancia Life*, p. 49; Sarmiento, *Facundo*, translated as *Life in the Argentine Republic*, p. 6.

12. Silvio R. Duncan Baretta and John Markoff, "Civilization and Barbarism," *Comparative Studies in Society and History* 20 (Oct. 1978): 592, 611.

13. Alberdi quoted in Gladys S. Onega, *La inmigración en la literatura argentina, 1880–1910*, p. 50; Manuel Gálvez, *La Argentina en nuestros libros*, pp. 43–44.

14. Ezequiel Martínez Estrada, *Muerte y transfiguración de Martín Fierro*, 1:303; Donald A. Yates, "The Model of Martín Fierro," in *Martín Fierro en su centenario*, pp. 14–15; Arturo Costa Alvarez, "Nuestro preceptismo literario," *Humanidades* 9 (1924): 85–164.

15. Horacio Jorge Becco, ed., *Antología de la poesia gauchesca*, pp. 28–32; Henry Alfred Holmes, *Martín Fierro*, p. 26; Edward Larocque Tinker, *The Horsemen of the Americas and the Literature They Inspired*, pp. 33–51; Williams Alzaga, *La pampa*, p. 93; Horacio J. Becco et al., *Trayectoria de la poesia gauchesca*, pp. 37–80.

16. Ezequiel Martínez Estrada, "Lo gauchesco," *Realidad* 1 (Jan. 1947): 45–48; Walter Sava, "A History and Interpretation of Literary Criticism of Martín Fierro," pp. 16–17; n. 32, p. 218.

17. Costa Alvarez, "Nuestro preceptismo," pp. 109–10; Ernesto Quesada, "El criollismo en la literatura argentina," *Estudios* 1:3 (1902): 277–78; Fernando E. Barba, *Los autonomistas del 70*, pp. 66–67; Ricardo Rodríguez Molas, "Elementos populares en la prédica contra Juan Manuel de Rosas," *Historia* 9 (Jan. 1963): 70, 72.

18. José Hernández, *The Gaucho Martín Fierro*, trans. Ward, pp. 185,

191, lines 65–66, 151–52; see also Martínez Estrada, *Muerte*, 1:31, 35–36.

19. José Hernández, *Vida de Chacho*, p. 19.

20. José Hernández, *The Gaucho Martín Fierro*, trans. Ward, p. 33, lines 412–14; see also Alvaro Yunque, "Prólogo," in José Hernández, *Instrucción del estanciero*, pp. 23–26.

21. Speech repr. in Antonio Pages Larraya, ed., *Prosas de Martín Fierro*, p. 282.

22. *El Río de la Plata*, Sept. 9, 14, 1869; also Hernández, *Martín Fierro*, trans. Ward, esp. pt. 1, sect. 5.

23. Quotation from *El Río de la Plata*, Sept. 1, 1869; Hernández, *Instrucción del estanciero*, pp. 30–31, 35.

24. Letter reprinted in Páges Larraya, *Prosas*, pp. 230–33; quotation from Hernández, *The Gaucho Martín Fierro: Adapted from the Spanish*, p. 294; Hernández, *Instrucción del estanciero*, p. 35; see also Ricardo Rodríguez Molas, "José Hernández," *Universidad* 60 (Apr. 1964): 101–3.

25. Barba, *Los autonomistas*, p. 115; Páges Larraya, *Prosas*, pp. 79–80; Horacio Zorraquín Becú, *Tiempo y vida de José Hernández, 1834–1886*, pp. 228, 233–34; quoted in Rodríguez Molas, "José Hernández," pp. 95–97.

26. Hernández, *The Gaucho Martín Fierro*, trans. Ward, lines 4631–36, 4643–72, 4745–50, 4851–52, 1395–1460, 2167–68; Emilio Alonso Criado, *El "Martín Fierro"*, pp. 33–34.

27. Adolfo Bioy Casares, *Memoria sobre la pampa y los gauchos*, pp. 20, 32, 40.

28. Enrique de Gandía, "La mitología del gaucho en la literatura argentina," in *Cultura y folklore en América* (Buenos Aires, 1947), pp. 170, 172; quotation from Herbert Gibson, "The Evolution of Live-Stock Breeding in the Argentine," in *Censo agropecuario nacional . . . 1908*, 3:73; Prudencio de la Cruz Mendoza, *Historia de la ganadería argentina*, p. 180.

29. Ricardo Güiraldes quoted in "Encuesta," *Crítica*, Aug. 26, 1926, p. 6 (repr. 1931), and "Encuesta," *Nativa* 3 (Mar. 31, 1931), unpag.; José A. de Basualdo, *El gaucho argentino*, p. 152; Latham quotation from Wilfred Latham, *The States of the River Plate*, pp. 325–27, 333.

30. Juan José de Lezica, "Lo que dice un gaucho viejo," *Revista nacional* 31 (Mar. 1901): 296–97; *Revista de policía* 2 (June 1902): 389–90.

31. Quesada, "El criollismo," pp. 295–97; Emilio Zuccarini, "Los exponentes psicológicos del carácter argentino: Evolución del gaucho al atorrante," *Archivos de psiquiatría y criminología aplicados a las ciencias afinas* 3 (Mar. 1904): 189–91; see also Manuel Bernárdez, *Tambos y rodeos*, p. 69.

32. Leopoldo Lugones, *El payador*, p. 81; Solberg, *Immigration and*

Nationalism, p. 141; Sava, "A History and Interpretation," pp. 30, 36–37; Ricardo Rojas, *La restauración nacionalista*, pp. 172–83, 339, 343.

33. Ricardo Güiraldes, *Don Segundo Sombra*, pp. 134, 203; Williams Alzaga, *La pampa*, p. 217; Carlos Astrada, *El mito gaucho* (Buenos Aires: Cruz del Sur, 1964), pp. 33–34.

34. Charles Darbyshire, *My Life in the Argentine Republic* (London: Frederick Warne, 1918), p. 78.

On the gaucho's continuing political and cultural significance through 1978, see Richard W. Slatta, "The Gaucho in Argentina's Quest for National Identity," *Canadian Review of Studies in Nationalism* 12:1 (1983).

Glossary

acción. License granted by colonial officials for permission to kill wild cattle for their hides.

aftosa. Hoof-and-mouth disease of cattle.

amargo. Bitter, unsweetened, as tea.

apartar. Dividing and sorting cattle into small herds during a roundup.

aquerenciar. Training cattle to graze within a certain pasturage—their accustomed range or "querencia."

argentinidad. Argentinity; the essential Argentine national character.

arrendatario. Agricultural renter.

asado. Barbeque; quick-roasted beef skewered on a metal frame (*asador*) and leaned next to an open fire.

Banda Oriental. "Eastern shore" of the Río de la Plata; modern-day Uruguay, which became a nation in 1826.

baqueano (also **baquiano**). Guide or scout.

blandengue. Frontier militiaman of the colonial era who guarded against Indian attack.

boleada. Ostrich hunt by gauchos using bolas.

boleadoras. Bolas, or weapon used by Indians and gauchos—consisting of two or, more often, three rawhide thongs, each tipped with a stone or metal ball, used to entangle the legs of a fleeing animal.

bombachas. Baggy trousers, taken in at the ankle to fit inside the boot; a garment of European origin that replaced the traditional gaucho chiripá.

bombero. Paramilitary fireman of the early twentieth century.

bombilla. Metal straw or tube for sipping *mate*.

botas de potro. Homemade boots fashioned from the skin of a colt's leg.

caballo criollo. See pingo.

cabaña. Stock-breeding ranch for raising purebred and mestizo animals.

calzonzillos blancos. Lace-fringed leggings worn under the chiripá.

camp. British corruption of "campo," meaning countryside.

capataz. Ranch foreman.

carne con cuero. Beef delicacy; meat wrapped in a cowhide and cooked slowly in a pit fire.

cautiva. Woman kidnapped and held captive by pampean Indians.

cepo. Stocks used for punishment.

chacra. Small rental farm run by a sharecropper (chacarero).

changador. One who illegally killed cattle for hides during the eighteenth century.

china. Native woman of the pampas, often mestiza.

chiripá. Diaper-like cloth worn by gauchos in lieu of trousers.

cimarrón. (a) Wild, untamed, as cattle; (b) unsweetened, as tea.

cinchada. Tug-of-war on horseback.

colono. Agricultural immigrant working on a colony or communal settlement; often extended to mean farmers in general.

criollo. Argentine native, especially a rural native.

cuatrero. Rustler, cattle thief.

curandero. Folk healer, medicine man or woman.

destinado. Military draftee.

domador. Horse tamer.

dulce de leche. Sweet, milk-based caramel dessert.

empanada. Meat pie.

emphyteusis. Land rental system used by the national government during the 1820s and 1830s.

enganchado. Enlistee, usually a foreigner who joined the military for bonus payment.

esquila. Sheep shearing.

estancia. Ranch of any size, owned or rented.

estero. Marshy lowland area of the pampa.

facón. Long, sword-like knife used by gauchos for work and fighting.

fortín. Small fort on the frontier.

frigorífico. Meat-chilling and processing plant.

galpón. Large barn.

gauchesco. Poetry, written in gaucho dialect, that depicts rural life on the pampas.

gauderio. Early pejorative term for pampean horseman.

golondrina. "Swallow," or migrant farm worker who crossed the Atlantic from Europe seasonally for the agricultural harvest.

guía. Legal writ granting permission to move cattle.

hierra. Branding season.

jagüel. Traditional well from which a horse raises water with bucket and rope.

jornalero. Day laborer.

lata. Metal disc or token given to sheep shearers for each one hundred animals sheared.

latifundio. Large ranch, usually defined as an estate, in excess of 1,000 or 2,500 hectares (2,471 to 6,178 acres).

liberto. Slave-born child who, according to an 1813 law, was to be freed upon marriage or coming of age.

madrina. (a) Belled heifer or mare used to lead and herd other animals; (b) godmother.

maroma. Dangerous gaucho game of dropping from a gate onto the back of a running steer or wild horse.

matadero. Slaughterhouse.

matambre. Meat between the ribs and hide; a beef delicacy.

matrero. Fugitive, outlaw, murderer of the frontier.

mayordomo. Ranch manager or overseer.

medianero. Sharecropper who splits the agricultural harvest half and half with the landowner.

minga. Traditional colonial communal harvest.

monte. Brushy, coarse grass region of the dry pampa.

montonera. Military raiding party composed of irregular cavalrymen, or montoneros, who followed a caudillo.

nighthawk. Rider who watches cattle at night.

ombú. Large twisted shrub of genus Phytolacca.

paisano. Rural native.

palomar. Dovecote, often found on ranches.

pampa gringa. Europeanized, modernized plains after the end of the frontier and open-range ranching.

pampero. Powerful windstorm.

papeleta. Military enrollment document required of rural males.

partido. County or parish; administrative unit of the province.

pato. Mounted game in which dozens of riders contest the possession of a duck stuffed in a rawhide bag.

patria. "Fatherland"; refers to the gaucho's native province.

pava. Small kettle used to heat water for brewing *mate*.

payador. Singer of improvisational songs, usually sung by two contestants in a form of duel.

pechando. "Breasting"; contest in which riders run their horses into one another.

peón de campo. Cowhand; ranch worker.

pialar. Roping the feet of an animal; also a gaucho equestrian game.

pingo. Native creole horse, usually ridden half-tamed.

porteño. Resident of Buenos Aires, the port city.

puchero. Stew of beef or mutton.

puesto. Pasture or grazing lands, often fenced, tended by a resident salaried renter or worker (*puestero*).

pulpería. General store and tavern, found in towns and in rural areas.

querencia. Accustomed range of a herd of cattle.

quinta. Orchards and cultivated areas surrounding a ranch house.

rancho. Simple adobe and thatch ranch house.

rastreador. Tracker.

rebenque. Quirt, horse whip of plaited leather.

recado. Soft, multilayered saddle.

recoger. Daily roundup of cattle.

resero. Cattle herder; one skilled at trailing cattle.

rincón. Confluence of two rivers, often a ranch site.

rodeo. Roundup of cattle, usually for branding.

ronda. Nightwatch of cattle herd.

Rosista. Supporter of Juan Manuel de Rosas.

saladero. Meat-salting plant.

sarna. Scab disease afflicting sheep.

sortija. Equestrian ring race.

sundown. Arrival of freeloading cowboy at mealtime.

taba. Gambling game in which the knuckle bone of a cow is thrown.

tasajo. Charqui.

terrateniente. Politically powerful rancher; latifundist controlling a large estate.

tirador. Broad leather belt.

toldería. Frontier Indian village.

tropero. See resero.

tropilla. Herd of horses, preferably matched.

truco. Popular gambling game of cards.

unitario. Centralist politician of Buenos Aires opposed to Rosas and the federalists of the countryside and interior.

vago y mal entretenido. Vagrant and ne'er-do-well; legal classification for the unemployed gaucho, making him subject to forced military service (*destinado*).

vaquería. Wild cattle hunt and slaughter of the colonial era.

velorio del angelito. Wake held for the death of a small child.

vicios. "Vices," or simple pleasures of tobacco and *mate* frequently included as part of the gaucho's wages.

vizcacha. Hare-like rodent living in burrows on the pampa.

yerra. See hierra.

Selected Bibliography

Archives

Archivo General de la Nación, Buenos Aires.
Archivo Histórico Municipal de San Antonio de Areco.
Archivo Histórico Municipal de Tandil.
Archivo Histórico de la Provincia de Buenos Aires "Ricardo Levene," La Plata.
Museo Fuerte Independencia, Tandil.
William Walker estancia papers, Instituto Torcuato Di Tella, Buenos Aires.

Government Publications

Argentine Republic. *Censo agropecuario nacional: La ganadería y la agricultura en 1908.* 3 vols. Buenos Aires, 1909.
————. Chamber of Deputies. *Investigación parlamentaria sobre agricultura, ganadería, industrias derivadas y colonización, anexo B, provincia de Buenos Aires.* Buenos Aires, 1898.
————. Comisión Directiva del Censo. *Segundo censo de la República Argentina, mayo de 1895.* 3 vols. Buenos Aires, 1898.
————. Comisión Nacional del Censo. *Tercer censo nacional levantado el 1° de junio de 1914.* 10 vols. Buenos Aires, 1916–19.
————. Departamento General de Inmigración. *Memoria.* Buenos Aires, 1879, 1890, 1893, 1896.
————. Dirección General de Estadística de la Nación. *La población y el movimiento demográfico de la República Argentina en el período 1910–1925.* Buenos Aires, 1926.
————. Dirección General de Inmigración. *Résumen estadístico del movimiento migratorio de la República Argentina, años 1857–1924.* Buenos Aires, 1925.

————. Superintendente del Censo. *Primer censo de la República Argentina, 1869.* Buenos Aires, 1872.

Buenos Aires Province. *Anuario estadístico*: Buenos Aires, 1896, 1897.

————. *Censo agrícolo-pecuario de la provincia de Buenos Aires levantado en el mes de octubre de 1888.* Buenos Aires, 1889.

————. *Censo general de la provincia de Buenos Aires, demográfico, agrícola, industrial, comercial, &, verificado el 9 de octubre de 1881.* Buenos Aires, 1883.

————. *Contribución directa: Registro catastral de la provincia de Buenos Aires con esclusión de la capital, año de 1863.* Buenos Aires, 1863.

————. Chamber of Deputies. *Diario de sesiones*, 1858–1915.

————. Comisión de Hacendados del Estado de Buenos Aires. *Antecedentes y fundamentos del proyecto de código rural.* Buenos Aires, 1864.

————. *Memorias de los diversos departamentos de la administración de la provincia de Buenos Aires y de las municipalidades de campaña.* 2 vols. Buenos Aires, 1867.

————. Ministro de Gobierno. *Memoria*: Buenos Aires, 1867–74.

————. *Registro estadístico:* Buenos Aires, 1854, 1856.

————. *Registro oficial:* Buenos Aires, 1822–24, 1829, 1831, 1852–54, 1857, 1884, 1888.

Municipality of Tandil. *Memoria de la municipalidad de Tandil de los años 1875 y 1876.* Buenos Aires, 1877.

————. Intendente Municipal. *Memoria del intendente al honorable Consejo Deliberante, 15 de junio a 31 de diciembre 1886.* Tandil, 1887.

Newspapers Cited (published in Buenos Aires unless otherwise indicated)

Agente comercial del Plata

El amigo del pueblo (Carmen de las Flores)

La aspiración (Mercedes)

La campaña

El centinela del norte (San Nicolás)

El correo ilustrado

El debate (San Pedro)

El eco de Tandil (Tandil)

El fraile

Giornale d'Italia

Herald

El hurón (Mercedes)

El industrial

El monitor de la campaña (Exaltación de la Cruz)

El municipio
El municipio (Tandil)
La nación
El nacional
El obrero
El oeste
El oeste de la provincia (Mercedes)
La opinión pública (Bahía Blanca)
El orden (Mercedes)
La organización
La palabra libre (Rojas)
La patria (Dolores)
La patria (Olavarría)
La prensa
La prensa (Belgrano)
El progreso de Flores (San José de las Flores)
El progreso de Quilmes (Quilmes)
El pueblo (Azul)
La reforma (Mercedes)
La reforma pacífica
La redención
La república
El Río de la Plata
La semana rural
South American Journal and Brazil and River Plate Mail (London)
Standard
La tribuna
La unión (Lomas de Zamora)
La unión del sud (Chascomús)
La vanguardia
La voz del Saladillo (Saladillo)

Books and Articles

Abad de Santillán, Diego. *La FORA: Ideología y trayectoria del movimiento obrero revolucionario en la Argentina*. 2d ed. Buenos Aires: Proyección, 1971.

Acevedo, Eduardo. "El sentimiento de lo cómico en el carácter argentino." *Revista de filosofía* 1 (November 1915): 450–57.

Alais, Octavio. P. *Libro criollo: Costumbres nacionales*. Buenos Aires: Brédahl, 1903.

Alberdi, Juan Bautista. *Bases y puntos de partida para la organización política de la República Argentina*. 1852. Reprint. Buenos Aires: Plus Ultra, 1974.

Allende, Andrés R. *Historia del pueblo y del partido de Lincoln en el siglo XIX: La conquista del oeste bonaerense*. La Plata: Archivo Histórico de la Provincia de Buenos Aires "Ricardo Levene," 1969.

Alsina, Juan A. *El obrero en la República Argentina*. Buenos Aires: Calle de México, 1905.

Alvarez, Juan. *Las guerras civiles argentinas*. 1912. Reprint. Buenos Aires: EUDEBA, 1972.

————. *Temas de historia económica aegentina*. Buenos Aires: El Ateneo, 1929.

Amaral Insiarte, Alfredo. *La Plata a través de los viajeros, 1882–1912*. Buenos Aires: Ministerio de Educación de la Provincia de Buenos Aires, 1959.

Andrews, George Reid. *The Afro-Argentines of Buenos Aires, 1800–1900*. Madison: University of Wisconsin Press, 1980.

Andrews, Joseph. *Journey from Buenos Ayres through the Provinces of Córdova, Tucumán and Salta, to Potosí*. 2 vols. London: John Murray, 1827.

Arena, José, Julio H. Cortés, and Alberto Valverde. *Ensayo histórico del partido de Olavarría:* Olavarría: Municipalidad de Olavarría, 1967.

Armaignac, Henri. *Viajes por las pampas argentinas: Cacerías en el Quequén Grande y otras adanzas, 1869–1874*. Translated by Isabel Molina Pico. French ed. 1883. Buenos Aires: EUDEBA, 1974.

Arnold, Samuel Greene. *Viaje por América del sur, 1847–1848*. Translated by Clara de Rosas. English ed. 1848. Buenos Aires: Emecé, 1951.

Assunção, Fernando O. *El gaucho*. Montevideo: Imprenta Nacional, 1963.

————. *El gaucho: Estudio socio-cultural*. 2 vols. Montevideo: Dirección General de Extensión Universitaria, 1978–79.

————. *Pilchas criollas: Usos y costumbres del gaucho*. Montevideo: Master Fer, 1978.

Avellaneda, Nicolás. *Estudio sobre las leyes de tierras públicas*. 1865. Reprint. Buenos Aires: Roldán, 1915.

Ayarragaray, Lucas. *La anarquía argentina y el caudillismo: Estudio psicológico de los orígenes argentinos*. 1904. 3d ed. rev. Buenos Aires: Rosso, 1935.

Azara, Félix de. *Descripción é historia del Paraguay y del Río de la Plata*. 2 vols. 1847. Reprint. Buenos Aires: Bajel, 1943.

————. *Memoria sobre el estado rural del Río de la Plata y otros informes*.

Edited by J. V. González. 1801. Reprint. Buenos Aires: Bajel, 1943.

Azeves, Angel Héctor. *Ayacucho: Surgimiento y desarrollo de una ciudad pampeana*. Buenos Aires: Municipalidad de Ayacucho, 1968.

Barba, Fernando Enrique. *Los autonomistas del 70: Auge y frustración de un movimiento provinciano con vocación nacional, Buenos Aires entre 1868 y 1878*. Buenos Aires: Pleamar, 1976.

————. "El desarrollo agrícolo-pecuario de la provincia de Buenos Aires (1880–1920)." *Investigaciones y ensayos* 17 (July 1974): 291–310.

Barrán, José Pedro. *Historia uruguaya: Apogeo y crisis del Uruguay pastoril y caudillesco, 1839–1875*. Vol. 4. 2d ed. Montevideo: Banda Oriental, 1975.

Barrán, José P., and Benjamín Nahum. *Historia rural del Uruguay moderno*. 6 vols. Montevideo: Banda Oriental, 1967–77.

Barros, Alvaro. *Fronteras y territorios de las pampas del sur*. 1871–72. Reprint. 2d ed. Buenos Aires: Hachette, 1975.

Basualdo, José Agustín de. *El gaucho argentino*. Buenos Aires: Quillet, 1942.

Bauer, Arnold J. "Reply." *Hispanic American Historical Review* 59 (August 1979): 486–89.

————. "Rural Workers in Spanish America: Problems of Peonage and Oppression." *Hispanic American Historical Review* 59 (February 1979): 34–63.

Beaumont, J. A. B. *Travels in Buenos Ayres, and the Adjacent Provinces of the Río de la Plata, with Observations Intended for the Use of Persons Who Contemplate Emigrating to That Country, or Embarking Capital in Its Affairs*. London: James Ridgeway, 1828.

Becco, Horacio Jorge, ed. *Antología de la poesia gauchesca*. Madrid: Aguilar, 1972.

Becco, Horacio Jorge, and Carlos Dellepiane Calcena. *El gaucho: Documentación, iconografía*. Buenos Aires: Plus Ultra, 1978.

Becco, Horacio Jorge, Félix Weinberg, Rodolfo A. Borello, and Adolfo Prieto. *Trayectoria de la poesia gauchesca*. Buenos Aires: Plus Ultra, 1977.

Beck-Bernard, Lina. *Cinco años en la Confederación Argentina, 1857–1862*. Translated by José Luis Busaniche. Buenos Aires: El Ateneo, 1935.

Bejarano, Manuel. "Inmigración y estructuras tradicionales en Buenos Aires, 1854–1930." In *Los fragmentos del poder: De la oligarquía a la poliarquía argentina*, comp. Torcuato S. Di Tella and Tulio Halperín Donghi. Buenos Aires: Alvarez, 1969.

Bernárdez, Manuel. *Tambos y rodeos: Crónicas de la vida rural argentina*. Buenos Aires: Argos, 1902.

Bialet Masse, Juan. *El estado de las clases obreras argentinas a comienzos del siglo.* 1904. Reprint. Córdoba: Universidad Nacional de Córdoba, 1968.

————. *Informe sobre el estado de las clases obreras en el interior de la República.* 2 vols. Buenos Aires: Adolfo Grau, 1904.

Billington, Ray Allen, ed. *The Frontier Thesis: Valid Interpretation of American History?* Huntington, N.Y.: Krieger, 1977.

Bioy Casares, Adolfo. *Memoria sobre la pampa y los gauchos.* Buenos Aires: Sur, 1970.

Bishop, Nathaniel Holmes. *The Pampas and the Andes: A Thousand Miles' Walk across South America.* 1854. 11th ed. Boston: Lee and Shepard, 1883.

Blanco Acevedo, Pablo. "El gaucho: Su formación social." *Revista del Instituto Histórico y Geográfico del Uruguay* 5 (August 1927): 433–44.

Bosco, Eduardo Jorge. *El gaucho a través de los testimonios extranjeros, 1773–1870.* Buenos Aires: Emecé, 1947.

Bossio, Jorge A. *Argentina: La historiografía en crisis.* Buenos Aires: Ediciones CICHAL, 1977.

————. *Historia de las pulperías.* Buenos Aires: Plus Ultra, 1972.

Brackenridge, Henry Marie. *Voyage to South America: Performed by Order of the American Government, in the Years 1817 and 1818, in the Frigate Congress.* 2 vols. Baltimore: Cushing and Jewett, 1819.

Brougnes, Augusto M. *Extinción del pauperismo agrícola por medio de la colonización en las provincias del Río de la Plata con un bosquejo geográfico é industrial de dichas provincias.* Translated by Ezequiel N. Paz. Paraná: Imprenta del Estado, 1855.

Brown, Jonathan C. "Dynamics and Autonomy of a Traditional Marketing System: Buenos Aires, 1810–1860." *Hispanic American Historical Review* 56 (November 1976): 605–29.

————. "A Nineteenth-Century Cattle Empire." *Agricultural History* 52 (January 1978): 160–78.

————. *A Socioeconomic History of Argentina, 1776–1860.* Cambridge: Cambridge University Press, 1979.

Bunge, Carlos Octavio. "El gaucho." In *El paisaje y el alma argentina: Descripciones, cuentos y leyendas del terruño,* ed. Carlos Ibarguren, Antonio Aita, and Pedro Juan Vignale. Buenos Aires: Consejo Argentino de Cooperación Intelectual, 1938.

Burgin, Miron. *The Economic Aspects of Argentine Federalism, 1820–1852.* Cambridge, Mass.: Harvard University Press, 1946.

Burmeister, Hermann. *Viaje por los estados del Plata.* Translated by Federico Burmeister and Carlos Burmeister. 3 vols. German ed., 1861. Buenos Aires: Unión Germánica de la Argentina, 1943.

Burns, E. Bradford. *The Poverty of Progress: Latin America in the Nineteenth Century.* Berkeley: University of California Press, 1980.

Caldcleugh, Alexander. *Travels in South America during the Years 1819–20–21: Containing an Account of the Present State of Brazil, Buenos Ayres, and Chile.* 2 vols. London: John Murray, 1825.

Cárcano, Miguel Angel. *Evolución histórica del régimen de la tierra pública, 1810–1916.* 1917. Reprint. Buenos Aires: EUDEBA, 1972.

Cárdenas de Monner Sans, María Ines. *Martín Fierro y la conciencia nacional.* Buenos Aires: Pléyade, 1977.

Carreño, Virginia. *Estancias y estancieros.* Buenos Aires: Concourt, 1968.

Carretero, Andrés M. *Los Anchorena: Política y negocios en el siglo XIX.* Buenos Aires: 8ª Década, 1970.

———. *La propiedad de la tierra en la época de Rosas.* Buenos Aires: El Coloquio, 1972.

Carril, Bonifacio del. *El gaucho a través de la iconografía.* Buenos Aires: Emecé, 1978.

Carrío de la Vandera, Alonso [Concolorcorvo]. *El lazarillo: A Guide for Inexperienced Travelers between Buenos Aires and Lima, 1773.* Translated by Walter D. Kline. Bloomington: University of Indiana, 1965.

Catlin, George. *Last Rambles amongst the Indians of the Rocky Mountains and the Andes.* London: Sampson, Low and Marston, 1868.

Chambliss, William J. "Functional and Conflict Theories of Crime: the Heritage of Emile Durkheim and Karl Marx." In *Whose Law? What Order? A Conflict Approach to Criminology,* ed. William J. Chambliss and Milton Mankoff. New York: John Wiley, 1976.

———. "A Sociological Analysis of the Law of Vagrancy." *Social Problems* 12 (Summer 1964): 67–77.

Chikhachev, Platon Alexandrovich. *A Trip across the Pampas of Buenos Aires, 1836–1837.* Translated by Jack Weiner. Lawrence: University of Kansas Center of Latin American Studies, 1967.

Coluccio, Félix. *Diccionario folklórico argentino.* 2 vols. Buenos Aires: Lasserre, 1964.

Coni, Emilio Angel. *El gaucho: Argentina, Brasil, Uruguay.* 1945. Reprint. Buenos Aires: Solar-Hachette, 1969.

———. *La verdad sobre la enfiteusis de Rivadavia.* Buenos Aires: EUDEBA, 1927.

Cordero, Carlos J. *Los relatos de los viajeros extranjeros posteriores a la Revolución de Mayo como fuentes de historia argentina: Ensayo de sistematación bibliográfica.* Buenos Aires: Coni, 1936.

Cortazar, Augusto Raúl. *Folklore argentino.* Buenos Aires: Nova, 1959.

Cortés Conde, Roberto. *The First Stages of Modernization in Spanish America.* New York: Harper & Row, 1974.

————. *El progreso argentino, 1880–1914.* Buenos Aires: Sudamericana, 1979.

Costa Alvarez, Arturo. *El castellano en la Argentina.* La Plata: Escuela San Vicente de Paúl, 1928.

————. "Nuestra preceptismo literario: Indianismo, americanismo, gauchismo, criollismo, nacionalismo." *Humanidades* 9 (1924): 85–164.

Crawford, Robert. *Across the Pampas and the Andes.* London: Longmans, Green, 1884.

Criado, Emilio A. *El "Martín Fierro": Estudio crítico.* Buenos Aires: Compañía Sud-Americana de Billetes de Banco, 1914.

Cross, Harry E. "Living Standards in Rural Nineteenth-Century Mexico: Zacatecas, 1820–80." *Journal of Latin American Studies* 10 (May 1978): 1–19.

Cuccorese, Horacio Juan. "La conservación de carnes en la Argentina: Historia sobre los orígenes de la industria frigorífica." *Trabajos y comunicaciones* 14 (1965): 61–99.

————. *Historia crítica de la historiografía socioeconómica argentina del siglo XX.* La Plata: Universidad Nacional de La Plata, 1975.

————. "Historia sobre los orígenes de la Sociedad Rural Argentina." *Humanidades* 35 (1960): 23–53.

Cunninghame Graham, Robert Bontine. *The Ipané.* 1899. Reprint. London: T. Fisher Unwin, 1925.

————. *Rodeo: A Collection of Tales and Sketches of Robert B. Cunninghame Graham,* comp. by A. F. Tschiffely. London: William Heinemann, 1936.

————. *The South American Sketches of R. B. Cunninghame Graham,* comp. by John Walker. Norman: University of Oklahoma Press, 1978.

Daireaux, Emilio. *Vida y costumbres en La Plata.* 2 vols. Buenos Aires: Lajouane, 1888.

Daireaux, Godofredo. *Costumbres criollos.* Buenos Aires: La Nación, 1915.

————. *La cría del ganado en la estancia moderna.* 1887. 3d ed. Buenos Aires: Prudent Brothers and Moetzel, 1904.

————. "Estancias in Argentina." In *Censo agropecuario nacional: La ganadería y la agricultura en 1908.* Vol. 3: *Stock-Breeding and Agriculture in 1908: Monographs.* Buenos Aires: Argentine Meteorological Office, 1909.

D'Amico, Carlos. *Siete años en el gobierno de la provincia de Buenos Aires.* Buenos Aires: Peuser, 1895.

Darwin, Charles. *Journal and Remarks, 1832–1836.* Vol. 3: *Narrative of the*

Surveying Voyages of Her Majesty's Ships Adventure and Beagle, between the Years 1826 and 1836 . . . London: Henry Colburn, 1839.

Delpech, Emilio. *Una vida en la gran Argentina: Relatos desde 1869 hasta 1944, anécdotas y finanzas.* Buenos Aires: Peuser, 1944.

Denhardt, Robert M. *The Horse of the Americas.* 1947. Rev. ed. Norman: University of Oklahoma Press, 1975.

Despontín, Luis A. *El derecho del trabajo: Su evolución en América, orígenes, colonia, independencia, organización.* Buenos Aires: Arga, 1947.

Díaz, Benito. *Juzgados de paz de la campaña de la provincia de Buenos Aires, 1821–1854.* La Plata: Universidad Nacional de La Plata, 1959.

―――. *Rosas, Buenos Aires y la organización nacional.* Buenos Aires: El Coloquio, 1974.

Duncan Baretta, Silvio R., and John Markoff. "Civilization and Barbarism: Cattle Frontiers in Latin America." *Comparative Studies in Society and History* 20 (October 1978): 587–620.

Durañona, Alberto A., ed. *Indice general de leyes, decretos y resoluciones desde el año 1810 a 1920.* 2 vols. La Plata: Taller de Impresiones Oficiales, 1922–24.

Dusenberry, William. "Juan Manuel de Rosas as Viewed by Contemporary American Diplomats." *Hispanic American Historical Review* 41 (November 1961): 495–514.

Earle, Peter G. *Prophet in the Wilderness: The Works of Ezequiel Martínez Estrada.* Austin: University of Texas Press, 1971.

Ebelot, Alfredo. *Frontera sur: Recuerdos y relatos de la campaña del desierto, 1875–1879.* Translated by Nina Dimentstein and Ecala Dimentstein. Buenos Aires: Kraft, 1968.

―――. *La pampa, costumbres argentinas.* 1890. 2d ed. Buenos Aires: Ciordia y Rodríguez, 1952.

Echeverría, Esteban. *Dogma socialista y otras páginas políticas.* 1837. Rev. ed. Buenos Aires: Estrada, 1970.

Elwes, Robert. *A Sketcher's Tour round the World.* London: Hurst and Blackett, 1854.

Estévez, Alfredo. "La contribución directa, 1821–1852." *Revista de ciencias económicas* 48 (April 1960): 123–234.

Estrada, Marcos. "Antecedentes para la historia del desarrollo agrícola y ganadero argentino." *Anales de la Sociedad Rural Argentina* 98 (September 1964): 42–58.

Etchepareborda, Roberto. "La estructura socio-política argentina y la generación del ochenta." *Latin American Research Review* 13:1 (1978): 127–34.

―――. *Rosas: Controvertida historiografía.* Buenos Aires: Pleamar, 1972.

Falkner, Thomas. *A Description of Patagonia and the Adjoining Parts of South America*. 1774. Facsimile ed. Chicago: Armann and Armann, 1935.

Fernández Latour de Botas, Olga. *Prehistoria de Martín Fierro*. Buenos Aires: Platero, 1977.

Fontana, Osvaldo L. *Tandil en la historia: Antecedentes completos de Tandil histórico, 1823–1883.* . . . Tandil: Parra, 1947.

Frers, Emilio. *Cuestiones agrarias y económicas*. 3 vols. Buenos Aires: Gadola, 1918–19.

Fugl, Juan. *Abriendo surcos: Memorias de Juan Fugl, 1811–1900*. Translated by Lars Baekhój. 2d ed. Buenos Aires: Altamira, 1973.

Gallo, Ezequiel. "Conflictos socio-políticos en las colonias agrícolas de Santa Fe, 1870–1880." Working paper 87. Buenos Aires: Instituto Torcuato Di Tella, Centro de Estudios Sociales, 1973.

————. *Farmers in Revolt: The Revolution of 1893 in the Province of Santa Fe, Argentina*. London: Athlone, 1976.

————. "Ocupación de tierras y colonización agrícola en Santa Fe, 1870–1895." Working paper 64. Buenos Aires: Instituto Torcuato Di Tella, Centro de Estudios Sociales, 1969.

Gallo, Ezequiel, and Roberto Cortés Conde. *Argentina: La república conservadora*. Buenos Aires: Paidos, 1972.

Gálvez, Manuel. *La Argentina en nuestros libros*. Santiago, Chile: Ercilla, 1935.

Gandía, Enrique de. "Sarmiento y su teoría de 'Civilización y Barbarie.' " *Journal of Inter-American Studies* 4 (January 1962): 67–87.

García, Juan Agustín. *La ciudad indiana*. 1900. 2d ed. Buenos Aires: EUDEBA, 1972.

Gerstaecker, Frederick. *Gerstaecker's Travels*. London: T. Nelson, 1854.

————. *Narrative of a Journey round the World*. New York: Harper, 1855.

Giberti, Horacio C. E. *El desarrollo agrario argentino*. Buenos Aires: EUDEBA, 1964.

————. *Historia económica de la ganadería argentina*. 1954. Reprint. Buenos Aires: Solar-Hachette, 1970.

Gibson, Herbert. "The Evolution of Live-Stock Breeding in the Argentine." In Argentine Republic, *Censo agropecuario nacional: La ganadería y la agricultura en 1908*. Vol. 3: *Stock-breeding and Agriculture in 1909: Monographs*. Buenos Aires: Argentine Meteorological Office, 1909.

————. *The History and Present State of the Sheep-Breeding Industry in the Argentine Republic*. Buenos Aires: Ravenscroft and Mills, 1893.

————. "Nuestras razas ovinas." *Revista de ganadería, veteranía y agricultura* 5 (March 1907): 129–50.

Girola, Carlos D. *Investigación agrícola en la República Argentina: Prelimi-*

nares. Buenos Aires: Compañía Sud-Americana de Billetes de Banco, 1904.

Glaubert, Earl T. "Ricardo Rojas and the Emergence of Argentine Cultural Nationalism." *Hispanic American Historical Review* 43 (February 1963): 1–13.

Gori, Gastón. *Ha pasado la nostalgia*. Sante Fe: Colmegna, 1950.

————. *La pampa sin gaucho: Influencia del inmigrante en la transformación de los usos y costumbres en el campo argentino en el siglo XIX*. Buenos Aires: Raigal, 1952.

————. *El pan nuestro: Panorama social de las regiones cerealistas argentinas*. Buenos Aires: Galatea, 1958.

————. *Vagos y mal entretenidos: Aporte al tema hernandiano*. 1951. 2d ed. Santa Fe: Colmegna, 1965.

Gorraiz Beloqui, Ramón. *Tandil a través de un siglo: Reseña geográfica, histórica, económica y administrativa, 1823–1923*. Buenos Aires: J. Héctor Matera, 1958.

Granada, Daniel. *Reseña histórico-descriptiva de antiguas y modernas supersticiones del Río de la Plata*. Montevideo: Barreiro y Ramos, 1896.

Grela, Plácido. *El grito de Alcorta: Historia de la rebelión campesina de 1912*. Rosario: Tierra Nuestra, 1958.

Guglieri, Pablo. *Las memorias de un hombre de campo: Treinta años de permanencia en la República Argentina*. Buenos Aires: Albasio, 1913.

Güiraldes, Ricardo. *Don Segundo Sombra: Shadows on the Pampas*. Translated by Harriet de Onís. Spanish ed., 1926. New York: Signet, 1966.

Guy, Donna J. *Argentine Sugar Politics: Tucumán and the Generation of 'Eighty*. Tempe: Arizona State University Press, 1980.

————. "The Rural Working Class in Nineteenth-Century Argentina: Forced Plantation Labor in Tucumán." *Latin American Research Review* 13:1 (1978): 135–45.

Guzmán, Yuyú. *Estancias de Azul*. Azul: Diario del Pueblo, 1976.

Hadfield, William. *Brazil and the River Plate in 1868: Showing the Progress of Those Countries since His Former Visit in 1853*. London: Bates, Hendy, 1869.

————. *Brazil, the River Plate, and the Falkland Islands, with the Cape Horn Route to Australia: Including Notices of Lisbon, Madeira, the Canaries, and the Cape Verdes*. London: Longman, Brown, Green, and Longmans, 1854.

Haigh, Samuel. *Bosquejos de Buenos Aires, Chile y Perú*. Translated by Carlos A. Aldao. English ed., 1829. Buenos Aires: Bibliotéca de la Nación, 1918.

Halperín Donghi, Tulio. "La expansión ganadera en la campaña de Buenos Aires, 1810–1852." *Desarrollo económico* 3 (April 1963): 57–110.

―――. *Politics, Economics and Society in Argentina in the Revolutionary Period.* Translated by Richard Southern. Cambridge: Cambridge University Press, 1975.

―――. *El revisionismo histórico argentino.* Mexico City: Siglo XXI, 1971.

Hannah, John. *Sheep-Husbandry in Buenos Ayres: A Continuation of the Discussion between Wilfred Latham, Esq., and the Author.* Buenos Aires: Imprenta Buenos Aires, 1868.

Hasbrouck, Alfred. "The Conquest of the Desert." *Hispanic American Historical Review* 15 (May 1935): 195–228.

Hay, Douglas. "Property, Authority and the Criminal Law." In *Albion's Fatal Tree*, by Douglas Hay, Peter Linebaugh, John G. Rule, E. P. Thompson, and Cal Winslow. New York: Random House, 1975.

Head, Francis Bond. *Rough Notes Taken during Some Rapid Journeys across the Pampas and among the Andes.* London: John Murray, 1826.

Helms, Anthony Zachariah. *Travels from Buenos Ayres, by Potosi, to Lima.* 1798. Reprint. London: Richard Phillips, 1807.

Hennessey, Alistair. *The Frontier in Latin American History.* Albuquerque: University of New Mexico Press, 1978.

Hernández, Ernesto Raúl. *Recopilación de leyes agrarias vinculadas a la ganadería: Período comprendido entre los años 1856 a 1952.* [La Plata?]: Ministerio de Asuntos Agrarios de la Provincia de Buenos Aires, 1952.

Hernández, José. *The Gaucho Martín Fierro.* Translated by C. E. Ward. Bilingual ed. Albany: SUNY Press, 1967.

―――. *The Gaucho Martín Fierro: Adapted from the Spanish and Rendered into English Verse by Walter Owen.* Buenos Aires: Pampa, 1960.

―――. *Instrucción del estanciero.* 1882. Buenos Aires: Peña, 1953.

―――. *Vida de Chacho.* 1863. Reprint. Buenos Aires: Rodolfo Alonso, 1973.

Herrera, Marcos A. "Martín Fierro y la ley penal." *Universidad* 86 (January 1977): 95–114.

Hinchliff, Thomas Woodbine. *South American Sketches; or, A Visit to Rio de Janeiro, the Organ Mountains, La Plata, and the Paraná.* London: Longman, Green, Longman, Roberts, and Green, 1863.

Hobsbawm, Eric J. *Bandits.* Harmondsworth, England: Penguin, 1969.

Holmes, Henry Alfred. *Martín Fierro: An Epic of the Argentine.* New York: Instituto de las Españas en los Estados Unidos, 1923.

Hopkins, Eduardo Augusto. *Memoria acompañando un proyecto de ley, proveyendo los medios de disponer de las tierras públicas de la Confederación Argentina, y otros objetos.* Rosario: El Nacional, 1857.

Hudson, William Henry. *Far Away and Long Ago: A History of My Early Life.* New York: E. P. Dutton, 1918.

――――. *The Naturalist in La Plata.* New York: E. P. Dutton, 1922.

――――. *Tales of the Pampa.* New York: Alfred A. Knopf, 1916.

Hutchinson, Thomas Joseph. *Buenos Ayres and Argentine Gleanings: With Extracts from a Diary of Salado Exploration in 1862 and 1863.* London: Edward Stanford, 1865.

――――. *The Paraná: With Incidents of the Paraguayan War, and South American Recollections, from 1861 to 1868.* London: Edward Stanford, 1868.

Inchauspe, Pedro. *Reivindicación del gaucho: Ensayos, disquisiciones folklóricos y cuentos.* Buenos Aires: Plus Ultra, 1968.

Jacob, Raúl. *Consequencias sociales del alambramiento, 1872–1880.* Montevideo: Banda Oriental, 1969.

Jefferson, Mark. *Peopling the Pampa.* New York: American Geographical Society, 1926.

Jones, Tom B. *South America Rediscovered.* Minneapolis: University of Minnesota Press, 1949.

Juan y Santacilia, Jorge and Antonio de Ulloa. *Noticias secretas de América, siglo XVIII.* 2 vols. Madrid: Editorial América, 1918.

Jurado, José María. "La estancia en Buenos Aires." *Anales de la Sociedad Rural Argentina (ASRA)* 9:2–3, 5–7 (1875): 33–38, 65–68, 153–55, 185–89, 217–21.

Justo, Juan Bautista, "La cuestión agraria." In *Discursos y escritos políticos.* Buenos Aires: W. M. Jackson, n.d.

――――. *El programa socialista del campo.* 2d ed. Buenos Aires: La Vanguardia, 1915.

King, John Anthony. *Twenty-four Years in the Argentine Republic.* London: Longman, Brown, Green, and Longmans, 1846.

Lan, Damián, and Pedro Cruz Mendoza. "Apreciación del costo de la producción de carne." *Boletín del Ministerio de Agricultura* 15 (January 1913): 105–46.

Larden, Walter. *Estancia Life: Agricultural, Economic, and Cultural Aspects of Argentine Farming.* 1911. Reprint. Detroit: Blaine-Ethridge, 1974.

Latham, Wilfred. *The States of the River Plate.* 1866. 2d rev. ed. London: Longmans, Green, 1868.

Lattes, Alfredo E. *La migración como factor de cambio de la población en la Argentina.* Buenos Aires: Instituto Torcuato Di Tella, 1972.

Leguizamón, Martiniano. "La cuna del gaucho." *Boletín de la Junta de Historia y Numismática Americana* 7 (1930): 161–71.

————. *El gaucho: Su indumentaria, armas, música, cantos y bailes nativos.* Buenos Aires: Compañía Sud-Americana de Billetes de Banco, 1916.

————. "Nueva noticia del gaucho." *Boletín de la Junta de Historia y Numismática Americana* 9 (1936): 163–68.

————. *Recuerdos de la tierra.* 1896. 2d ed. Buenos Aires: Solar-Hachette, 1957.

Lemée, Carlos. *La agricultura y la ganadería en la República Argentina: Origen y desarrollo.* La Plata: Sola Brothers, Sesé and Company, 1894.

————. *El domador: Instrucciones para la cría y la educacíon de los caballos.* Buenos Aires: Coni, 1889.

————. *El estanciero: Instrucciones para la organización y dirección de un establecimiento de campo.* 2d ed. Buenos Aires: Peuser, 1888.

————. *El paisano: Reflexiones sobre la vida del campo.* Buenos Aires: El Censor, 1887.

Levene, Ricardo. *A History of Argentina.* Translated by William Spence Robertson. Spanish ed., 1937. New York: Russell and Russell, 1963.

Liceaga, José V. *Las carnes en la economia argentina.* Buenos Aires: Raigal, 1952.

Lichtblau, Myron I. *The Argentine Novel in the Nineteenth Century.* New York: Hispanic Institute of the United States, 1959.

Lima, Miguel A. *El estanciero práctico: Manual completo de ganadería.* Buenos Aires: Río de la Plata, 1876.

————. *El hacendado del porvenir.* Buenos Aires: Juan Kidd, 1885.

López Osornio, Mario A. *Viviendas en la pampa.* Buenos Aires: Atlántida, 1944.

Loveman, Brian. "Critique of Arnold J. Bauer's 'Rural Workers in Spanish America: Problems of Peonage and Oppression.' " *Hispanic American Historical Review* 59 (August 1979): 478–85.

Lugones, Leopoldo. *El payador.* 1916. 4th ed. Buenos Aires: Huemul, 1972.

Lynch, John. *Argentine Dictator: Juan Manuel de Rosas, 1829–1852.* Oxford: Clarendon, 1981.

Lynch, Ventura R. *Folklore bonaerense.* 1881. Buenos Aires: Lajouane, 1953.

MacCann, William. *Two Thousand Miles' Ride through the Argentine Provinces.* 2 vols. 1853. Reprint. New York: AMS Press, n.d.

McGann, Thomas F. *Argentina: The Divided Land.* Princeton: D. Van Nostrand, 1966.

————. *Argentina, the United States and the Inter-American System, 1880–1914.* Cambridge, Mass.: Harvard University Press, 1957.

———— . "The Generation of 'Eighty." *The Americas* 10 (October 1953): 141–58.

Mafud, Julio. *Psicología de la viveza criolla: Contribuciones para una interpretación de la realidad social argentina y americana.* 3d ed. Buenos Aires: Américalee, 1968.

Magariños Cervantes, Alejandro. *Estudios históricos, políticos y sociales sobre el Río de la Plata.* 2 vols. 1854. Reprint. Montevideo: Artigas, 1963.

Magnanini, Nicanór. *El gaucho "surero" de la provincia de Buenos Aires: Relatos de una época.* Buenos Aires: La Facultad, 1943.

Manning, William R., ed., *Diplomatic Correspondence of the United States: Inter-American Affairs, 1831–1860.* 12 vols. Washington D.C.: Carnegie Endowment for International Peace, 1932.

Mansfield, Charles B. *Paraguay, Brazil, and the Plate: Letters Written in 1852–1853.* Cambridge, Eng.: Macmillan, 1856.

Marmier, Xavier. *Buenos Aires y Montevideo en 1850.* Translated in 1 vol. by José Luis Busaniche. 3 vols. French ed., 1851. Montevideo: ARCA, 1967.

Marotta, Sebastián. *El movimiento sindical argentino: Su génesis y desarrollo.* 4 vols. Buenos Aires: Calomino, 1960–61, 1970.

Martínez Estrada, Ezequiel. *Muerte y transfiguración de Martín Fierro: Ensayo de interpretación de la vida argentina.* 2 vols. Mexico City: Fondo de Cultura Económica, 1948.

———— . *X-Ray of the Pampa.* Translated by Alain Swietlicki. Spanish ed., 1933. Austin: University of Texas Press, 1971.

Mawe, John. *Travels in the Interior of Brazil: With Notices on Its Climate, Agriculture, Commerce, Population, Mines, Manners, and Customs.* London: Longman, Hurst, Rees, Orme, and Brown, 1823.

Mayer, Ruben Franklin. *El país que se busca a si mismo: Historia social argentina.* 2d ed. Buenos Aires: Claridad, 1970.

Mendoza, Prudencio de la Cruz. *Historia de la ganadería argentina.* Buenos Aires: Rosso, 1928.

Miatello, Hugo. *El hogar agrícola.* Buenos Aires: Oceana, 1915.

Miers, John. *Travels in Chile and La Plata: Including Accounts Respecting the Geography, Geology, Statistics, Government, Finances, Agriculture, Manners, and Customs, and the Mining Operation in Chile . . . .* 2 vols. 1826. Reprint. New York: AMS Press, 1970.

Miller, William. *Memoirs of General Miller: In the Service of the Republic of Peru.* Edited by John Miller. 2 vols. 2d ed. London: Longman, Rees, Orme, Brown, and Green, 1829.

Moncaut, Carlos Antonio. *Estancias bonaerenses*. City Bell, Argentina: Aljibe, 1977.

————. *Pampas y estancias: Nuevas evocaciones de la vida pastoril bonaerense*. City Bell, Argentina: Aljibe, 1978.

Montoya, Alfredo J. *La ganadería y la industria de salazón de carnes en el período 1810–1862*. Buenos Aires: El Coloquio, 1971.

————. *Historia de los saladeros argentinos*. Buenos Aires: El Coloquio, 1970.

Mulhall, Marion McMurrough. *Between the Amazon and the Andes; or, Ten Years of a Lady's Travels in the Pampas, Gran Chaco, Paraguay and Mato Grosso*. London: Edward Stanford, 1881.

Mulhall, Michael G., and Edward T. Mulhall. *Handbook of the River Plate Republics*. London: Edward Stafford, 1875.

Muñiz, Diógenes, Luis Ricardo Fors, and Agustín B. Gambier, eds. *La policía de la provincia de Buenos Aires: Su historia, su organización, sus servicios*. La Plata: Impresiones Oficiales, 1910.

Muñiz, Rómulo. *El gaucho*. Buenos Aires: Roldán, 1934.

Napoli, Rodolfo A. *El trabajador rural en la República Argentina*. Buenos Aires: Abelardo-Perrot, 1958.

Napp, Ricardo, et al. *La République argentine: Ouvrage escrit par ordre du comité central argentin pour l'exposition de Philadelphie*. Buenos Aires: Courrier de la Plata, 1876.

Nario, Hugo. *Tata Dios: El mesías de la última montonera*. Buenos Aires: Plus Ultra, 1976.

Naylor, Bernard. *Accounts of Nineteenth-Century South America*. London: Athlone, 1969.

Nichols, Madaline Wallis. "The Argentine Theatre." *Bulletin hispanique* 42 (January 1940): 39–53.

————. "The Gaucho." *Pacific Historical Review* 5 (March 1936): 61–70.

————. *The Gaucho: Cattle Hunter, Cavalryman, Ideal of Romance*. 1942. Reprint. New York: Greenwood Press, 1968.

————. "The Historic Gaucho." *Hispanic American Historical Review* 21 (August 1941): 417–24.

————. "Pastoral Society on the Pampa." *Hispanic American Historical Review* 19 (August 1939): 367–71.

Oddone, Jacinto. *La burguesía terrateniente argentina*. 1936. 3d ed. Buenos Aires: n.p., 1956.

Onega, Gladys S. *La inmigración y la literatura argentina, 1880–1910*. Buenos Aires: Galerna, 1969.

Orbigny, Alcides d'. *Viaje a la América meridional realizado de 1826 a 1833*. 2 vols. Buenos Aires: Futuro, 1945.

Ortega y Gasset, José. "Intimidades." In *Obras completas de José Ortega y Gasset.* Vol. 2. 7th ed. Madrid: Revista de Occidente, 1966.

Ortíz, Ricardo M. *Historia económica de la Argentina.* 4th ed. Buenos Aires: Plus Ultra, 1974.

Páez, Jorge. *Del truquiflor a la rayuela: Panorama de los juegos y entretenimientos argentinos.* Buenos Aires: Centro Editor de América latina, 1971.

Pagano, José León. *Criminalidad argentina.* Buenos Aires: Depalma, 1964.

Page, Frederick Mann. "Remarks on the Gaucho and His Dialect." *Modern Language Notes* 8 (January 1893): 18–27.

Páges Larraya, Antonio, ed. *Prosas de Martín Fierro.* Buenos Aires: Raigal, 1952.

Paladino Giménez, José M. *El gaucho: Reseña fotográfica, 1860–1930.* Buenos Aires: Palsa, 1971.

Pallière, Jean León. *Diario de viaje por la América del sud.* Translated by Miguel Sola and Ricardo Gutiérrez. Buenos Aires: Peuser, 1945.

Panettieri, José. *La crisis ganadera: Ideas en torno a un cambio en la estructura económica del país, 1866–1871.* La Plata: Universidad Nacional de La Plata, 1965.

————. *Los trabajadores en tiempos de la inmigración masiva en Argentina, 1870–1910.* La Plata: Universidad Nacional de La Plata, 1965.

Parish, Woodbine. *Buenos Ayres, and the Provinces of Río de la Plata: Their Present State, Trade, and Debt, with Some Accounts from Original Documents of the Progress of Geographical Discovery . . . .* London: John Murray, 1839.

Patroni, Adrián. *Los trabajadores en la Argentina.* Buenos Aires: n.p., 1897.

Paullada, Stephen. *Rawhide and Song: A Comparative Study of the Cattle Cultures of the Argentinian Pampa and the North American Great Plains.* New York: Vantage, 1963.

Peabody, George Augustus. *South American Journals, 1858–1859.* Edited by John Charles Phillips. Salem, Mass.: Peabody Museum, 1937.

Pérez Amuchástegui, Antonio Jorge. *Mentalidades argentinas, 1860–1930.* 2d ed. Buenos Aires: EUDEBA, 1970.

Perkins, William. *The Colonies of Santa Fe: Their Origin, Progress and Present Condition, with General Observations on Emigration.* Rosario: Ferrocarril Santa Fe, 1864.

Pescatello, Ann M. *Power and Pawn: The Female in Iberian Families, Societies, and Cultures.* Westport, Conn.: Greenwood, 1976.

Peyret, Alexis. *Une visite aux colonies de la république argentine.* Paris: Mouillot, 1889.

Pinto, Luis C. *Entre gauchos y gaúchos: Argentinismos y brasilerismos:*

idioma nacional argentina (ensayos lingüísticos). Buenos Aires: Nueva Vida, 1963.

————. *El gaucho rioplatense, frente a los malos historiadores: Refutación a Enrique de Gandía*. Buenos Aires: Ciordia y Rodríguez, 1944.

————. *El gaucho y sus detractores: Defensa de las tradiciones argentinas, reivindicación del gaucho*. Buenos Aires: Ateneo, 1943.

Podestá, José P. *La pequeña propiedad rural en la República Argentina: Estudio económico, jurídico y social*. Buenos Aires: Baiocco, 1923.

Potter, David M. *People of Plenty: Economic Abundance and the American Character*. 1954. Reprint. Chicago: University of Chicago Press, 1973.

Prado, Manuel. *La guerra al malón*. 6th ed. Buenos Aires: EUDEBA, 1970.

Prado y Rojas, Aurelio, comp. *Leyes y decretos promulgados en la provincia de Buenos Aires desde 1810 a 1876*. Vol. 6. Buenos Aires: Mercurio, 1878.

Proctor, Robert. *Narrative of a Journey across the Cordillera of the Andes, and of a Residence in Lima, and Other Parts of Peru, in the Years 1823 and 1824*. London: Constable, 1825.

Pulley, Raymond H. "The Railroad and Argentine National Development, 1852–1914." *The Americas* 23 (July 1966): 63–75.

Quesada, Ernesto. "El criollismo en la literatura argentina." *Estudios* 1:3 (1902): 251–322, 396–453.

————. *El "criollismo" en la literatura argentina*. Buenos Aires: Coni, 1902.

————. *El problema del idioma nacional*. Buenos Aires: Revista Nacional, 1900.

Quinney, Richard. "Crime Control in Capitalist Society: A Critical Philosophy of Legal Order." In *Critical Criminology,* ed. Ian Taylor, Paul Walton, and Jock Young. London: Routledge and Kegan Paul, 1975.

————. *The Social Reality of Crime*. Boston: Little, Brown, 1970.

Ramos Mejía, José María. *Las multitudes argentinas*. 1899. Reprint. Buenos Aires: Tor, 1956.

Reber, Vera Blinn. *British Mercantile Houses in Buenos Aires, 1810–1880*. Cambridge, Mass.: Harvard University Press, 1979.

Recchini de Lattes, Zulma, and Alfredo E. Lattes. *Migraciones en la Argentina: Estudio de las migraciones internas é internacionales basado en datos censales, 1869–1960*. Buenos Aires: Instituto Torcuato Di Tella, 1969.

Repetto, Nicolás. *Mi paso por la política*. 2 vols. Buenos Aires: Santiago Rueda, 1956–57.

Rodríguez, Augusto G. *Reseña histórica del Ejército Argentino, 1862–1930*.

Buenos Aires: Secretaría de Guerra, Dirección de Estudios Históricos, 1964.

Rodríguez Molas, Ricardo. "Algunos aspectos de la economia rural bonaerense en los siglos XVII y XVIII." *Revista de la universidad* 8 (May 1959): 148–52.

―――. "Antigüedad y significado histórico de la palabra 'gaucho,' 1774–1805." *Boletín del Instituto de Historia Argentina "Dr. Emilio Ravignani"* 1 (April 1956): 144–64.

―――. "Elementos populares en la prédica contra Juan Manuel de Rosas." *Historia* 9 (January 1963): 69–101.

―――. "El gaucho y la modernización." *Polémica* 22 (October 1970): 37–56.

―――. "El gaucho rioplatense: Origen, desarrollo y marginalidad social." *Journal of Inter-American Studies* 6 (January 1964): 69–89.

―――. *Historia social del gaucho.* Buenos Aires: Marú, 1968.

―――. "José Hernández: Discípulo de Sarmiento." *Universidad* 60 (April 1964): 93–113.

―――. "Realidad social del gaucho rioplatense, 1653–1852." *Universidad* 55 (January 1963): 99–152.

Rojas, Ricardo. *La restauración nacionalista.* 1909. 2d ed. Buenos Aires: La Facultad, 1922.

Romero, José Luis. *A History of Argentine Political Thought.* Translated by Thomas F. McGann. 2d ed. Stanford: Stanford University Press, 1968.

Rosas, Juan Manuel de. *Instrucciones a los mayordomos de estancias.* Notes by Carlos Lemée. Buenos Aires: Plus Ultra, 1968.

Rossi, Vicente. *El gaucho: su origen y evolución.* Córdoba: Río de la Plata, 1921.

Sáez, Justo P., Jr. *Equitación gaucha en la pampa y mesopotamia.* 4th ed. Buenos Aires: Peuser, 1959.

Salas, Carlos P. *Elementos para un estudio de la demografía de la provincia de Buenos Aires.* La Plata: Impresiones Oficiales, 1913.

Salaverría, José María. *Vida de Martín Fierro: El gaucho ejemplar.* Madrid: Espasa-Calpe, 1934.

Sánchez, Florencio. *La gringa.* Translated by Alfred Coester. In *Plays of the Southern Americas.* Spanish ed., 1904; English ed., 1942. Freeport, N.Y.: Books for Libraries, 1971.

Sánchez-Albornoz, Nicolás. "Rural Population and Depopulation in the Province of Buenos Aires, 1869–1960." In *Population and Economics,* ed. Paul Deprez. Winnipeg: University of Manitoba Press, 1970.

Sánchez Zinny, E. F. *Integración del folklore argentino: Ensayo sobre el folklore en las zonas bonaerense, pampeana y patagónica.* Buenos Aires: Stilcograf, 1968.

Santos Gómez, Susana E. *Primera contribución para la bibliografía de viajeros a la Argentina.* Buenos Aires: EUDEBA, 1959.

Sarmiento, Domingo Faustino. *Cartas de Sarmiento a la Señora María Mann.* Buenos Aires: Academia Argentina de Letras, 1936.

———. *El Chacho: Ultimo caudillo de la montonera de los llanos.* Buenos Aires: Rodolfo Alonso, 1973.

———. *Condición del extranjero en América.* Compiled by Augusto Belín Sarmiento. Buenos Aires: La Facultad, 1928.

———. *Facundo.* 1845. Buenos Aires: Estrada, 1940.

———. *Inmigración y colonización.* Vol. 23: *Obras de D. F. Sarmiento.* Buenos Aires: Luz del Día, 1951.

———. *Life in the Argentine Republic in the Days of the Tyrants: Or, Civilization and Barbarism.* Translated by Mrs. Horace Mann. Spanish ed., 1845; English ed., 1868. Reprint. New York: Hafner, 1971.

———. *Obras de D. F. Sarmiento.* Vols. 13, 14, 21, 38, 44. Buenos Aires: Mariano Moreno, 1896–1900.

Sbarra, Noél H. *Historia de las aguadas y el molino.* La Plata: El Jagüel, 1961.

———. *Historia del alambrado en la Argentina.* 1955. 3d ed. Buenos Aires: EUDEBA, 1973.

———. "Historia de un pionero: Don Francisco Halbach fue el primero en alambrar en todo su perimetro una estancia argentina." *Boletín de la Academia Nacional de Historia* 35 (1964): 361–72.

Scardin, Francisco. *La Argentina y el trabajo: Impresiones y notas.* Buenos Aires: Peuser, 1906.

Scarlett, Peter Campbell. *South America and the Pacific: Comprising a Journey across the Pampas and the Andes . . . .* 2 vols. London: Henry Colburn, 1838.

Scenna, Miguel Angel. *Los que escribieron nuestra historia.* Buenos Aires: La Bastilla, 1976.

Schneider, Samuel. *Proyección histórica del gaucho.* Buenos Aires: Procyón, 1962.

Schopflocher, Roberto. *Historia de la colonización agrícola en Argentina.* Buenos Aires: Raigal, 1955.

Scobie, James R. *Argentina: A City and a Nation.* 2d ed. New York: Oxford University Press, 1971.

———. *La lucha por la consolidación de la nacionalidad argentina, 1852–1862.* Buenos Aires: Hachette, 1964.

———. *Revolution on the Pampas: A Social History of Argentine Wheat, 1860–1910.* Austin: University of Texas Press, 1964.

Scrivner, John H. *Memorias de Dr. Juan H. Scrivner: Impresiones de viaje, Londres—Buenos Aires—Potosí*. Translated by Lola Tosi de Dieguez. Buenos Aires: López, 1937.

Sebreli, Juan José. *Apogeo y ocaso de los Anchorena*. 2d ed. Buenos Aires: Siglo Veinte, 1974.

Seymour, Richard Arthur. *Pioneering in the Pampas; Or, The First Four Years of a Settler's Experience in the La Plata Camps*. London: Longmans, Green, 1869.

Shaw, Arthur E. *Forty Years in the Argentine Republic*. London: Elkin Mathews, 1907.

Slatta, Richard W. "Cowboys and Gauchos." *Américas*, 33 (March 1981): 3–8.

——— . "Gaúcho and Gaucho: Comparative Socio-economic and Demographic Change in Río Grande do Sul and Buenos Aires Province, 1869–1920." *Estudos Ibero-Americanos* 6 (December 1980): 191–202.

——— . "Pulperías and Contraband Capitalism in Nineteenth-Century Buenos Aires Province." *The Americas* 38 (January 1982): 347–62.

Sociedad Rural Argentina. *Tiempos de epopeya, 1866–1966*. Buenos Aires: EGLO, 1966.

Socolow, Susan Migden. *The Merchants of Buenos Aires, 1778–1810: Family and Commerce*. Cambridge: Cambridge University Press, 1978.

Solberg, Carl E. "Decline into Peonage: The Fate of Argentina's Gaucho Population, 1860–1930." In *Martín Fierro en su centenario*. Washington, D.C.: Embajada de la República Argentina en los Estados Unidos, 1973.

——— . "Farm Workers and the Myth of Export-Led Development in Argentina." *The Americas* 31 (October 1974): 121–38.

——— . *Immigration and Nationalism: Argentina and Chile, 1890–1914*. Austin: University of Texas Press, 1970.

——— . "Rural Unrest and Agrarian Policy in Argentina, 1912–1930." *Journal of Inter-American Studies and World Affairs* 13 (January 1971): 18–52.

Solomonoff, Jorge N. *Ideologías del movimiento obrero y conflicto social: De la organización nacional hasta la Primera Guerra Mundial*. Buenos Aires: Proyección, 1971.

Spalding, Hobart A., Jr., comp. *La clase trabajadora argentina: Documentos para su historia, 1890–1912*. Buenos Aires: Galerna, 1970.

Stabb, Martin S. *In Quest of Identity: Patterns in the Spanish American Essay of Ideas, 1890–1960*. Chapel Hill: University of North Carolina Press, 1967.

Storni, Carlos Mario, "Acerca de la 'papeleta' y los juzgados de paz de la campaña bonaerense." *Revista del Instituto de Historia del Derecho "Ricardo Levene"* 20 (1969): 153–71.

————. "Las disposiciones de los códigos rurales en materia laboral y sus raíces históricas." *Revista de historia del derecho* 7 (1973): 177–204.

Strickon, Arnold. "Class and Kinship in Argentina." *Ethnology* 1 (October 1962): 500–515.

————. "The Euro-American Ranching Complex." In *Man, Culture, and Animals: The Role of Animals in Human Ecological Adjustments*, ed. Anthony Leeds and Andrew P. Vayda. Washington, D.C.: American Association for the Advancement of Science, 1965.

Tanzi, Héctor José. *Historiografía argentina contemporánea*. Caracas: Instituto Panamericano de Geografía é Historia, 1976.

Tapson, Alfred J. "Indian Warfare on the Pampa during the Colonial Period." *Hispanic American Historical Review* 42 (February 1962): 1–28.

Taylor, Carl C. *Rural Life in Argentina*. Baton Rouge: Louisiana State University Press, 1948.

Tejedor, Carlos. *Manuel de jueces de paz en las demandas civiles y asuntos administrativos: Edición oficial*. Buenos Aires: La Tribuna, 1861.

Temple, Edmond. *Travels in Various Parts of Peru: Including a Year's Residence in Potosi*. 2 vols. 1833. Reprint. New York: AMS Press, 1971.

Thompson, Edward P. *Whigs and Hunters: The Origin of the Black Act*. New York: Pantheon, 1975.

Thompson, I. A. A. "A Map of Crime in Sixteenth-Century Spain." *Economic History Review* 21 (August 1968): 244–67.

Tinker, Edward Larocque. "The Horsemen of the Americas." *Hispanic American Historical Review* 42 (May 1962): 191–98.

————. *The Horsemen of the Americas and the Literature They Inspired*. 1952. 2d rev. ed. Austin: University of Texas Press, 1967.

Tobal, Federico. "Los libros populares de Eduardo Gutiérrez: El gaucho y el árabe." 5 pts. *La nación*. February 16, 18, 28; March 2, 4, 1886.

Trifilo, S. Samuel. *La argentina vista por viajeros ingleses, 1810–1860*. Buenos Aires: Gure, 1959.

————. "A Bibliography of British Travel Books on Argentina, 1810–1860." *The Americas* 16 (October 1959): 133–43.

————. "British Travel Accounts on Argentina before 1810." *Journal of Inter-American Studies* 2 (July 1960): 239–56.

Turk, Austin T. *Criminality and Legal Order*. Chicago: Rand McNally, 1969.

Turner, Frederick Jackson. "The Significance of the Frontier in American History." In *The Frontier in American History*. 1893. Reprint. New York: Henry Holt, 1958.

Valle, Antonio G. del. *Recordando el pasado: Campañas por la civilización*. 2 vols. [Azul]: n.p. [1926].

Vásquez-Presedo, Vicente. *El caso argentino: Migración de factores, comercio exterior y desarrollo, 1875–1914*. Rev. ed. Buenos Aires: EUDEBA, 1971.

Vicuña MacKenna, Benjamín. *Páginas de mi diario durante tres años de viaje, 1853–1854–1855*. Vol. 2 of *Obras completas*. Santiago: University of Chile, 1936.

Vidal, Emeric Essex. *Picturesque Illustrations of Buenos Ayres and Montevideo, Consisting of Twenty-four Views: Accompanied with Descriptions of the Scenery, and of the Customs, Manners, &c. of the Inhabitants of Those Cities and Their Environs*. 1820. Reprint. Buenos Aires: Viau, 1943.

Villafañe Casal, María Teresa. "Antecedentes del código rural de la provincia de Buenos Aires." *Comunicaciones: Serie campaña bonaerense*, no. 1. La Plata: Instituto Bonaerense de Folklore e Historia, 1961.

———. La guerra del Paraguay: Su repercusión en la campaña bonaerense." *Communicaciones: Serie campaña bonaerense*, no. 2. La Plata: Instituto Bonaerense de Folklore e Historia, 1961.

Villalobos R., Sergio. *Comercio y contrabando en el Río de la Plata y Chile, 1700–1811*. Buenos Aires: EUDEBA. 1965.

Villanueva, Amaro. *El mate: Arte de cebar*. Buenos Aires: Fabril, 1960.

Walter, Richard J. *The Socialist Party of Argentina, 1890–1930*. Austin: University of Texas Press, 1977.

———. "The Socialist Press in Turn-of-the-Century Argentina." *The Americas* 37 (July 1980): 1–24.

Walther, Juan Carlos. *La conquista del desierto: Síntesis histórica de los principales sucesos ocurridos y operaciones militares realizados en La Pampa y Patagonia, contra los indios, años 1527–1885*. 2d ed. Buenos Aires: EUDEBA, 1973.

Webb, Walter Prescott. *The Great Frontier*. Austin: University of Texas Press, 1964.

Williams Alzaga, Enrique. *La pampa en la novela argentina*. Buenos Aires: Estrada, 1955.

Wright, Winthrop. *British-Owned Railways in Argentina: Their Effect on the Growth of Economic Nationalism, 1854–1948*. Austin: University of Texas Press, 1974.

Yates, Donald A. "The Model of Martín Fierro." In *Martín Fierro en su centenario*. Washington, D.C.: Embajada de la República Argentina en los Estados Unidos, 1973.

Yunque, Alvaro. "Estudio preliminar." In *Fronteras y territorios federales de las pampas del sur*, by Alvaro Barros. 2d ed. Buenos Aires: Hachette, 1975.

———. *La literatura social en la argentina: Historia de los movimientos literarios desde la emancipación nacional hasta nuestros días*. Buenos Aires: Claridad, 1941.

Zeballos, Estanislao S. *Callvucurá y la dinastía de los piedra*. 1886. Reprint. Buenos Aires: Hachette, 1961.

————. *La conquista de quince mil leguas: Estudio sobre la traslación de la frontera sud de la República al Río Negro dedicado a los jefes y oficiales del Ejército Expedicionario*. 2d ed. Buenos Aires: La Prensa, 1878.

————. *Descripción amena de la República Argentina*. 3 vols. Buenos Aires: Peuser, 1881, 1883, 1888.

Zorraquín Becú, Horacio. *Tiempo y vida de José Hernández, 1834–1886*. Buenos Aires: Emecé, 1972.

Unpublished Works

Castro, Donald S. "The Development of Argentine Immigration Policy, 1852–1914." Ph.D. dissertation, University of California at Los Angeles, 1970.

Cortés Conde, Roberto. "The Different Role of the Frontier in Argentine History." Center for International Studies, New York University, n.d. Mimeographed.

Hernando, Diana. "Casa y familia: Spacial Biographies in Nineteenth-Century Buenos Aires." Ph.D. dissertation, University of California at Los Angeles, 1973.

Lobb, Charles G. "The Historical Geography of the Cattle Regions Along Brazil's Southern Frontier." Ph.D. dissertation, University of California, Berkeley, 1970.

Perry, Richard Owen. "The Argentine Frontier: The Conquest of the Desert, 1878–1879." Ph.D. dissertation, University of Georgia, 1971.

Pisano, Juan M. "El proletariado rural." Master's thesis, Facultad de Derecho, Buenos Aires, 1907.

Rodríguez, Manuel Chavez. "El gaucho: Bios a mitos." Ph.D. dissertation, University of Arizona, 1978.

Sava, Walter. "A History and Interpretation of Literary Criticism of Martín Fierro." Ph.D. dissertation, University of Wisconsin, 1973.

Shelton, Leroy R. "The Gaucho in the Works of Sarmiento." Ph.D. dissertation, University of Colorado at Boulder, 1969.

Sternberg, Rolf. "Farms and Farmers in an Estanciero World, 1856–1914: Origin and Spread of Commercial Grain Farming on the Humid Pampa—with Emphasis on Santa Fe Province." Ph.D. dissertation, Syracuse University, 1971.

Strickon, Arnold. "The Grandsons of the Gauchos: A Study in Subcultural Persistence." Ph.D. dissertation, Columbia University, 1960.

Svec, William R. "A Study of the Socio-Economic Development of the Modern Argentine Estancia." Ph.D. dissertation, University of Texas at Austin, 1966.

Index